Heaven Is My Fatherland

Heaven Is My Fatherland

The Life and Work of Michael Praetorius

Siegfried Vogelsänger

Translated and edited by Nathaniel J. Biebert

RESOURCE *Publications* · Eugene, Oregon

Enraptured by love for the lute,
I patiently overcome the most difficult hardships.
There is no salvation with the world;
heaven is my sweet fatherland.

—MICHAEL PRAETORIUS OF CREUZBURG

Contents

List of Illustrations

List of Illustrations

Translator's Preface

The Anniversary

FEBRUARY 15, 2021, WILL mark the four hundredth anniversary of the death of the Lutheran organist, composer, court music director, and music theorist Michael Praetorius (1571–1621). Also, if my research and inferences are correct (see Appendix II), September 27 or 28, 2021, will mark the four hundred and fiftieth anniversary of the birth of Michael Praetorius, and September 29, the Feast of St. Michael and All Angels, the four hundred and fiftieth anniversary of his baptism. Oxford University Press has called Praetorius "one of the most versatile, wide-ranging, and prolific German composers of the seventeenth century," "also important as a theorist," and "the most often quoted and excerpted writer on performance practice."[1] The fact, then, that these anniversary dates were approaching without any biography of this important and fascinating historical figure available in English was little short of a tragedy in need of immediate remedy.

Thus the book you hold in your hands—an English translation of the German book *Michael Praetorius. Hofkapellmeister und Komponist zwischen Renaissance und Barock. Eine Einführung in sein Leben und Werk* (Michael Praetorius, Court Music Director and Composer between Renaissance and Baroque: An Introduction to His Life and Work). This book was written by Siegfried Vogelsänger in collaboration with Winfried Elsner, and published by the Karl Heinrich Möseler Verlag of Wolfenbüttel in 2008.

---

1. *Syntagma Musicum III*, "Description" tab, Oxford University Press website, accessed Dec. 16, 2019, https://global.oup.com/academic/?lang=en&cc=us.

Why Did I Undertake This Project?

My diary entry for "Ascension, Thursday, May 10 (written on Sunday, May 13)" in the year 2018 reads in part:

> At about 5:55 [my wife Katie and I] went down to wait for [Winfried Elsner] in the entryway [of the Landhaus Dürkop in Wolfenbüttel]. At one point we thought he had arrived and was coming in, but the man only looked at us briefly and walked right past us to the desk. But after a few minutes, we heard the man talking to the man behind the desk and it sounded like he was waiting for someone, so I went in and said, "Herr Elsner?" And he said that it was indeed he. So we introduced ourselves and took a seat in the breakfast room (the man behind the desk kindly cleared a table for us) and we began to talk. Well, he did most of the talking, as was appropriate, since he was the Praetorius expert.
>
> I didn't get every last little detail, but I did glean this: In 2003, the [Michael Praetorius] Collegium [of Wolfenbüttel] had asked him to help produce an exhibition to celebrate the four hundredth anniversary (in 2005) of Praetorius beginning his work as court music director (*Hofkapellmeister*) in Wolfenbüttel. The seed of that request has produced much fruit since then, and continues to do so. The resulting exhibition, which we had already seen, was obviously still on display in the main church. He was continuing to work with the city's cultural institute to help produce more frequent concerts of Praetorius' music, which have also resulted in more Praetorius recordings and CDs. (He gave me the programs from the three annual January concerts that had taken place thus far.) He had helped to produce a biography of Praetorius, *Michael Praetorius. Hofkapellmeister und Komponist zwischen Renaissance und Barock. Eine Einführung in sein Leben und Werk*. His ultimate goal is to help facilitate a yearlong celebration of Praetorius' life and work in 2021, the four hundredth anniversary of his death. He also talked about his contact with Dr. Margie Boudreaux, a professor in America who had also already made contact with me via my blog. The conversation confirmed what I had already suspected: He is one of the leading Praetorius authorities of our time and has done as much as anyone to help promote awareness of his life and music. It was an honor to talk with him. It was also an honor to purchase a new copy of Gurlitt's biography from him, which he had procured for me, and to purchase a copy of the much shorter biography that he had helped to author (he signed the title page for me); he said it was "the only book of its kind in the world."

Though I did not record it in my diary, it was either at some point during this conversation, or during the private tour of the *Hauptkirche* (main church) that he gave us the following day, that he encouraged me to translate the book he had helped Siegfried Vogelsänger to produce. He said it would be a much better place to start than the Gurlitt biography, which he knew I had already started. And he was right.

Winfried Elsner was born in 1936 in East Prussia. After studying school music in Berlin and Freiburg im Breisgau, he taught music and mathematics at the secondary school (*Gymnasium*) in Dannenberg (Elbe), at the German school in Tehran, and at the secondary school in the Wolfenbüttel Palace. Since his retirement, he has occupied himself with the person and work of Michael Praetorius. Vogelsänger details some of Elsner's work in Chapter 6.

The excitement of conversing with Mr. Elsner that evening in May 2018 is still fresh in my memory. If there is one event I can point to in answer to the question, "How did you come to undertake this project?", it would be that conversation. It occurred during a three-week European vacation my wife and I took, during which we not only visited Wolfen-büttel, but also Praetorius' birth city of Creuzburg.

But of course, a person does not deliberately include Praetorius' birth- and work-city as destination stops on his European vacation without other events leading up to that. Most notable among these other factors:

- My classmates, now colleagues, Joshua Zarling and Mark Tiefel, blew me away with the Praetorius Christmas music coming from their dorm rooms in high school and college. (Archiv's glorious album *Praetorius: Mass for Christmas Morning* came out the year before we entered high school.)

- I had the privilege of singing no. 5 in Installment II of Praetorius' *Musae Sioniae*—an eight-part, two-choir setting of "In dulci jubilo [Now Sing We, Now Rejoice]"—twice in college, first in December 2001 with the Martin Luther College Chorale and then in December 2003 and on tour in the spring of 2004 with the Martin Luther College Choir. "A solemn blast" is the best way I can describe it.

- I also had the privilege of singing no. 43 in Installment VI of the *Musae Sioniae*—a relatively simple yet hauntingly beautiful four-part setting of "Parvulus nobis nascitur [See, Born for Us a Precious Child]"—together with the eleven other men of Chorus Cantans Latine at several churches in December 2004.

- After discovering the first two chapters of Wilibald Gurlitt's Praetorius-disseration online (see WGD in Annotated Abbreviations), I started translating it on November 8, 2013. Though I did not get very far, it definitely increased my interest in Praetorius' life.

- After working on Gurlitt's dissertation for less than two weeks, I was impelled to attempt to start a joint Praetorius Choir at the two rural parishes in Wisconsin then in my pastoral care. I owe the members who joined the choir an extraordinary amount of gratitude. After over-ambitiously trying to rehearse a two-choir Easter setting with them, I came to my senses and, with the gracious, via-email assistance of the Martin Luther College Library staff (who had access to the *Gesamtausgabe* or complete edition of Praetorius' works), we made use of Praetorius' two-, three-, and four-part settings. The settings proved quite lovely and gave me valuable firsthand experience with Praetorius' style. (This experience is directly responsible for n. 57 in Chapter 4.)

- My email correspondence with Winfried Elsner about Gurlitt's biography in February 2014 quickly resulted in him loaning me his copy of the new 2008 edition of Gurlitt's work via mail. (He offered to do so in just his second email to me—a testament to his generosity.)

- Dr. Margaret Boudreaux's comment on my translation blog on October 29, 2015. This led to a fairly regular email correspondence in which I benefitted from her musical expertise, especially as I began translating Vogelsänger's Praetorius biography.

All this and more led to me translating the book in your hands, the book Winfried Elsner affectionately referred to as "the only book of its kind in the world."

Notes on the Translation

Translators don't always have the same purpose in translating their source material, and purpose directly affects translation. If, for instance, I were to translate a sermon by Martin Luther, my goal would be to reproduce what Luther preached as faithfully and intelligibly as possible, at the same time attempting to keep some of the German style and flavor of his words. That was not my goal in taking up Vogelsänger's work. My goal, first and foremost, was to provide an accurate and readable biography

of Michael Praetorius to the English-speaking public. Translating Vogelsänger's 2008 biography of Praetorius just so happened to be the most
efficient way for me to do so.

In the course of my work, however, I discovered that Vogelsänger's
content was not always accurate. To cite one notable example, on pages
33–35 of the original book, Vogelsänger says that Praetorius' purpose in
Installments V–IX of his *Musae Sioniae* was to rework the hymns that
had appeared in Installments I–IV, scoring them "in motet style with five
parts in imitation of Orlando di Lasso," "in madrigal style with five parts
in imitation of Luca Marenzio," and "with six parts in the style of [Tomás]
Luis de Victoria, just as if they were scored for multiple choirs." But these
quotes, which Vogelsänger took from Praetorius' remarks in Installment
IX, do not actually describe what Praetorius did anywhere in Installments
V–IX. Praetorius is rather describing one of his many unrealized plans.

What to do with Vogelsänger's inaccuracies? Keeping in mind my
primary purpose, I decided early on not to make this a pure translation,
but a translation with corrections and improvements. I was strengthened in this decision by a clause in my contract with Wipf and Stock
Publishers: "The Translator hereby warrants to the Publishers . . . that all
statements contained therein purporting to be fact are to the best of the
Translator's knowledge and belief true." Thus the words "Translated and
edited by" on the title page.

But I do not hereby intend in *any* way to undermine Vogelsänger's
work or his contribution to Praetorius scholarship. In writing his book, he
certainly consulted a wealth of sources and did his best to keep everything
straight in an outline that functions well. The skeleton is excellent and, for
that matter, so is the majority of the flesh. It's just that, in some cases, there
are serious flesh wounds, so to speak, that need careful attention. If I did
not have his foundation, there is no way I could have fulfilled my goal,
and I am guessing that we would still be waiting for a good Praetorius
biography in English long after 2021. Not to mention that in some places
Vogelsänger (rightly) cites some of his own previous and indispensable
scholarly works. These works detail, among other things, Praetorius' and
Schütz's respective roles in the centennial celebration of Luther's Reformation in 1617, and works of Praetorius that appear to have been published
during his lifetime but which have yet to be located today.

Moreover, as it turns out, Vogelsänger's inaccuracies—and the
research and extra primary source and other translation work I had to
do as a result—have made this book better than it would have been if

Vogelsänger had simply authored a completely accurate overview-biography of Praetorius' life. It had the effect of putting me, the translator, into immediate and intimate contact with the primary sources that Vogelsänger and his sources were using. As I translated Vogelsänger's work, therefore, I could often do so with the freshness and originality of a true author, and not just a translator. I also ended up with more primary source material to include in the appendices.

But how to document my editing changes?

Please note in advance that you can ignore what follows, you can skip ahead to the "Assessment of Praetorius," and you can ignore the asterisks in the main body of the present work if you have no interest in comparing the present work to Vogelsänger's original.

I basically made three kinds of changes to Vogelsänger's work. First, in a number of cases, his content was accurate but he failed to cite a source. If I found one or more credible sources, I documented that source(s) in a footnote. Asterisks (*) appearing in footnotes identify my own source citations. Though I did not mark English-source references or references to the Glossary and Annotated Abbreviations, the reader should know that any of these are also my own. I also did not mark footnotes occurring in content that I added and identified in Major Corrections and Improvements (see two paragraphs below); I considered that to be superfluous.

Second, I made minor alterations and additions here and there when I thought I could improve on Vogelsänger's clarity or that the additions were too valuable to be foregone. Some of these I did not feel required to document, e.g. if Vogelsänger only had a composer's last name and I added his first name, or if I added a lifespan in parentheses next to a person's name. If these minor changes occurred in the main text itself and I did judge them important enough to document, I did so in a footnote concluding with "—Trans." (I tried to anticipate when a reader might raise his or her eyebrows in confusion when looking at the German and English editions side by side.) If I only added supplementary material in a footnote that I myself created, I concluded the footnote with "—Trans." If I added material of interest to one of Vogelsänger's already existing footnotes, or it proved easier to document minor alterations and additions to a paragraph in one of his already existing footnotes, I put my original notes in parentheses and concluded with "—Trans." A number of times, this results in a footnote concluding: "(I translated more of the original quote than the author did.—Trans.)" I kindly ask the reader not to read any boastful tone into these; I simply want you to know when I made changes to the author's original text. I observed the same practices with captions.

Third, where I judged his content to be inaccurate, insufficient, or confusing to an extent requiring major corrections and improvements, I indicate this with asterisks in the main text. If I altered Vogelsänger's text and/or added text of my own, I put an asterisk before the word at the start of the altered and/or added text, and a corresponding asterisk at the end. (If an asterisk appears before a word, like *this, there is *always* a corresponding asterisk and it is *always* the next one that appears in the main text.) In cases where content was omitted or moved, I put just one asterisk after the word or sentence immediately preceding the omitted or moved text (like this*). I then documented all of these alterations, additions, omissions, and transpositions more carefully in the section titled Major Corrections and Improvements (see Table of Contents).

Finally, note that I always refer to Vogelsänger as "the author" in any notes documenting my changes, so that his name would not be repeated *ad nauseam.*

None of the appendices nor the Glossary appeared in Vogelsänger's original.

Assessment of Praetorius

The final section of his biography Vogelsänger labeled "Praetorius in the Assessment of Posterity." Permit me to add my own assessment here.

Friedrich Blume says that one of the traits we find in Praetorius is "the most pretentious parading of the beloved self." If one reads enough of Praetorius' dedications, prefaces, and book content, one can see where Blume gets this idea. But two things may be said in response.

First, to make such a judgment, one must also treat the places where Praetorius insists that he is presenting his work "*not* from ambition nor to achieve a great name and reputation"[2] as disingenuous. But to do so arbitrarily is itself an instance of catering to "the beloved self."

Second, one must keep in mind the problem that every talented Christian wrestles with at some point after becoming aware of his or her talent. Permit me to phrase this problem in the form of an internal conversation: God wants me not to keep my talents to myself or to use my talents only for my own benefit and satisfaction, but to use them to

---

2. *SM* 3E:9 (emphasis added).

benefit my fellow Christians and, ultimately, as many people as possible within the scope of my daily callings. At what point, though, am I no longer selflessly making my talent known and available to others, but instead simply trumpeting myself and feeding my own ego? At what point does it become less about others and more about me? And if I sense both influences at work in me at the same time (Rom 7:21), does that mean that I should just abandon my work entirely and put my talent on the shelf?

While one can make the argument, as apparently Blume did, that Praetorius leaned more on the side of "self-promotion" than service, I must say in Praetorius' defense that at least he recognized and confessed his shortcomings and sins, as evidenced, among other things, by Pastor Peter Tuckermann's graveside remarks at his funeral. The man after God's own heart in the Scriptures is not the one without blemishes. It is the one "who is humble and contrite in spirit, and who trembles at [God's] word" (Isa 66:2; cf. Luke 18:9–14), and who trusts in God's mercy in Christ to cover his unrighteousness. By that standard, Praetorius was certainly no egotist. The fact that his work has stood the test of more than 400 years shows that he was not wrong in judging his skill and work worthy of exhibition, publication, and promotion. He was no reincarnation of Catullus' Suffenus, inaccurately appraising his own skill. He most certainly had a God-given responsibility not to hide his talent away, but to share it as broadly as possible. Did he sometimes take himself too seriously? Yes. Was his activity stained with sin and selfishness? Yes. We may elaborate on this at greater length when we ourselves have learned the secret of overcoming it. Praetorius' own stated intention was to glorify God and to serve his fellowman. We have no firm grounds on which to dismiss that intention; in fact, we must acknowledge that it is still bearing rich and abundant fruit into the present.

The other fact often ignored not just in Praetorius studies, but also in other academic biographical studies, is that, for those who take Christianity seriously, as Praetorius certainly did, their religious impulses are always the strongest and most determinative ones. If you want to understand Praetorius, you ultimately have to understand his confessional Lutheran faith and the religious context in which he lived. This assertion would already be true if we knew nothing else about the man. The fact that he had one staunch, battle-tested, confessional Lutheran pastor for a father and another for a grandfather, and two staunch, confessional Lutheran pastors for brothers—all of whom he admired—only strengthens the assertion all the more.

Did Praetorius, for example, desire to introduce the new Italian concerto manner of singing and playing into his German fatherland? Absolutely, but that desire proceeded from a conviction that this manner was a powerful tool for impressing God's saving word on the hearts of its listeners. Did Praetorius desire to systematically master the entire field of music? Absolutely, but this particular desire proceeded from his broader and deeper desire to glorify God his Savior and to ready himself and his fellow believers for the far more glorious music of their true and eternal fatherland.

That is precisely why his music still matters and is widely appreciated far beyond his German fatherland more than 400 years later. As goes the soul, so goes the music, since music is a spiritual affair. And when the listener hears in Praetorius' music a soul filled up with Christ, and thus filled with truly supernatural integrity, stability, peace, and exultation, his or her own soul cannot help but be touched, even if not conquered by his conviction.

But what distinguishes Praetorius from other composers, such as J. S. Bach (1685–1750)? Not as much as one might initially think. Yes, Bach was a born and bred musician, while Praetorius was one abnormally born, a man raised and trained to be a theologian and always regretful of the fact that he never became one. But both were men of the same sincere religious conviction. Both had natural, God-given musical talent and worked hard to develop it. Both loved their work and were convinced of its objective value, and could therefore get testy with those who stood in its way. Both were men of great learning and capable of musical complexity on a breathtaking level.

Putting aside any distinguishing traits of a technical nature, I think that Praetorius himself put his finger on the chief trait that distinguishes his music from any other: In his compositions we find a "singular force emanating from the alternating or interchanging variation" of the music.[3] That's a fancy way of saying that Praetorius' sacred music is uniquely, strikingly robust, and a key aspect of its robustness is his jaw-dropping, spine-tingling sound architecture. There are certainly notable exceptions—such as Praetorius' popular, lulling setting of "Es ist ein Ros entsprungen [Lo, How a Rose E'er Blooming *or* Behold, a Branch Is Growing]")—but comparatively speaking, Bach's music typically floats to

3. Appendix IV, A, p. 172.

our ears from the performance stage, while Praetorius' is more liable to be driven there, and often from multiple directions.

Praetorius himself, with his constant fascination with new developments in music, would probably give a ready nod to Bach as the better composer. But listen sometime to Praetorius' final setting of "In dulci jubilo [Now Sing We, Now Rejoice]" for twenty parts divided among five choirs.[4] If you do not know German or Latin, follow along using a CD booklet or online translation. Listen as the separately positioned instrumentalists and singers echo the words *"Eya wären wir da* [Oh, that we were there]*!"* Experience it for yourself as the composer's own intense longing for heaven becomes your own. Experience it for yourself, even if only for a fleeting second, as the composer actually transports you there. Experience it for yourself as the composer's conviction crystallizes in your own heart:

Mihi patria coelum. Heaven is my fatherland.

No one—not even the inimitable Bach—can give you that experience like Michael Praetorius of Creuzburg.

Nathaniel J. Biebert

January 24, 2020

Feast of St. Timothy, Pastor and Confessor

Austin, TX

---

4. E.g., track 23 on *Praetorius: Christmette (Christmas Mass)*, Gabrieli Consort & Players, conducted by Paul McCreesh, Deutsche Grammophon, 1994, compact disc.

Original Acknowledgments

THE AUTHOR IS INDEBTED to the following:

- Mr. Prof. Dr. Paul Raabe (Wolfenbüttel), for supporting this work and generously overseeing its development;

- Mr. Prof. Dr. Rainer Schmitt (Wolfenbüttel), for constructive suggestions regarding the layout of the content of this work;

- Mrs. Heike Schmitt-Monreal (Salzgitter), for extensive critical feedback on the literary style;

- Mr. Winfried Elsner (Wolfenbüttel), for encouraging me to take up this work and for his advice and support in many stimulating conversations as it developed, and for the editorial preparation of the pictures, artwork, and documents included in this work;

- The women and men on the staff of the Herzog August Library and the Public Archives of Lower Saxony in Wolfenbüttel, for always being ready to offer their kind help and expertise in the development of this work; and

- Mr. Prof. Dr. Josef Kopperschmidt (Erkelenz), for the friendly advice and guidance he has given me for many years, and not just related to my academic work.

Siegfried Vogelsänger
November 2007
Wolfenbüttel

[Vogelsänger dedicated his book "to Mr. Prof. Dr. Arno Forchert."—Trans.]

Translator's Acknowledgments

I WISH TO ACKNOWLEDGE all of my Latin and German professors from high school and college, in the order in which I encountered them: Thomas Lindloff, Robert Krueger, Ronald Hahm, Phoebe Lawrenz, James Danell, Joel Fredrich (who also helped me with a couple difficult Latin questions related to the present work), and Daniel Deutschlander. Without the education they gave me in these languages, I could not have pursued my interest in Praetorius' person and work in a serious way.

I also wish to acknowledge my high school, college, and seminary music professors and choir directors, in the order in which I encountered them: Steven Biedenbender, Randy Bode, Jodi Hermanson (now Rowe), Roger Hermanson, Kermit Moldenhauer, and James Tiefel. Without the education and practical experience they gave me in music, the richness and beauty of music, including Praetorius' music, would be lost on me.

More specific to this project, I wish to thank the following:

- Winfried Elsner, for his generosity and encouragement, as detailed in my Translator's Preface;

- Dr. Margaret Boudreaux, Professor Emerita of Music at McDaniel College, for her scholarly interaction and musical expertise;

- Keith Womer, Dr. Boudreaux, Rev. M. John Dermé, Anne Grimes, and my wife, for proofreading my manuscript (any mistakes in spelling, grammar, and/or content should, however, be placed squarely at my feet, not theirs);

- the libraries of the University of Texas at Austin, through whose Courtesy Borrower program I was able to access and consult many of the works cited in this book;

- Wipf & Stock Publishers, for accepting my manuscript for publication and working patiently and genially with me to get it to press;

- Mark Tiefel, Kirk and Sarah Lahmann, Joe and Debbie Dietrich, Paul Prange, Victor and Ana Prange, and Dave Backus, for their generous support of this project, without which it could not have proceeded;

- Schott Music of Mainz, Germany, for the right to translate and edit Siegfried Vogelsänger's Praetorius biography;

- the congregation I serve in South Austin, for their support of my ministry, continuing education, and well-being; and

- my dear wife Katherine, for her unremitting love, support, and care.

Finally, I must thank the triune God himself. He is the one ultimately responsible for my confessional Lutheran faith, upbringing, formation, education, spiritual care, and worship life. Because of this, reading Praetorius' dedications, prefaces, letters, books, and other documents and listening to his music is, in some ways, like recalling a meaningful conversation with a close friend or a memorable classroom lecture, even when it is my first encounter.

But more importantly, because (and only because) of the saving work of Jesus Christ, the Son of God, I can confidently and wholeheartedly say with Praetorius: Heaven is my fatherland, my true home.

To God alone be the glory.

Annotated Abbreviations

NOTE: IF AN ENTRY does not contain complete bibliographic information, see Bibliography. Also see Bibliography for URLs (if available). If abbreviations representing original foreign-language works are cited after an English quote or quotes in this book, the translation is mine (NJB).

- *DWB—Deutsches Wörterbuch von Jacob und Wilhelm Grimm.* 33 vols. Leipzig, 1854–1971.

  Begun by the Brothers Grimm in 1838 and concluded with a source index volume in 1971, *DWB* is the most comprehensive dictionary of the German language, and indispensable for work in fifteenth, sixteenth, and seventeenth century German. Also available online at http://woerterbuchnetz.de/cgi-bin/WBNetz/wbgui_py?sigle=DWB.

- FS—Tuckermann. *Leichpredigt. Des Ehrnvesten/ Achtbarn vnd Kunstreichen Herrn. Michaelis Praetorii* etc. (Funeral Sermon for the Distinguished, Estimable, and Accomplished Gentleman, Michael Praetorius, the Late Music Director for the Duke of Brunswick, Who Fell Asleep Blessedly in God on February 15, and Was Buried on February 23 in the Heinrichtown Church).

  This work, translated in its entirety in Appendix III, includes Pastor Tuckermann's marvelous sermon on Genesis 32:24b–32, his graveside remarks, Tobias Herold's tribute, and Friedrich Hildebrand's epitaph and tribute.

- GA—Blume. *Gesamtausgabe der Musikalischen Werke von Michael Praetorius* (The Complete Musical Works of Michael Praetorius). Vols. 1–19. Wolfenbüttel: Georg Kallmeyer Verlag, 1928–1940. (In

1947, Kallmeyer Verlag became Möseler Verlag, which continued to print vols. 1–19 under the new name.) Vol. 20 and index. Wolfenbüttel: Möseler Verlag, 1960.

These volumes can be found in many university and college libraries. The index volume also contains, among other things, excerpts from Duke Julius' Church Order of 1569.

- *LSL*—Praetorius. *Leiturgodia Sionia Latina* etc. (The Latin Liturgody of Zion, Comprising under this General Title All the More Familiar and Selected Latin Church Songs That Are Usually Repeated in Church Throughout the Year in the Morning, Main, and Evening Services *etc.*).

  This is the general introduction Praetorius composed for the Latin installments of his series *Musae Sioniae*. It contains a short foreword to the reader, an illustrative table, an extensive observation about the author's purpose and goal for the collection, some remarks on "certain musical vices that occur in older choral works," and some extensive quotes from the first Lutheran cantor, Johann Walther. Like most of Praetorius' Latin works, it remains woefully understudied.

- *LW*—Pelikan, Jaroslav, Hilton C. Oswald, Helmut T. Lehmann, et al., eds. *Luther's Works*. Vols. 1–30. St. Louis: Concordia Publishing House, 1955–1976. Vols. 31–55. Philadelphia: Fortress Press, 1957–1986.

  In other works this series is sometimes abbreviated AE for "American Edition."

- *MGG*—*Die Musik in Geschichte und Gegenwart* (Music Past and Present). 2nd ed., edited by Ludwig Finscher. 27 vols. Kassel: Bärenreiter, 1994–2007.

  This musical encyclopedia, founded by Friedrich Blume, is divided into two groups—Sachteil (Things) (ten volumes, including an index volume; 1994–1999) and Personenteil (People) (seventeen volumes; 1999–2007).

- *Miss.*—Praetorius. *Missodia Sionia* etc. (The Missody of Zion, Containing the Sacred Songs Customarily Used in Church in the Forenoon Service Known as the Main Service).

Reprinted in GA 11. This work's importance for Praetorius biographical research is touched on in Appendix I.

- *MS* 1—Praetorius. *Musae Sioniae* etc. (The Muses of Zion, or Concerted Religious Songs Based on the Most Prominent German Psalms by Mr. Luther and Others). Erster Theil (First Installment).

  Reprinted in GA 1. See also *MS* Coll.

- *MS* 2—Praetorius. *Musae Sioniae* etc. (The Muses of Zion: Concerted Religious Songs Based on the Most Prominent German Psalms and Hymns). Ander Theil (Second Installment).

  Reprinted in GA 2. See also *MS* Coll.

- *MS* 3—Praetorius. *Musae Sioniae* etc. Dritter Theil (Third Installment). Cantus I. Chori. Helmstedt: Jacob Lucius, 1607.

  Reprinted in GA 3. See also *MS* Coll.

- *MS* 4—Praetorius. *Musae Sioniae* etc. Vierdter Theil (Fourth Installment). Cantus I. Chori. Helmstedt: Jacob Lucius, 1607.

  Reprinted in GA 4. See also *MS* Coll.

- *MS* Coll.—*Musae Sioniae Michaëlis Praetorii C. Darinnen Deutsche Psalmen und geistliche Lieder / wie sie durchs gantze Jar in der Christlichen Kirchen breuchlich* etc. (The Muses of Zion by Michael Praetorius of Creuzburg, Containing German Psalms and Hymns, As They Are Customarily Sung in the Christian Church Throughout the Year *etc.*).

  In 1607 *MS* 1–4 were published together. This special edition included a portrait, special prefaces, and a general index. It is viewable on the Royal Danish Library's website: http://www5.kb.dk/en/nb/samling/ma/digmus/pre1700_indices/praetorius.html.

- *MSL*—Praetorius. *Musarum Sioniarum Motectae et Psalmi Latini* (Latin Motets and Psalms of the Muses of Zion).

  Reprinted in GA 10. This too is available on the Royal Danish Library's website at the same link as at *MS* Coll.

- PG—Migne, J.-P., ed. *Patrologiae Cursus Completus*. Greek series. 161 vols. Paris, 1857–1886.

- PL—Migne, J.-P., ed. *Patrologiae Cursus Completus*. Latin series. 217 vols. Paris, 1844–1855.

  Migne did continue publishing volumes of the PL after 1855, but since these editions often have different page numbering, some publishing handbooks encourage writers to cite his original volumes.

- *Pol. Cad.*—Praetorius. *Polyhymnia Caduceatrix & Panegyrica* etc. (The Peacemaking and Celebratory Polyhymnia, Containing Solemn Concertos of Peace and Joy). Bassus-Generalis seu Continuus (Thorough Bass).

  Reprinted in GA 17. The other part-books (Primus–Decimus-quartus, or Parts 1–14) have a slightly altered title: *III. Polyhymnia Panegyrica Michaëlis Praetorii C. Darinnen XL Solennische Friedt-und Frewdens-Concert* (Polyhymnia III by Michael Praetorius: Celebratory, Containing Forty Solemn Concertos of Peace and Joy). The publication date given on their title pages is 1618, even though they too were published in 1619. These are all viewable on the Royal Danish Library's website: http://www5.kb.dk/en/nb/samling/ma/digmus/pre1700_indices/praetorius_polyhym.html.

- *SM 1*—Praetorius. *Syntagmatis Musici Tomus Primus* (First Volume of the Musical Compendium).

  See Chapter 4 for more information about Praetorius' *Syntagma Musicum* series.

- *SM 1E*—Fleming. "Michael Praetorius, Music Historian: An Annotated Translation of *Syntagma Musicum* I, Part I."

  Fleming translated pages i–xxiv (from the title page through the dedicatory epistle), xliv–xlv (Foreword to the Benevolent Reader), 1–152, and 447–57. This dissertation has also been microfilmed by University Microfilms International (now ProQuest LLC); the microfilm can be accessed at many university libraries. While this translation does a fine job introducing English-speaking readers to this largely ignored work by Praetorius, its deficiencies have led me usually to cite *SM 1* and provide my own translation.

- *SM 2*—*Syntagmatis Musici Michaelis Praetorii C. Tomus Secundus De Organographia* (Second Volume of the Musical Compendium of Michael Praetorius of Creuzburg: On Instrumentography). 1619.

Later published with *Theatrum Instrumentorum Seu Sciagraphia Michaëlis Praetorii C.* (Exhibition of Instruments or Shadow Drawing of Michael Praetorius of Creuzburg). 1620.

Sciagraphia or "Shadow Drawing" refers to the use of shadows to create the illusion of depth; today we would call this three-dimensional illustration. The title at least suggests that Praetorius did the "shadow drawing" of these instruments himself, which would certainly add another dimension to his character. However, "of Michael Praetorius of Creuzburg" could also simply refer to his careful oversight of the project and his organization of the illustrations. A 1929 reprint including both parts can be viewed here: https://books.google.com/books?id=yqsIAQAAIAAJ&printsec=frontcover.

- *SM* 2E1—Praetorius. *Syntagma Musicum II: De Organographia, Parts I & II.*

  This volume includes the instrument exhibition.

- *SM* 2E2—Praetorius. "Syntagma Musicum II: De Organographia, Parts III—V with Index."

  This work is formatted so that each original page from *SM* 2 appears on the left and the translation of that page appears opposite it on the right.

- *SM* 3—*Syntagmatis Musici Michaelis Praetorii C. Tomus Tertius* (Third Volume of the Musical Compendium of Michael Praetorius of Creuzburg).

- *SM* 3E—Praetorius. *Syntagma Musicum III.*

  This edition includes the page numbers of the original edition in the margins. This translation's approach and deficiencies often led me to cite *SM* 3 and provide my own translation, but I then included "cf." with the corresponding page number(s) in this volume.

- WA—Knaake, J. K. F., Gustav Kawerau, Carl Bertheau, et al., eds. *D. Martin Luthers Werke: kritische Gesamtausgabe* (Complete Works of Dr. Martin Luther: Critical Edition). Vols. 1–57 and partial General Index. Weimar: Hermann Böhlaus Nachfolger, 1883–1948.

  WA stands for *Weimarer Ausgabe* (Weimar Edition) and is the standard abbreviation for this definitive series. Though this edition also includes other divisions (*Tischreden* or Table Talk, *Deutsche Bibel* or German Bible, and *Briefwechsel* or Correspondence), and more volumes were also added to this division (*Schriften/Werke* or Writings/Works), these original volumes comprise this edition's core.

- WBB—Nolte. *Chronicon Der Stadt und Vestung Wolffenbüttel, in sich haltend des seel. Herrn Ober-Amtmanns Christoph Woltereck Begräbniß-Buch der Kirchen B. M. V. zu Wolffenbüttel* etc. (Chronology of the City and Stronghold of Wolfenbüttel, Containing the Late Chief Officer Christoph Woltereck's Burial Book for the Church of the Blessed Virgin Mary in Wolfenbüttel).

  Pages 89–90 confirm the date of Praetorius' burial, identify the location of his burial, and describe his memorial slab in detail. Page 101 documents the burial of Praetorius' widow. Nolte reports in his Introduction (*Vorbericht*) that Woltereck started to have his *Begräbniß-Buch* (Burial Book) printed in Blankenburg in 1731. But he passed away "over the completed print copy" in 1735. Nolte was commissioned in 1740 by Woltereck's surviving widow to complete his intended work, which was finally issued in 1747.

- WGD—Gurlitt. *Michael Praetorius (Creuzbergensis).*

  This book consists of *a*) an unaltered reprint of the inaugural dissertation Gurlitt submitted to the philosophical faculty of the University of Leipzig in 1914 (Chapters 1 & 2; Leipzig: Breitkopf & Härtel, 1915; https://books.google.com/books?id=VqEUAQAAIAA J&printsec=frontcover), plus *b*) the first printing of Chapters 3 and 4 with appendices on the basis of Breitkopf & Härtel's galley proofs from Gurlitt's estate. See Chapter 6 of the present work for more information. Gurlitt's work not only remains the single most useful reference work for the life and work of Praetorius, but also contains the only biography of Praetorius' father, Michael Schulteis.

Original Introduction

The creative work of Michael Praetorius strikingly reflects the shift in music history from the Late Middle Ages to the Early Modern Age in Germany. One encounters both prevailing traditions of the German music scene—on the one hand the civic, ecclesiastical-religious, Dutch-German choristry[1] tradition, rooted in the Latin schools and municipal parish churches, and on the other hand the courtly, Italian-German concerto tradition, tailored to the self-distinguishing needs of the nobility and the rising principalities. Both traditions unite in the grand musical form of Praetorius' time, the choral concerto.[2]

WHEN ONE SURVEYS THE almost fifty years of Michael Praetorius' life, three distinct stages present themselves:

- His youth and schooling in Creuzburg, Torgau, and Zerbst and his studies in Frankfurt an der Oder[3] and Helmstedt, from 1571[4] until approximately 1593/94 (about twenty-two years);

- His time in the service of Heinrich Julius, bishop of Halberstadt and duke of Brunswick and Lüneburg, as chamber organist and court music director in Gröningen and Wolfenbüttel, from approximately 1593/94 until the death of the duke in 1613 (about twenty years);

---

1. See Glossary.

2. Gurlitt, afterword to *Syntagma Musicum III* (1958), 1–2.

3. Some German cities end with "an der," "am" (short for "an dem"), or "ob der," followed by the name of the river on or above which they are situated, in order to distinguish them from other cities with the same name. In this case, Frankfurt an der Oder distinguishes it from Frankfurt am Main.—Trans.

4. The author had 1572; see Appendix II. I also accordingly adjusted the figure in the parentheses at the end of the bullet.—Trans.

- The time of his continued activity at the court in Wolfenbüttel in the service of Duke Friedrich Ulrich of Brunswick and Lüneburg and as nonresident music director at the courts of Dresden and Halle, in addition to numerous duties at other princely courts, accompanied by trips that led him as far as the royal court in Denmark (about eight years).

From 1915 to 2005, a number of musicological works were published with different approaches to and findings on Praetorius' life and work. What follows is a summary of these. This book is meant to be a compendium in layperson's terms for music lovers and music scholars alike, acquainting them with the life and work of Michael Praetorius and inciting them to further studies. The volumes of the GA[5], available in numerous libraries, can also help to that end. They offer a wealth of additional information beyond the musical notation and lyrics.

5. See Annotated Abbreviations.

— 1 —

Childhood and Youth

The Father, Michael Schulteis

MICHAEL PRAETORIUS WAS THE youngest child of the Lutheran pastor Michael Schulteis and probably his third wife Gertrud, the daughter of the Torgau pastor Gabriel Zwilling (also called Didymus).[1] The difference in names between father and son is due to the custom of scholars and artists at the time of Latinizing German names. Thus Schulteis (Schultheiß, Schultes, Schultz) was changed to Praetorius.[2] Michael's father, however, appears to have stuck to the German form his whole life, so that all of his children[3] were most likely baptized with the name Schulteis. This is confirmed by the chronicle of the Torgau Latin School, in which Michael Praetorius is listed as "Michael Schultes" among the

1. Zwilling (German) and Didymus (Greek) both mean "twin." The author's original reads: "Michael Schulteis and his second (or third) wife Magdalena, the daughter of the Torgau patrician Andreas Leicher." See Appendix I.—Trans.

2. According to DWB, Schultheisz is a compound noun formed from Schuld, "debt, obligation," and Heisz, the old agent noun of heiszen, "to command, enjoin." It thus denotes someone who commands or imposes an obligation or duty. The word "consistently denotes a local authority with predominantly judicial and executive power, as a subordinate official/officer or representative of the centenar or the count." From the sixteenth century onward, the title usually denoted a village judge or magistrate. Michael Praetorius likely elected to Latinize his family name as Praetorius (Latin for "magistrate-related, one with the rank of magistrate") instead of Praetor ("magistrate") because, although his family name perhaps indicated descent from one or more magistrates, neither he nor his father had actually been magistrates themselves.—Trans.

3. The author's original has: "all seven children from this marriage." See Appendix I.—Trans.

189 (!) pupils of the fifth or entry-level class for 1576.[4] (The same spelling was also occasionally used to identify his father.) In the chronicle his oldest brother Andreas is already identified with the name Prätorius, as a former "Doctor of Theology, Pastor and Professor in Frankfurt."[5]*

Michael Schulteis was born around 1515 in Bunzlau in Silesia (today Bolesławiec, Poland). He obtained his bachelor's degree, the lowest academic degree, from the University of Wittenberg, and was employed in 1534 as a teacher at the Latin school in Torgau.[6] There he was a colleague of the first Lutheran cantor[7] Johann Walther, the man who advised Martin Luther in music-related questions.[8] At Luther's recommendation, Schulteis received a stipend in 1538 from the Saxon elector Johann Friedrich (John Frederick) the Magnanimous for the continuation of his studies in Wittenberg, and in 1539 he returned to Torgau as a chaplain.[9] His ministerial colleague at the parish church, Gabriel Zwilling, characterized him as "well disciplined" in his studies, "a fine, learned, God-fearing, diligent, and pious man."[10]

During his studies in Wittenberg, Michael Schulteis had become a staunch adherent of the theological teachings of Martin Luther. This put him into a number of very difficult situations in the following years, during the infighting among the Lutheran theologians.

*Luther died in 1546, and in 1547 Holy Roman Emperor Charles V defeated the Schmalkaldic League, an alliance of Lutheran princes, at the Battle of Mühlberg. Charles then attempted to bring the subdued Lutheran territories back into the Roman Catholic fold. He issued the "Declaration of the Sacred Imperial Majesty as to How Religious Affairs Shall Proceed in the Empire Until the Decision of the General Council," or Augsburg Interim for short, in May 1548. This decree put good works back into the doctrine of justification and undermined the natural bondage of the human will in spiritual affairs that Luther had emphasized. It also commanded the formerly Lutheran churches to reintroduce invocation of the departed saints, prayers for souls in purgatory, processions,

---

4. Böhm, *Chronik der Oberschule Torgau*, 100.

5. *Ibid.*, 102.

6. *Foerstemann, *Album Academiae Vitebergensis*, 133b, #30; WGD, 7–10.

7. See Glossary.

8. *See *SM* 1:451ff; *SM* 1E:314ff.

9. *WGD, 16–18, 29. On "chaplain," see Glossary.

10. Letter to Elector Johann Friedrich (August 4, 1544); cited in WGD, 30.

festivals, consecrations, traditional Roman Catholic vestments (articles of liturgical clothing), votive masses, and seven sacraments.[11] It did allow the laypeople to receive the wine in the Lord's Supper and the priests to marry, but no one explained that even these concessions were invalid without an official dispensation from the pope.[12]

Philipp Melanchthon, who had been Luther's colleague and was now generally viewed as his successor and the new leader of the Reformation movement, initially yielded to the emperor's demands. This marked the beginning of a noticeable pattern of indecision on his part.[13] The reaction to the Interim in the formerly Lutheran territories was overwhelmingly negative, and two opposing camps developed within Lutheranism. Their irreconcilable positions focused in large part on *Mitteldinge* ("middle things") or adiaphora—things which, in and of themselves, God neither commands nor forbids in the Scriptures.

The one camp, called Philippists after Philipp Melanchthon, were much more willing to yield to the emperor's authority in adiaphora, especially in liturgical matters. They claimed that "the liturgy, as an external matter, had no doctrinal significance," and that "Christ determines the doctrine, the government the church order."[14]

The other camp consisted of the so-called Gnesio Lutherans (from the Greek word γνήσιος/*gnesios*, "genuine"), also called Flacians after the most prominent member of their camp, Matthias Flacius. They continued to advocate a position consistent with Luther's doctrine that the only way to salvation was through faith in the grace of God exhibited in Jesus Christ. They claimed that liturgical practices should be consistent with one's doctrine, and that there were no adiaphora in situations where one's confession of faith was involved.[15] So in this context, where secular princes and even prominent theologians were trying to placate the emperor, and the emperor was trying to return them to the Roman Catholic fold with its false doctrine, the Gnesio Lutherans maintained

---

11. Lutherans only acknowledge two sacraments when a sacrament is defined as a) a rite instituted by Christ b) in which the grace of God and the forgiveness of sins are given c) together with and in one or more earthly elements (water, bread, wine). If clause *c* is omitted, then they add absolution and acknowledge three. See Article 13 of the *Apology of the Augsburg Confession*.

12. Olson, *Matthias Flacius*, 84–85.

13. *Ibid.*, 85–86, 93–97.

14. *Ibid.*, 117.

15. *Ibid.*, 112–15, 121.

that one should not yield even to the demand that the clergymen wear the surplice—a white vestment, similar to the alb, but of a wider and shorter cut. Though an adiaphoron in itself, it would pose a stumbling block to ordinary believers and give a false impression to the opponents of Lutheranism, encouraging them in their continued efforts to suppress Lutheran doctrine.[16]

In April 1549, during a conference held in Torgau to discuss new liturgical practices, Gabriel Zwilling, Michael Schulteis' colleague, preached two strong sermons against the winds of change in the air. Elector Moritz (Maurice) of Saxony promptly dismissed him from office and imprisoned him. His replacement, Georg Mohr, insisted that Schulteis wear a surplice. Schulteis refused and was also arrested.[17] On June 3, Schulteis submitted a defense of his refusal to Elector Moritz, and on June 6, to the elector's representatives and counselors in Torgau:

> For since the confession of our faith is demanded of us, no change should be made at this time. And if I would approve or accept the most inconsequential thing, I would have to abandon God the Almighty, deny the Lord Christ, worship the devil and serve him, and deceive and mislead Your Electoral Grace and everyone else, burdening you all with innumerable sins and God's eternal and temporal wrath. That I ought not, will not, and cannot do.[18]

After being mistreated by the guards, being summoned to a hearing on June 12 conducted by Wittenberg theologians, being denounced by them as a "fanatic" and "mentally unbalanced," and yet refusing to alter his position, Schulteis was banned from the country.[19]*

That same year he was able to find a pastoral position in Creuzburg an der Werra in Thuringia (in the vicinity of Eisenach). The congregation there was clearly happy with him. A visitation report from the year 1554

16. *Ibid.*, 131–38.

17. *Ibid.*, 133–34.

18. Clemen, *Beiträge zur Reformationsgeschichte*, 42.

19. Olson, *Matthias Flacius*, 134–35. Matthias Flacius himself commented on this "Torgau Affair" eleven years later: "Now it is certainly true that [Gabriel Zwilling] and his deacon assistant, Master Michael Schulteis, did an excellent work with their confession and cross, and it contributed greatly to the preservation of the pure religion in Meissen, but they were poorly rewarded for it. For the leaders of the adiaphoristic heresy tortured them horribly . . . They cast off [Zwilling's] chaplain into poverty" (Flacius, *Gründliche Verlegung*, fol. Aa iii verso).—Trans.

reads: "The pastor Michael Schulteis is a learned man; his teaching and conduct are sufficiently known and acclaimed."[20] Here he could also en-

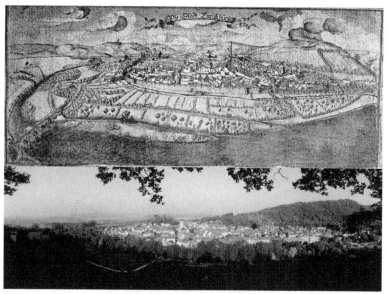

Fig. 1. Above: J. G. Busch, *Die Stadt Creutzburg*, c. 1717, drawing. Below: Panorama of Creuzburg, 2018, photo. Both views are from the east. Note the prominent steeple of St. Nicholas' Church (much taller in Busch's drawing) and the castle for which the city is named SW of the church (marked with a D in Busch's sketch, surrounded by trees in the photo).—Trans.

joy, at least at first, an undisturbed family life with his wife.[21] After their son Andreas, who was born before 1549 while they were still in Torgau, their second son Johannes (c. 1552) and their daughters Maria (1554) and Brigitte (1562) were all born in Creuzburg.[22]

*In 1555, Charles V signed the Peace of Augsburg, which permitted the free practice of Lutheranism in the Holy Roman Empire and established the principle of *cuius regio, eius religio*—whoever rules the territory determines its religion. But the Lutherans were still divided by controversies, and political power played an increasingly significant role

20. Cited in WGD, 40.

21. By this time he had perhaps already married his second wife, Magdalena Leicher. See Appendix I.—Trans.

22. Ludewig, "Genealogische Forschungen zur Familie Praetorius." (The author also included "Sabine [c. 1556]," but see Appendix I. Sabine seems to have been born in Torgau in 1558 to a Mr. Leicher and Gertrud née Zwilling, Schulteis' eventual third wife.—Trans.)

Fig. 2. Looking east toward St. Nicholas' Church in Creuzburg from the site of the former parsonage, 2018, photo. See also Fig. 3.—Trans.

in them. The Protestant princes were attempting to codify the various confessional statements in their territorially controlled church governments. These governments obligated their subjects to side with their respective territorial prince in religious matters, including matters of controversy. Those primarily affected by this were, not surprisingly, the pastors. For they had to publicly represent the position prescribed at any given time—with their sermons and official acts—and they were examined on this during visitations. If the examination turned up any deviations from the religious confession enforced in that territory, the pastor only had one of two choices—to submit or to leave the territory and look elsewhere for a position corresponding to his confession.

Thus in 1562 the theological battles between the Gnesio Lutherans and Philippists caught up with Schulteis once again, in particular the controversy about free will.* In 1563 he had to leave the territory with his family on this account, and he found a new pastoral position in Roben (by Gera) in 1565.[23] But by 1569 the situation in Thuringia had already changed again and Schulteis was able to return to Creuzburg that same year, since the "[city] council together with the entire community" had

23. *WGD, 45–56.

"lost [him] against their will."[24] The Schulteis couple's daughter Magdalena was born there circa 1570, and in 1571 their youngest son Michael, probably on September 27 or 28.[25] But already in 1573 Schulteis lost the pastoral position in Creuzburg for the second time. Even so, the city

Fig. 3. Above: Historical marker: "Here stood the birth house of Michael Praetorius. It was destroyed by fire on Sept. 24, 1634. Michael Praetorius was born on Feb. 15 [incorrect; see Appendix II], 1571, in Creuzburg and died on Feb. 15, 1621, in Wolfenbüttel. He was the preeminent court music director and composer of his time in Protestant Germany. He has bequeathed to posterity a comprehensive compositional and musicological body of work." The last word—*gegenüber*, added after the marker was moved—informs the reader that the site is actually across the street opposite the marker. Bottom: Birth site of Michael Praetorius. Ruins of the old city wall can be seen along the hill in the background.—Trans.

burgomasters and council drew up a moving testimonial for "their faithful and steadfast spiritual shepherd," which reports that he had "been dismissed from his office and ministry without cause and expelled in spite of prior pleading.

> For he has faithfully taught and preached the saving Word of God purely, clearly, and undistorted, according to the prophetic and apostolic Scriptures and the writings of Luther; he has discharged his ministry [*Predigtamt*] with teaching, rebuking, admonishing, and, attendant to all of this, with all diligence. He

24. Creuzburg City Council, letter to Duke Johann Wilhelm of Saxe-Weimar (May 26, 1569); cited in WGD, 56.

25. The author's original sentence concluded: "and circa 1572 their youngest son Michael, whose exact birthdate is still unknown." See Appendix II.—Trans.

has also conducted himself among us at all times irreproachably, honorably, and well, with all Christian propriety, both for his own part and on the part of his family. We consequently do not know how to talk about and praise his doctrine and ministry [*Amt*] or his and his family's good Christian life and conduct in any manner other than a fitting one, with all respect, affection, and approval. And since it is the will of our dear God to entreat him for this and possible to do so: We would be very glad to put up with and endure him as our pastor, and to keep him and his family among us. We nevertheless leave the matter in the hands of our dear God.[26]

Nevertheless, the congregation and their pastor had to conform to the regulations of their territorial prince, and Schulteis had fourteen days to leave the territory.

Fig. 4. *Torgau*, engraving in Matthäus Merian's heirs, eds., *Topographia* for Upper Saxony, Thuringia, Meissen, and Lusatia (1650).

He returned to Torgau, to the city in which he had first begun his activity as a teacher. He was now about sixty years old, without job or income; he and his family were dependent on the help of relatives and friends. In a 1578 visitation report for Torgau by Polycarp Leyser, one can read about Schulteis' religious conduct by that point:

There is a man in the city named Michael Schultz [*sic*]; he was formerly a pastor in Thuringia. He is currently staying in the city, is an overt Flacian, and is already going on three years of abstaining from Communion and the ministry as a whole. There is also a concern that he might have secret disciples, and

26. Notice (*Kundschaft*) of the Creuzburg City Council (August 21, 1573); cited in WGD, 62. (I included more of the original quote than the author did.—Trans.)

the pastor [Caspar Heidenreich] does not know what he should do with him when he dies.[27]

Schooling in Torgau and Zerbst[28]

The foregoing describes the circumstances in which the younger Michael grew up in Torgau. He obviously would have received a strict Lutheran upbringing under the direction of his father. In Torgau Michael attended the Latin school, whose condition is described as follows in a report from 1578: "The school is in good order. The schoolteachers are pure and accurate in their teaching and have good gifts for instruction, keep good discipline and are diligent."[29] The cantor Michael Voigt gave the music instruction; the pupils learned to sing "choral and figural music" (one-part hymns and multi-part motets).[30] This prepared the students for singing in the choristry[31], which Michael Voigt directed as Johann Walther's successor. One of Michael Praetorius' fellow pupils, Jacob Bornitz, later reported that he had seen and heard songs composed by Michael himself while attending school with him[32]—evidence of Michael's musical talent at an early age.

After the two sons Andreas and Johannes had already taken up the study of theology in Jena in 1570 and 1572, respectively,[33] the Schulteis family apparently reorganized itself around 1582.[34] The precise motives for this can no longer be ascertained. Whatever the case, the members of the family thereby escaped the Torgau plague years of 1584–85, to which numerous Latin schools also fell victim. Schulteis and his wife moved

27. Cited in WGD, 64; corresponds to Pallas, *Die Registraturen der Kirchenvisitationen*, 46, where, however, this part of the report is excerpted and Schultz is misprinted as Schütz.

28. See also Aumüller, "Lebens- und Arbeitsbedingungen hessischen Organisten," 100–103.

29. Pallas, *Die Registraturen der Kirchenvisitationen*, 45; also cited in WGD, 75, n. 4.

30. *Pallas, 44,45.

31. See Glossary.

32. *Bornitz, *Tractatus Politicus*, 210 (ch. 101). Bornitz became a legal doctor and imperial councilor in Schweidnitz (today Świdnica, Poland) and gained some renown as a political economist.

33. *Mentz and Jauernig, *Die Matrikel der Universität Jena*, 243. Andreas obtained his master's degree on July 15, 1572 (*ibid.*, 571).

34. Ludewig, "Genealogische Forschungen zur Familie Praetorius."

with their unmarried daughters to Treuenbrietzen to live with their daughter Sabine and her husband Andreas Lussovius, who had been the superindendent and head pastor there since 1580. Michael Schulteis and his wife died and were buried in Treuenbrietzen,[35] though their death dates are unknown.

The younger Michael went to live with his oldest sister Maria in Zerbst around 1582. She had entered into her second marriage there in 1580, to the burgomaster and city councilor Jacob von Jena. There Michael most likely attended the Nicolai School affiliated with the Nicolai Church. The school order was oriented according to Melanchthon's pedagogical ideal.[36] Along with the biblical writings—including a psalter in the form of hymns—the pupils were instructed in the writings of antiquity. The school order prescribed that they speak Latin even outside of instruction, and violations were punished. The musical instruction imparted the fundamentals of basic music theory, which in many Latin schools of the time was taught using a systematically constructed music theory manual by Heinrich Faber that had appeared in numerous editions.[37] The singing prepared the students for participation in the school choir and the soliciting street choir (*Kurrende*), the *chorus musicus*. Here Michael Praetorius was "involved in a musical environment that, as in Torgau, stood in the tradition of Johann Walt[h]er, but was also open to . . . modern developments and could provide him at least as much stimulation as the rather conservative Torgau."[38]

Studies in Frankfurt an der Oder and Helmstedt

In the spring of 1583, at age eleven, Michael Praetorius matriculated as "Kruciburgensis [of Creuzburg]" at the Viadrina, the famed university in Frankfurt an der Oder.[39] The goal of his studies seemed prescribed: He

35. *See point 3 in Praetorius' will on p. 112.

36. Arbeitsgruppe am Francisceum Zerbst, *Philipp Melanchthon und Zerbst*, 23ff. (See also WA 26:236ff; *LW* 40:314ff.—Trans.)

37. First edition: *Compendiolum musicae pro incipientibus* (Nuremberg: Johann Montanus [vom Berg] and Ulrich Neuber, 1548).

38. Aumüller, "Lebens- und Arbeitsbedingungen hessischen Organisten," 102; see also *MGG* Sachteil, 9:2381, s.v. "Zerbst."

39. *Friedlaender, *Aeltere Universitäts-Matrikeln*, 303b, line 30, #180. A Latin note beneath Praetorius' name says, "This enrollee and the preceding four did not take the oath on account of age." Gurlitt explains: "No one was permitted to take the university

wanted (or was supposed) to become a pastor like his father and his two brothers Andreas and Johannes. He was able to take up this course of study in 1585 at age thirteen, which was not unusual in those days. He probably did not move from Zerbst to Frankfurt by himself, but was accompanied by his sister Maria and her husband. Perhaps they traveled via Treuenbrietzen, in order to visit their parents and other siblings there. Later Michael abbreviated his name using the initials MPC, in which the C stands for *Creuzburgensis,* "of Creuzburg," and from this he formulated his motto M*ihi* P*atria* C*oelum*—"Heaven is my fatherland."

Fig. 5. Franz Friedrich, *Portrait of Andreas Musculus*, 1577, woodcut.

Andreas and Johannes Praetorius had continued their theological studies in Frankfurt an der Oder after their semesters in Jena;[40] at both universities the theological teaching was governed by the influence of the Gnesio Lutherans.[41] Andreas had obtained his doctor's degree in theology on May 15, 1576. That same day he married Theodora, the daughter of Andreas Musculus,[42] the famed professor of theology, rector of the university, and general superintendent of the Margraviate of Brandenburg, who had studied in Wittenberg together with Michael Schulteis from 1538–39. After receiving his doctorate, Andreas Praetorius was appointed by Elector

---

oath until he had reached age thirteen" (WGD, 77).

40. *For the conclusion of Andreas' studies at Jena, see WGD, 82 (though the date should be June 9, 1573, not June 5). For Andreas' and Johannes' enrollments at the Viadrina in the fall of 1573 and spring of 1575, respectively, see Friedlaender, *Aeltere Universitäts-Matrikeln*, 234, lines 1–2, #89, and 245, lines 11–12, #102. For Johannes' bachelor's (Apr. 17, 1578) and master's (Oct. 13, 1580) degrees in philosophy, see Bauch, *Das älteste Decanatsbuch*, 75,78.

41. The author has "Old Lutherans," but he uses this label anachronistically, since it was not coined until the infamous Prussian Union of 1817, when it was used to refer to those who were against union with the Reformed and wished to remain Lutheran.—Trans.

42. *Becman, *Notitia Universitatis Francofurtanae*, 56b.

Johann Georg (John George) of Brandenburg to be his court preacher. After the death of Andreas Musculus in 1581, he was appointed to be Musculus' successor "for the duration of his life," with the exception of the general superintendency, which was given to Christoph Cornerus.[43]

Andreas saw it as his primary preaching task "to have an effect 'in these last, evil times with warnings and admonitions to repentance and reform' and 'to discharge faithfully not just the Holy Spirit's ministry of comforting but also that of rebuking people in stations high and low.'"[44] In doing so, he not only took on various common citizens in his sermons, including prominent ones, but also city councilors, so that he gained a reputation as the "Frankfurt pope." Michael Praetorius initially lived with this brother and his wife and their three children. One might wonder whether Andreas' family life was just as dominated by such an austere mood focused on repentance and the end times, as his sermons were. If so, it certainly would have had an impact on the adolescent Michael. Through Andreas, however, he also became acquainted with numerous important persons from the religious and public spheres. This included several professors at the university with whom Andreas enjoyed friendly ties.

Michael also became acquainted with life in a large city for the first time. The Frankfurt townspeople had already reached a level of considerable prosperity in the fourteenth and fifteenth centuries, which facilitated the development of a diverse musical life. This included the religious music in the Protestant churches, led by the University Church of St. Mary (*Unser lieben Frauen* or Our Dear Lady's Church), with its thirty-six altars and the picture Bible in its colorful windows from the late fourteenth century.

In addition, there was the secular music at social and public events. Occupying a special position was the lute music cultivated among the students and in the patricians' homes, which was influenced by Italian madrigals and villanelle and by Polish, French, and English dances.[45] One can thus safely assume that "in the atmosphere of the university city, which was an extraordinarily vibrant one both intellectually and especially musically, [Michael Praetorius] was exposed to significant musical impressions and influences that were crucial to his personal development."[46]

---

43. WGD, 83–85. (I added everything from "with the exception" to the end.—Trans.)

44. WGD, 85, citing Andreas Praetorius, BPABEION (1584), fol.)(i verso.

45. *MGG* Sachteil, 3:665ff, s.v. "Frankfurt an der Oder."

46. Grimm, *Meister der Renaissancemusik an der Viadrina*, 179.

Unfortunately we have no testimonies from him or anyone else about the effect that life in his brother's house and in the large city had on him, nor about the effect of his studies in the various disciplines—philosophy and theology chief among them—or of his regular attendance at church services. In the large University Church he was able to experience the organ playing of organist Georg Bruck and the choristry under the direction of the cantor Christoph Richard. We do not know, however, what impression their music made on him or whether he put the singing skills he had already acquired in Torgau and Zerbst to use in the choristry.

It did not take long before his adolescent life in Frankfurt was overshadowed by deeply affecting events. On October 27, 1585, his brother Johannes died at the age of not much more than thirty.[47] Johannes had become pastor at the St. Georg Church in Frankfurt as a result of his brother Andreas' influence, and had married Elisabeth, the daughter of Johannes Knobloch, the professor of medicine. In the city council minutes for September 15, 1585, Johannes is described as "reserved and quiet, also a good preacher."[48]

The year 1586 initially brought a happier event: His sister Brigitte and Daniel Sachse, the rector of the school at St. Martin, married on November 28. (We do not know if the parents and siblings from Treuenbrietzen and Zerbst made the journey to attend this celebration.) But just four weeks later, on December 20, 1586, his brother Andreas died at the age of less than forty after being in frail health for some time.[49]

How did Michael deal with these events, and how was he now going to continue with his studies? He later wrote about this:

> As for me, I cannot fail to mention that, when I was still quite young, I was permitted to devote myself to and engage in literary training both publicly and privately under the university's flags— nobly set up by the elector of Brandenburg—in the philosophical school. And I did so fruitfully, up until I was into my third year of filling the organist position in Frankfurt. Without me conceiving anything of the sort, this position was entrusted to me by the Frankfurt congregation, in order that I might be able to finish my studies more easily and successfully, which would have otherwise been interrupted by the demise of my brother. It was a

47. Gurlitt gives his death year as 1586 (WGD, 88). I was unable to verify either.—Trans.

48. Cited in WGD, 87.

49. WGD, 88.

position to which I was attracted more by the inclination of my
nature than by any instruction I ever received in it.[50]

This immediately raises the question: Where did Michael learn to
play the organ and achieve such proficiency in it that he was considered
capable of performing this task at approximately sixteen? There is no evidence to answer the question. One can only guess that he had perhaps received organ instruction in Zerbst from one of the organists active there
(Thomas or Lucas von Ende).[51] An additional question remains: Which
three years did he serve as the organist in Frankfurt? The first reference
point we have for this is the death of his brother Andreas on December
20, 1586. This means that Michael could not have taken up the position
before 1587, but it does not prove that he actually did so that year. In
the financial record books of St. Mary's, his predecessor Georg Bruck is
still mentioned one more time in 1587.[52] We can therefore infer that Michael's service likely began in the course of 1588 and lasted until 1590/91.
Oddly enough, however, Michael's name doesn't appear anywhere in the
financial records for those years. Not until later, in connection with the
employment of his successor, does it say, "after the departure of Michael
Praetorius," without any indication of date.[53]

Whatever the case, his subsistence was secured during those three
years: For his service as organist he received an annual honorarium of "at
least 70 florins, [in addition to] free housing, firewood, and clothing."[54]
(*Florin* is the French term for gulden; the monetary amount would perhaps have corresponded to the yearly income of a master craftsman in
those days.)[55] But what form did Michael's life now take after the death

---

50. *Miss.*, fol.)(4 verso; reprinted in GA 11:viii. (I translated this directly from the
Latin original rather than from the author's German translation, and included more of
the original quote than he did.—Trans.)

51. Aumüller, "Lebens- und Arbeitsbedingungen hessischen Organisten," 99ff.

52. Wolfgang Töppen, excerpt from the Church Records of St. Mary's Church in
Frankfurt an der Oder, graciously placed at the author's disposal in 2003.

53. Grimm, *Meister der Renaissancemusik an der Viadrina*, 181.

54. *Ibid.*, 176.

55. In approximate terms, this would have equalled $21,000 of current American
currency in Luther's time, about half a century earlier. Since prices rose on average by
1–1.5 percent per year in the sixteenth century and currency was coin- rather than
note-based, the free housing, firewood, and clothing was a considerable bonus. See
also Chapter 2, n. 24.—Trans.

of his brother? We only know that, starting in 1589, he lived in the "small organist's house" that had recently been rebuilt.[56]

What then could have prompted him to leave Frankfurt around 1590/91, apparently without completing his studies? Probably purely familial reasons: The widows of his two brothers had remarried in 1586 and 1588, and in 1591 his sister Brigitte had moved with her husband Daniel Sachse to Halberstadt, where he had taken up the position of head cathedral preacher. Michael thereby lost his last direct contacts with family members in Frankfurt. So he too made the sensible decision to move—to Halberstadt with his sister and brother-in-law. This would ensure the approximately nineteen-year-old young man of a family connection and that he would be provided for. But what would now become of his studies and career plans?

In a letter dated September 16, 1608, with no clear indicator of location, Praetorius writes that "it is now going on fifteen years since I hung up my studies here."[57] That means that he continued them after moving on from Frankfurt (1590/91), since by "here" he cannot mean Frankfurt. *Investigations have uncovered that Praetorius continued his studies in Helmstedt,[58] which was now home to the historian Reiner Reineccius. From 1578–1582, Reineccius had taught at the Viadrina in Frankfurt and had been a friend of Andreas Praetorius. In 1582, Reineccius was appointed to the University of Helmstedt, which had been founded in 1576 by Duke Julius of Brunswick (Braunschweig) and Lüneburg. Reineccius accepted the appointment, but he was exempted from all public classroom instruction at his own request. Instead he had to provide written instructions for the university's historical studies and privately train professors and students how to implement them. His special assignment was to supervise the historical studies of the young Duke Heinrich Julius. (In those days the university was about a day's journey from Halberstadt.) Reineccius could have also given Michael Praetorius private instruction, or assisted him in taking up his studies at the university.* He also could have made arrangements for his lodging there.

In a dedicatory epistle dated January 1605, Praetorius reports that he had already been associated with the court chapel ensemble of Duke Heinrich Julius of Brunswick and Lüneburg for more than ten years,

---

56. Grimm, 179.

57. Deeters, "Alte und neue Aktenfunde über Michael Praetorius," 107.

58. Forchert, "Musik zwischen Religion und Politik," 109.

that is, since the latter part of 1594.[59] He had thus stopped pursuing the career goal of becoming a pastor since that time. One must ask what circumstances could have prompted him to do so. It was probably the duke's connection to Reineccius. Moreover, the duke was looking for a successor to his chamber organist Antonius Ammerbach, after the latter's death circa 1590. The duke had commissioned an organ for his palace chapel in Gröningen in 1592—an extraordinary instrument in every respect and one of the largest in Germany. In this context Reineccius could have made the duke aware of the young, talented Praetorius. However, it is also conceivable that Praetorius' brother-in-law Daniel Sachse was the key connection. The duke, as bishop of Halberstadt, was Sachse's superior, and Sachse was already acquainted with Praetorius' organ skills from their time in Frankfurt.

In this context, however, a note in the ducal chamber accounts dated June 10, 1593, is worthy of mention: "To Carl Loff, organist, for the trip to Hamburg he was ordered to take: 20 thalers."[60] What else can this signify but the duke's intention to have the Gröningen town organist, Carl Loff, trained as his chamber organist by the famous Hamburg organist Hieronymus Praetorius? From this one can conclude that, at this point in time, there was probably not yet any connection between Duke Heinrich Julius and Praetorius.[61]

In the previously mentioned letter dated September 16, 1608, Praetorius writes (regretfully?): "Never in my life have I aspired to great honor and dignities; at the time when I became an organist, I could have easily become a great doctor"—of theology, like his brother Andreas?—"but it has always been better for me to live in fear and humility than in honor and distinction."[62] Pastor Tuckermann also reported in his graveside

59. *MSL*, dedication (dated Jan. 1605), fol. (2) verso; reprinted in GA 10:viii. (I added the final clause for clarification.—Trans.)

60. Cited in WGD, 113.

61. Cf. Forchert, "Musik zwischen Religion und Politik," 108ff, where he demonstrates that Praetorius entered the duke's service in 1593, and initially in a non-musical capacity, "apparently" occupying himself "with menial chancellery tasks, possibly also with clerical work." Also cf. WGD, 113, n. 4, where Gurlitt documents Carl Loff's dubious reputation. It was reported of him on April 24, 1589: "[He] is harshly accused of being very lazy in his work [and] of having no qualms about taking off somewhere for an entire half-year without permission."—Trans.

62. Deeters, "Alte und neue Aktenfunde über Michael Praetorius," 108. (The author's citation ends with "a great doctor"; I thought the rest of the quote also worthy of inclusion as a window into Praetorius' character. Most of the quote is in German, but

remarks at Praetorius' funeral that Praetorius had "greatly desired to pursue that profession [i.e. to become a pastor like his father and brothers], and he often regretted the fact that he did not devote himself to the public ministry."[63] In other words, this decisive turning point in his life surely did not take place without conflict.

---

after "better for me," Praetorius concludes the sentence in Latin.—Trans.)

63. Appendix III, p. 164.

– 2 –

At the Courts of Gröningen
and Wolfenbüttel

IN THE TWENTY YEARS that followed, from about 1593 to 1613, Praetorius was employed by Heinrich Julius, the bishop of Halberstadt and duke of Brunswick (Braunschweig) and Lüneburg—from 1594 as his chamber

organist and from 1604 as his court music director.[1] Heinrich Julius also charged him with various tasks unrelated to music. Due to his background and training, Praetorius was a young man of wide-ranging talents and knowledge. In seeking to put his qualifications to use, Heinrich Julius occasionally engaged him in activities characteristic of a private secretary.[2] As a result of this close and diverse collaboration, he and the duke developed a relationship of trust between intellectual equals, one that went beyond the employee-employer, servant-master relationship of a musician to his prince. We must

Fig. 6. Elias Holwein, *Wahrhafftige Contrafactur Des . . . Herrn Heinrichen Julii*, 1603, woodcut, Herzog Anton Ulrich Museum, Brunswick, courtesy of Winfried Elsner.

1. I added the final clause for more precise clarification.—Trans.
2. Appendix IV, D, p. 183.

18

therefore start by taking a closer look at the life of Heinrich Julius, for much of Praetorius' life from this point on can only be understood if one understands his collaboration with the duke.

Duchess Elisabeth (1573–1626) was also involved in this relationship of trust. She took care of government business when her husband was absent, especially when he spent time in Prague, where he attempted to assert his rights over the rebellious city of Brunswick. The duchess, like Praetorius, was given a strict Lutheran upbringing, and according to one tradition he was also her private secretary.[3] "She was apparently the one interested in him being appointed as a conventual of the Amelungsborn Abbey in 1608—the first conventual in the history of this abbey who was not an ordained

Fig. 7. Elias Holwein, *Wahre und eigentliche Contrafactur Der . . . Frawen Elisabethen*, 1603, woodcut, Herzog Anton Ulrich Museum, Brunswick, courtesy of Winfried Elsner.

clergyman. Praetorius' appointment as prior of the Ringelheim Abbey, which took place in 1614 at the latest, could also be traced back to her considerable influence in the religious affairs of the territory."[4]

Heinrich Julius (1564–1613), Bishop of Halberstadt and Duke of Brunswick-Lüneburg

*Johannes Bugenhagen, Martin Luther's fellow reformer in Wittenberg, helped to implement the Reformation in the city of Brunswick during an extended visit in 1528.[5] The city was able to facilitate this transition against the wishes of its territorial ruler, Duke Heinrich the Younger of

3. *Johann Caspar Wetzels Historische Lebens-Beschreibung Der berühmtesten Lieder-Dichter*, 315–16.

4. Forchert, "Musik zwischen Religion und Politik," 113. (I included more of the original quote than the author did.—Trans.)

5. Hendel, *Johannes Bugenhagen*, 33–37; Preus, *The Second Martin*, 103–4.

Brunswick-Lüneburg (1489–1568), because of the wealth, influence, and independence it had gained as a prominent member of the Hanseatic

League, an association of German traders. Thus developed a distinction between the religious organization of the *city* of Brunswick and that of the *principality* of Brunswick-Wolfenbüttel, which initially remained Roman Catholic, like its ruler.[6]

In 1542 the Duchy of Brunswick-Lüneburg, which included the just-mentioned principality, fell into the hands of the Lutheran Schmalkaldic League, which immediately sought to implement the Reformation in the territory. However, the defeat of

Fig. 8. Statue of Johannes Bugenhagen in Brunswick, 2018, photo.—Trans.

the Schmalkaldic League in 1547 by the forces of Emperor Charles V resulted in the restoration of the duchy to Duke Heinrich, who immediately sought to suppress the Reformation.[7]

In the Battle of Sievershausen in 1553, the two older, Roman Catholic sons of Duke Heinrich were killed, leaving Heinrich's neglected and crippled son Julius (1528–1589) in direct line to the throne. Julius had become a zealous Lutheran, so Heinrich initially sought various avenues of replacing Julius as his successor. However, Heinrich "finally recognized the impossibility of converting his son or even of keeping the duchy out of the Lutheran church, and father and son were reconciled." He began to tolerate Lutheranism toward the end of his reign and even came out publicly in support of the Augsburg Confession not long before his death on July 11, 1568.[8]

---

6. Hendel, 66–67; Preus, 101–3.

7. Hendel, 67,69; Preus, 139–40.

8. Preus, 139–41 (quote on p. 141).

Heinrich's grandson, Heinrich Julius, was born to Julius and his wife Hedwig on October 14, 1564. Heinrich loved this grandson dearly and in 1566, when the boy was only two, had him elected bishop of Halberstadt by the cathedral chapter[9]. Halberstadt was not just a city (about forty miles southeast of Brunswick); the city was the capital of a territory with the same name, ruled by the bishop of the city. Thus Heinrich Julius' appointment (which was not confirmed by the pope) would also make him the *de facto* ruler of this territory neighboring the duchy. The only condition was "that the administration of the office should for the next 12 years be allowed to remain with the [cathedral] chapter, which was still Roman Catholic."[10]

After Duke Heinrich passed away in 1568, his son Julius' first order of business was the reformation of the Duchy of Brunswick-Lüneburg. For this he employed the services of the brilliant Lutheran theologian Martin Chemnitz, the superintendent of the city of Brunswick, whom the duke eventually made the chairman of his consistory. The subsequent collaboration between Duke Julius and Chemnitz became well known, and resulted in the production of the Formula of Concord, which had a reconciling and unifying effect on Lutheranism at large.[11]

Fig. 9. *Collegium in Helmstett*, engraving in Matthäus Merian's heirs, eds., *Topographia* for Brunswick-Lüneburg (1654).

On October 15, 1576, the newly founded Julian University in Helmstedt was formally opened. That day marked the twelfth birthday of Prince Heinrich Julius, and he was in fact named the rector, though Timothy Kirchner was the head of the school in practice.[12] The young prince memorized and delivered a speech in Latin for the occasion, which he admittedly did not compose himself,[13] and then took up his studies there.

9. See Glossary.

10. Preus, 141–42.

11. *Ibid.*, 142,148,167ff.

12. *Ibid.*, 208–9; Leuckfeld, *Antiquitates Gröningenses*, 58.

13. *Bodemann, "Herzog Julius von Braunschweig," 327–28.

Two years later, Heinrich Julius was installed into his office as bishop of Halberstadt in an ostentatious ceremony in the Huysburg Abbey north of the city of Halberstadt.[14]

> It had been the request of the old duke [Heinrich Julius' grand-
> father, Heinrich the Younger], with the consent of the Lutheran
> son [Heinrich Julius' father, Julius], that the grandson [Heinrich
> Julius] be chosen as bishop of Halberstadt . . . and that the con-
> secration take place according to the Roman rite. Duke Julius, in
> keeping with his original promise, complied, although the boy
> had been brought up to be neither a Catholic nor a clergyman.
> A particularly vehement Roman abbot was used to perform
> the ceremony that took place on Nov. 27, 1578, in the Abbey of
> Huesburg [Huysburg] and involved the especially offensive use
> of the first tonsure, a haircut used in connection with ordination
> and installation into the priesthood and involving the complete
> or partial shaving of the head. Furthermore, the entire ritual was
> according to the Roman rite at the request of the local cathedral
> chapter that had requested a ceremonial mass as part of the in-
> duction and enthronement.[15]

Although "the entire proceeding took place with the greatest possible secrecy," the secret was impossible to keep. It caused great offense not
only throughout Julius' duchy, but in other Lutheran territories as well.[16]

> There was no objection from the Lutheran side that a 14-year-
> old boy become a bishop. Everyone realized that he would be
> bishop in name only and that it was perhaps for the income that
> the whole episode took place. Nor was there any Lutheran ob-
> jection to the office of bishop. The only objection lay in the fact
> that the duke and his sons took part in a Roman mass. There was
> no talk about the young prince becoming a Roman Catholic,
> and in fact shortly after Henry [Heinrich] Julius took over, the
> entire operation became Lutheran. Nor was there any pressure
> on Julius from any of his courtiers or fellow princes. It was quite
> the opposite. It seems to have been an entirely independent ac-
> tion of Julius, who must have felt some qualms about it, because
> he did not consult Chemnitz and kept the matter so secret . . . It
> appears that the best explanation for his Halberstadt action lies
> in the fact that he felt bound to the promise he had made to his

14. WGD, 98.

15. Preus, *The Second Martin*, 196; see also Leuckfeld, *Antiquitates Gröningenses*, 58.

16. Leuckfeld, 58–59.

father, and Julius was a man who once having made up his mind could not be moved, even if he made a mistake in the process.[17]

Martin Chemnitz wrote a long letter to Duke Julius, protesting the action and calling the duke to repentance, which caused him to be dismissed from the duke's consistory and to fall out of his favor.[18]

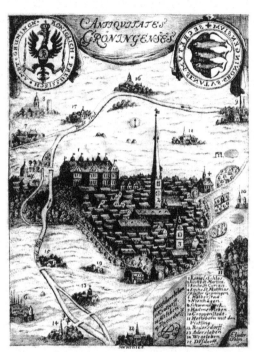

Fig. 10. Erasmus Andresohn, *Gröningen* (oriented northward), c. 1710, engraving. (St. Martin's Church and the royal palace (formerly the ducal palace) are most prominently featured. Praetorius also had dealings with Kroppenstedt, no. 10 on the engraving. See also Fig. 13.—Trans.)

Heinrich Julius was a pawn in these affairs to a large extent, but the strong and widespread reaction to his installation doubtless left some sort of impression on him. He may have felt some need to make amends and to validate his Lutheranism through his court appointments. As Michael Praetorius was only about seven years old at the time, he probably remained largely unaware of the scandal.*

Heinrich Julius moved into the palace of Gröningen by Halberstadt, along with his younger brothers Philipp Sigismund and Joachim Karl. There he also received his own court. His father, Duke Julius, had him go through a carefully prescribed program of education and culture. This included the study of the classical languages, the Bible, other writings of antiquity, and Roman law and architecture, as well as exercises in writing and music (playing on a keyboard instrument). Later riding, fencing, and

17. Preus, 197–98.

18. Leuckfeld, 59; Chemnitz's letter is reprinted in an addendum at the end of the book, pp. 1–9; see also Preus, 198–203.

other physical activities were added. However, during repeated visits to Gröningen, his father frequently found occasion to object to his son's inclination to luxury and ostentation.[19]

In 1585/86, the Gröningen court consisted of about 160 persons: two court preachers, six chamber advisers, seven at-large and chancery advisers, eleven courtiers and country squires, seven pages, seven bodyguards, seventeen persons in the royal stables with nearly a hundred horses and several carriages, and numerous personnel for kitchen, cellar, table, etc.[20] All the members of the court were subject to a strict code of court regulations, which was read to them every quarter-year as a reminder.[21]

After Heinrich Julius got married in 1585, to Princess Dorothea, a daughter of Elector August of Saxony, he developed an ambitious plan for construction activity in Gröningen. He wanted to have the existing palace complex expanded according to his own needs and desires. For this he appointed the architect Christoph Tendler of Electoral Saxony to his court in 1586, and they drew up the construction plans together.[22] These pursuits came to a standstill, however, when Heinrich Julius' wife died at just twenty-three years old on February 13, 1587, while giving birth to a daughter.

Heinrich Julius had also already begun to set up a chapel ensemble in Gröningen, which in 1585/86 consisted of two leaders (one of which was designated as music director [*Kapellmeister*]), seven cantors, and "the small boy with the sackbut."[23] His ensemble was thus larger than his father's in Wolfenbüttel. In 1589 Duke Julius died and his son took over government business. But at first he continued to reside predominantly in the Gröningen palace.

---

19. WGD, 97–99.

20. Liebe, "Der Hofhalt des Bischofs Heinrich Julius von Halberstadt," 743–44. (The stable numbers are a little misleading, since the personnel listed belonged to Heinrich Julius alone, while the number of horses includes those belonging to his wife and the staff; "several carriages" can also only be said with certainty if one includes his wife's carriage[s]. Princess Dorothea's male staff consisted of a major-domo, cupbearer, three pages, a court tailor, two coachmen, two carriage servants, a fire-stoker, and a personal attendant [*Jungfrauenknecht*]. Her female staff consisted of a governess, four pages, a chamberlady, two chambermaids, a cook, and a laundress.—Trans.)

21. *Ibid.*, 745–50. (The opening regulations of the code deal with the regular hearing of God's word and attending of church services.—Trans.)

22. *WGD, 101.

23. Liebe, 743.

On April 19, 1590, he married the seventeen-year-old Princess Elisabeth of Denmark. The wedding was celebrated with great pomp at

the Kronborg Castle near Helsingør. The chamber accounts from the year 1590 reveal that Heinrich Julius also took along his chapel ensemble to Denmark. An entry for this trip, dated April 8, 1590, under the expenditures for "Provisions [*Zehrung*]" (the traveling and feeding expenses for the court officials), reads: "To Thomas Mancinus, Music Director, for his and all the musicians' provisions for the trip to Denmark, since they have to follow My Gracious Prince and Lord: 210 thalers."[24] Note that this entry also shows that Thomas Mancinus was directing the ensemble at this time.

Fig. 11. Georg Scharffenberg, *Thomas Mancinus*, 1585, woodcut. Mancinus, here pictured at age thirty-five, served as court music director in Wolfenbüttel and Gröningen from 1584–1604. Praetorius was active as organist and member of the chapel ensemble under his direction.

As one can see from Eitner's index of Thomas Mancinus' compositions, Mancinus composed a now-lost five-part wedding song in 1589, using the text "Quam pulchrae sunt [How Beautiful Are]" from the Song of Solomon.[25] But pieces from Mancinus' *Das erste Buch Newer Lustiger und Höfflicher Weltlicher Lieder* (The First Book of New Cheerful and Stately Secular Songs) for four to five parts from 1588 could also have been sung at the wedding feast.[26] It is also conjectured that the occasion was used as an opportunity to perform the duke's own drama *Susanna*.

24. "Kammerrechnungen des Herzogtums zu Braunschweig und Lüneburg," Public Archives of Lower Saxony in Wolfenbüttel, 17 III Alt Nr. 62a,134; also cited in WGD, 108, n. 6. (On p. 45 of the present work, a hundred thalers is listed as equivalent to 312 gulden; see also Chapter 1, n. 55.—Trans.)

25. *Eitner, Biographisch-Bibliographisches Quellen-Lexikon der Musiker und Musikgelehrten, 6:296a. If this were composed using an English translation, it would most likely be titled "How Beautiful *or* Delightful Is [Your Love]." The Latin Vulgate, however, contains a more vivid translation (as does Luther's German Bible).

26. *MGG* Personenteil, 11:955, s. v. "Mancinus, Thomas."

The duke liberally distributed 14,500 thalers' worth of jewelry to those who attended the wedding celebration, including a large diamond ring worth 2,100 thalers as a gift to his bride. After the festival, Elisabeth moved to Wolfenbüttel in a gilded carriage in the company of her mother, arriving on June 20, 1590. Heinrich Julius had gone on ahead of her and

Fig. 12. *Fürstl. Brunsw: Lüneb: Residentz Statt und Vestung Wolfenbüttel*
(oriented northward), engraving printed in Matthäus Merian's heirs, eds.,
***Topographia* for Brunswick-Lüneburg (1654), after a drawing by Conrad Buno.**
Cf. Fig. 48.—Trans.

welcomed her there. On the two following days banquets were held there with a princely table of forty-eight persons.[27]*

Around the time of the wedding, Heinrich Julius also witnessed the work of English comedy actors in Copenhagen.[28] In 1592, at his invitation, they put on their first guest performance in Wolfenbüttel, and he himself wrote theater pieces for them.[29] This guest performance turned into a multi-year stay, so that the first permanent theater in Germany now existed at the Wolfenbüttel court, in contrast to the conventional traveling theaters. The duke himself possessed a great affinity for costuming and drama. A particular masterstroke in this field is reported in connection with his wedding: On the way to Denmark he went on ahead of his wedding guests and appeared at the Danish court disguised as a jewelry salesman. The seventeen-year-old princess Elisabeth took an interest in the jewelry and wanted to know the price of an especially beautiful item. In response, the unrecognized bridegroom asked her for a kiss, which immediately got him thrown into prison. Not until his company arrived and vouched for him was he released.[30]

27. Lietzmann, *Herzog Heinrich Julius zu Braunschweig und Lüneburg (1564–1613),* 12–13.

28. WGD, 109, n. 5.

29. *Ibid.*, 110.

30. Lietzmann, 12.

During the wedding in Denmark the duke also became acquainted with the royal chapel ensemble there—one of the most distinguished in Protestant lands. It was probably the impression it left on him that led him, after returning to his residence, to enlarge his own chapel ensemble by five musicians, primarily instrumentalists, so that he could also have purely instrumental music performed at his court. In 1590, his ensemble was already a force of sixteen musicians from various nations, not including the music director Thomas Mancinus, the organist Antonius Ammerbach, or the ten trumpeters and two drummers.[31]

Fig. 13. Maler Gustav, *Gröninger Schloss* (oriented northeast-ward), painting, https://www.malergustav.de. For this painting, the painter obtained very detailed specifications from a local researcher who had researched the palace extensively for a couple years. The beautiful chapel was housed in the palace's northern wing.—Trans.

After taking over the reins of government in 1589, the duke continued his construction in Gröningen. He had the building expanded and turned into a magnificent Renaissance palace.[32] For example, the ballroom on the fourth floor, "the golden hall," was about thirty-five by twelve meters (112 by thirty-seven feet) large with fifteen windows each

31. Ruhnke, *Beiträge zu einer Geschichte der deutschen Hofmusikkollegien im 16. Jahrhundert*, 64–65, 89, 91. (Here I cited more pages of this work than the author did, and in the text I added the final clause.—Trans.)

32. WGD, 101ff.

on the east and west sides. It was decorated with richly gilded wainscot-
ing and paintings, which featured the pagan Roman emperors on the side
walls and the exploits of Hercules in ten panels on the ceiling.[33]

The jewel was the palace chapel, two stories high with dimensions of about twenty-three by eleven meters (seventy-five by thirty-six
feet). It didn't take long for it to be renowned as "the beautiful church in
Gröningen." It was decorated with painted scenes from the Old and New
Testaments, and in a semicircle above the arch on the chancel balcony
the name and title of the duke were printed in gold-plated Latin script.[34]
The showpiece of the palace chapel was an organ with fifty-nine stops,
including fourteen reed stops, the third-largest in Germany at the time.
The Halberstadt organ builder David Beck constructed it from 1592–96
for a price of 10,000 thalers. Concerning this instrument it is reported:

> Inside this church there can also found on the evening side [west
> side] a splendid organ, unequaled in Germany, which on account
> of its size and exceptionally beautiful gilding is not a little to be
> admired, just as it can also provide supreme delight to a music-
> loving ear and heart when it is played. And although some of the
> pipes in the organ are as much as eight full ells high [about sixteen
> feet] and several of them are very wide and heavy, so that each of
> the most solid of them weighs up to one and half hundredweight
> [about 165 lbs.] or more, their tone is disposed so proportionally
> that it conforms to the size of the church building.[35]

The organ was adorned "with verses written in golden letters in the
Rückpositiv[36]," which translate as follows:

> Heinrich Julius, prelate of Halberstadt, prince of two duchies—
> Duke of the stronghold established by Bruno [i.e. Brunswick] and
>   likewise of Luen'burg—
> Gladly devoted these piercing pipe-muses, in shrines neatly gilded,
> Unto your honor, O Christ; pray, in turn, this duke and his offspring
> Furnish with health and long life and enjoyment of peace in their
>   homeland [*Patriae*],
> Also, when welcomed to heaven as promised, with parts in its music.[37]

33. *Leuckfeld, *Antiquitates Gröningenses*, 85.

34. *Ibid.*, 79–80.

35. *Ibid.*, 80–81.

36. See Glossary.

37. Leuckfeld, 81. (I translated this directly from the Latin original rather than
from the author's German translation. I also attempted to reflect the original strophe's

The organ was fitted with a monumental, magnificently designed case of unparalleled significance for art history, though its builder remains unknown. The organ rated "as a widely celebrated marvel in the world of music and art on account of its extraordinary size, glorious showcase of visual artwork, and gorgeous development of tone. Over the centuries the chapel, in which the organ represented the main attraction, became the focal point of an early 'educational tourism.'"[38]

At the time of the organ's construction, Praetorius was already very likely the duke's chamber organist and therefore would surely have had frequent opportunity to acquaint himself with his future instrument down to the finest details. This might also account for how he acquired some of his profound organ expertise. After the instrument was dedicated, the duke entrusted him with its playing and maintenance.[39] Unfortunately no records have been preserved from which one might learn exactly when he was appointed as chamber organist or the particulars of his service.[40] He also continued to function in this capacity after he was appointed court music director in 1604. He thus played the Gröningen organ for more than ten years, so that it can also rightly be termed the Gröningen Praetorius Organ. Today the organ is located in St. Martin's Church in Halberstadt.

The duke organized a great festival in 1596 for the testing and dedication of the instrument. He invited fifty-three (!) organists from all of Germany to the festival, including celebrities like the Hassler brothers and the Hamburg organist Hieronymus Praetorius (not related to Michael Praetorius, who also participated). It turned into a festival of the century and a tremendous organ marathon, since each of the participants naturally did not wish merely to see and hear the large, new instrument, but also to test and play it himself. As a reward the duke distributed 3,000 thalers among them.[41]

---

dactylic hexameter.—Trans.)

38. Brülls, "Stellungsnahme zur kunsthistorischen Bedeutung und denkmalpflegerischen Behandlung des Renaissance-Orgelprospektes von 1596 in der Stadtkirche St. Martini zu Halberstadt," 1.

39. WGD, 118–19, 130.

40. All we have are Praetorius' own later calculations of when he moved to Wolfenbüttel, entered the duke's service, and became a member of the duke's ensemble. See Forchert, "Musik zwischen Religion und Politik," 107–9, esp. #6 on p. 108, which puts his appointment as court organist in the latter part of 1594.—Trans.

41. *WGD, 127–30; Werckmeister, *Organum Gruningense redivivum*, 11–12, §§ 9–11.

The biographer Hilda Lietzmann characterizes Duke Heinrich Julius as follows:

> [He] was German prince to the core, stout and—as they say—
> from the right stock. He had an irascible temper, yet there also
> must have been periods of pensive melancholy. The duke had
> his heart in the right place, but it was also frequently to be found
> on his tongue. Heinrich Julius was accustomed to saying what
> was on his mind; diplomatic maneuvering seems not to have
> been his concern . . . He was also a Christian prince and a con-
> vinced adherent of the doctrine of Martin Luther up to his dying
> hour . . . Besides Landgrave Moritz of Hesse-Kassel, he was the
> most learned prince of his time in the German-speaking world.
> It is undisputed that his legal knowledge made him a celebrity.
> He likewise devoted himself to both astrology and alchemy with
> great interest. He had a horoscope prepared for himself until his
> final days.[42]

He was also fond of craftsmen's activities, hiking, and hunting. The
hunting room in his Gröningen palace was decorated with many stun-
ning hunting trophies.

Michael Praetorius as Chamber Organist and Organ Specialist

Fundamental to Michael Praetorius' church music are Luther's
statements on the dialogical structure of the church service:
"God speaks to us through his Word and we respond to him
through prayer and praise" (Church Dedication Sermon in
Torgau).[43] Luther restores to the organ its original task as a par-
ticipant in the praise, standing next to the priest and the choir
on equal footing. He values the organ not as an accompanying
or compensational instrument, but as a liturgical factor capable
of performing worship tasks on its own (Christhard
Mahrenholz).[44] . . . For Michael Praetorius the harmony of

---

42. Lietzmann, *Herzog Heinrich Julius zu Braunschweig und Lüneburg (1564–
1613)*, 13–14. (Horoscopes of the time should not rashly be equated with those of
today. The early Lutheran view of the heavenly bodies is a subject worthy of its own
treatment.—Trans.)

43. *See WA 49:588; *LW* 51:333.

44. This seems to impart to the organ an almost personal character, as if the very
playing of the organ in worship by itself gave praise to God. Luther actually says the

congregation, organ, choir, and instruments in the service furnishes a picture of the eschatological praise of God: "It is a very lovely and pleasant thing to hear when the entire assembly joins in together with the choir and the organ like this, and shows and portrays to some extent what it's going to be like in heaven when all the dear angels and saints of God intone and take up the *Sanctus, Sanctus, Sanctus* ['Holy, Holy, Holy'] and *Gloria in Excelsis Deo* ['Glory to God in the Highest'] with us."[45]

Praetorius had his first intensive encounter with the organ as the young organist of the University Church of St. Mary in Frankfurt an der Oder. One can easily imagine what kind of impression the instrument made on him after reading his effusive later statements on "The Dignity and Excellence of Organs, and How Those Designed Only and Especially for Service to the Church and for Worship Are to Be Preferred to All Other Instruments":

Fig. 14. Plates II and XXVI from the *Theatrum Instrumentorum* appended to *SM* 2. Left: A pipe organ with a Rückpositiv. Right: Two bellows treaders working the bellows of the large organ in the Halberstadt cathedral.—Trans.

Indeed, this lovely polyphonic mechanism contains just about everything that can be devised and invented in music, and it produces such a genuine, natural sound, tone, and timbre—not unlike an entire choir full of musicians, where a number of different melodies are heard from the voices of both boys and men. In summary, the organ alone contains and encompasses all other musical instruments, large and small, whatever names they

---

opposite in multiple places, including such an idea among the papal errors (e.g. *LW* 21:307; 34:55; 35:80–81; 44:31–32). He does say that "if these things [including organ playing] are done with such faith that we believe that they please God, then they are praiseworthy, not because of their virtue, but because of that very faith by which all works are of equal value" (44:32). He also says that if it would help to educate Christians in God's word and impress its truths upon their hearts, he "would have all the bells pealing, and all the organs playing, and have everything ring that can make a sound" in the worship rite (53:62).—Trans.

45. Niemann, "Michael Praetorius als Organist," 19–20; the Praetorius quote can be found in GA 14:x–xi.

might have. If you wish to hear a timpanum, trumpet, sackbut,[46] cornet, recorder, flutes, bombards, shawms,[47] dulcians,[48] racketts, sorduns, crumhorns, viols, violins, lyras, etc., you can have all of these, and many other whimsical delights besides, in this ingenious mechanism. Thus, when you have and hear this instrument, you cannot help but imagine that you have and are hearing all the other instruments at once. Not to mention that on the organ a person with only basic experience in the art can often outdo outstanding masters on other instruments, since proper control of this mechanism's muzzle requires the simultaneous use of hands and feet. And it is not an exaggeration to say that no art has advanced as far as the art of the organ, for mankind's clever ingenuity and diligent reflection have brought it to the point that it can continue to exist just fine in its current state without any further additions whatsoever, and one gets the impression that its perfection and completeness leave nothing to be desired and cannot be increased or augmented in any way.[49]

Already during his organist activity in Frankfurt (c. 1588–c. 1591) he must have sufficiently proved himself in this position; when it became vacant again in 1601, the Frankfurt congregation tried to get him back.[50]

His experience there now served him well in his occupation in Gröningen, so that Heinrich Julius was pleased with his diligent, indefatigable chamber organist. In this capacity Praetorius, as a member of the court chapel ensemble and player of all keyboard instruments, was responsible for the following tasks:

- Performing the opening prelude and closing postlude during the service
- Playing the introductions and closings for the sung portions of the liturgy and for the choir music
- The interchange with the choir during the *Kyrie, Gloria in Excelsis,* etc.

46. Early form of trombone

47. Bombards and shawms, forerunners of the oboe, are in the same class. When distinguished from each other, bombards are larger and of lower pitch and shawms are smaller and of higher pitch (*SM* 2E1:47).

48. Early type of bassoon

49. *SM* 2:82,85; cf. *SM* 2E2, same pages. (I added the quote and the three accompanying footnotes.—Trans.)

50. Grimm, *Meister der Renaissancemusik an der Viadrina,* 171.

- The music during Communion[51]

These were carried out improvisationally for the most part, which Praetorius was already familiar with from his time in Frankfurt. The congregational singing, however, was not accompanied by the organ.

For the other obligations of the court ensemble, he had to play the clavicymbal or portative (portable miniature organ) either as a soloist or as an accompanist for solo or multi-part recitals by other ensemble members. As one can gather from several compositions written by various musicians and dedicated to the duke, this kind of "musical catering at the table and in the private chamber" consisted of the performance of "German songs; Italian madrigals and canzonette; English lute and spinet music; and French dances and instrumental processional pieces."[52]

As Praetorius reports, he himself "collected many splendid toccatas by the foremost Italian and Netherlandish organists—and in my own modest way even added some myself" for this activity as chamber organist.[53] (He perhaps had works by Claudio Merulo, Girolamo Frescobaldi, Andrea Gabrieli, and Jan Pieterszoon Sweelinck in mind.) He wanted to complete this collection with "many . . . psalms, toccatas, . . . fugues, fantasies, and concertos, for two keyboards."[54] He also received twenty-four thalers from the court treasury in 1602 "for the fabrication of some stamps and dies to give to the print shop for instrumental notation," so that he could print this collection.[55] But the publication was never realized; parts of it might later have been absorbed into his series of secular works.

Praetorius did incorporate some of his organ compositions into the volumes of his religious vocal works "at the persistent pleading of several organists."[56] These comprise three large-scale choral fantasies, two choral variations, and six compositions based on ancient Christian hymns, which were to be played in alternation with the singing of the choir.[57]

51. *See WGD, 123–26.

52. Forchert, "Michael Praetorius und die Musik am Hof von Wolfenbüttel," 626.

53. *SM* 3E:40.

54. *GA 7:vii.

55. WGD, 126, n. 2.

56. *GA 7:vii.

57. These organ compositions were recorded in 2005 on the Scherer Organ (built in 1624) in Tangermünde, Germany, by Jean-Charles Ablitzer, titular organist of the Belfort Cathedral in France (album released by Alpha in 2007). Ablitzer has also been pushing for some time for the restoration of the organ that once served as the palace chapel organ in Gröningen and is now located in St. Martin's Church in Halberstadt.

They are "characterized by compositional mastery, high demands on playing technique, and great resonant beauty, but also by his incredibly inventive employment of temporal expansion, quite considerable in some parts."[58] They are especially prized as early specimens of Protestant organ music.

Not long after its dedication, the chapel organ in Gröningen began showing some deficiencies, which necessitated an overhaul. The organ builder Esaias Compenius was tasked with the job. He carried it out in the years 1603–4 and in 1605, at Praetorius' recommendation, was appointed by Duke Heinrich Julius as the Ducal Organ and Instrument Maker of Brunswick. During this collaboration he and Praetorius culti-

vated a friendship that lasted to the end of Compenius' life. In a letter Praetorius even calls him his *Gefatter*, a now antiquated German word for "godfather," often with connotations of close personal friendship.[59] This label might suggest that Compenius was a sponsor for one of Praetorius' sons.

Following the job in Gröningen, Duke Heinrich Julius tasked Compenius with another project in 1605. As a counterpart to the palace chapel organ in Gröningen, he was to build a house organ in Hessen Castle, about seventeen miles southeast of

Fig. 15. Nicolas de Clerck (?), *Christian IV, King of Denmark and Norway*, engraving after a drawing (c. 1606) by Remmert Petersen, courtesy of Winfried Elsner.

Wolfenbüttel, for the duke's consort Elisabeth. Praetorius contributed significantly to its design and execution. This instrument received nine

As a result of his efforts, a Beck Organ Initiative Group has been founded in Halberstadt. (See https://www.praetorius–beckorgel.de/en/aktuelles.php for more.—Trans.)

58. Aumüller, "Lebens- und Arbeitsbedingungen hessischen Organisten," 99.

59. *Letter to the City Council of Kroppenstedt (Feb. 13, 1610); cited in "Der Orgelbau in Kroppenstedt durch Esaias Compenius," Die Compenius-Orgel der St. Martini-Kirche zu Kroppenstedt (website), https://www.compenius-orgel.de/geschichtederorgel.htm.

stops each for the upper manual, lower manual, and pedalboard. The pipes were constructed purely out of wood, without the use of metal, and the façade pipes were veneered with ivory. About this instrument Praetorius writes: "Its unusual, gentle, subtle sound and charm . . . cannot be described so accurately in writing."[60] Compenius worked on this organ for five years. In 1616 the duchess gifted it to her brother, King Christian IV of Denmark, a skilled organ player, for his silver wedding anniversary. Compenius supervised the transportation of the instrument to Denmark and set it up in Frederiksborg Castle himself. He died the following year and was buried there. This Compenius Organ is the only Renaissance organ preserved in its original state, and it is still regularly played.

Fig. 16. Ib Rasmussen, *Compenius Organ*, 2007, photo, all rights released.—Trans.

The collaboration between Praetorius and Compenius also produced the organ in the Bückeburg Palace Chapel in 1612.[61] It experienced a checkered history, ended up in the Bückeburg Parish Church, was completely destroyed in 1962 as a result of arson, and was replaced in 1997 by a large, new instrument.[62]

Praetorius also continued to occupy himself intensively with questions of organ construction in his later years, as can be gathered from volume II of his *Syntagma Musicum* (Musical Compendium; 1619). In addition to a description "of all ancient and modern musical instruments,"[63] it contains a history of ancient and modern organs, along with their stops,

60. *SM* 2:141; cf. *SM* 2E2, same page.

61. *Ibid.*, 185–86. (Praetorius says that the organ was completed in 1615, so perhaps its construction began in 1612. However, he also says the organ mentioned in the previous paragraph was finished in 1612, even though other sources say 1610.—Trans.)

62. *Festschrift zur Einweihung der Orgel in der Stadtkirche zu Bückeburg.*

63. **SM* 2, title page; *SM* 2E1:1.

on eighty pages.[64] Esaias Compenius "afforded [him] much good counsel" in composing it.[65] For his own part, Praetorius in turn provided him "with counsel and assistance"[66] in composing a book on "Organ contracting, construction, and delivery, in both the production of new organs and the renovation of old organs,"[67] which was supposed to warn and protect congregations against the practices of dishonest organ builders. Volume II of the *Syntagma Musicum* also contains the dispositions of thirty-three "Distinguished Organs in Germany,"[68] some of which Praetorius either looked up himself or obtained by letter. With the number of organs, one must keep in mind that some cities had more than one and that Praetorius also included seven of his own proposed designs.

Another intensive collaboration developed beginning in 1614, this time between Praetorius and Gottfried Fritzsche, an organ builder from Dresden. That year Praetorius gave his expert advice on the construction of an organ with thirty-three stops for the palace chapel in Dresden. The organ had been designed by Hans Leo Hassler before he died. The Praetorius-Fritzsche collaboration eventually produced the organs in the following places:

- Church of the Holy Trinity in Sondershausen: thirty-three stops (1616/17)

- Schöningen Castle: twenty stops (1617; built for the widowed Duchess Elisabeth)

- Parish Church in Bayreuth: thirty-five stops (1618/19; Praetorius, Samuel Scheidt, Heinrich Schütz, and Johann Staden jointly participated in its dedication)

The last organ that Praetorius designed together with Gottfried Fritzsche was intended for the new Church of the Blessed Virgin Mary (usually simply called the *Hauptkirche* or Main Church) in Wolfenbüttel, which had been under construction since 1608. The list of stops signed in Praetorius' own hand can be found in the Public Archives of Lower Saxony in Wolfenbüttel.[69] However, Praetorius did not live to see its comple-

64. *SM* 2:89ff; *SM* 2E2, same pages.

65. *Ibid.*, 160.

66. *Ibid.* (translation mine, not *SM* 2E2).

67. *SM* 3:224, no. 8; cf. *SM* 3E:209; actual work reprinted in WGD, 307ff.

68. *SM* 2:161ff; *SM* 2E2, same pages.

69. Signatur 100 N 1277.

Fig. 17. Sebastian Furck, interior of the Church of the Blessed Virgin Mary in Wolfenbüttel, before 1650, engravings printed in Martin Gosky, *Arbustum vel Arboretum Augustaeum* (1650), after drawings by Albert Freyse. Left: Facing east. Note the beautiful Ditterich altar. Praetorius' memorial slab (see Chapter 6) was located in the gallery behind the first partial pillar on the left. Right: Facing west. Note the beautiful Fritzsche organ. Praetorius is buried beneath the organ balcony on the left side. Today one can find a commemorative plaque on the wall near the site (installed later).—Trans.

tion, though he did find his final resting place beneath the organ loft on February 21, 1621, after his death on February 15. It is touching to imagine the organ builder and his assistants going about their work above Praetorius' grave, constructing the mechanism and bringing its thirty-five stops to life one after the other, until its completion in 1624. This organ experienced a checkered history too; it was replaced in 1960 by an organ with fifty-three stops built by Karl Schuke's Berlin Organ Building Studio. The new instrument still has six of Fritzsche's original stops.[70]

70. *Die Orgel der Hauptkirche Beatae Mariae Virginis Wolfenbüttel.*

$-3-$

Marriage and Children

DURING HIS TIME AS chamber organist at the Gröningen court, Praetorius became acquainted with his future wife. Her name was Anna, the daughter of the Halberstadt councilman Wolfgang Lakemacher and his wife Dorothea. She had been born in Halberstadt on September 17, 1579. Anna's two brothers, Wolfgang and Stephan, also served in Duke Heinrich Julius' court—the former as feed marshal for the ducal stables and the latter as a lawyer and ducal councilor in Halberstadt.[1] Anna had been previously married once, to Master Johann Wernighof, head preacher at St. Peter and Paul in Halberstadt. They had one daughter together before Johann died in 1602.[2] Since Anna's first husband had been a pastor in Halberstadt like Praetorius' brother-in-law Daniel Sachse, it is quite possible that both families were already acquainted, which might explain how Michael Praetorius and Anna became acquainted with each other.

They married on September 3, 1603, and it is likely that Michael's brother-in-law Daniel Sachse officiated at the wedding at St. Martin's Church in Halberstadt.[3] Sachse had shifted to that church from the cathedral in 1601 and had become the superintendent of Halberstadt. One can still view his lifesize memorial slab in St. Martin's Church. It is possible that some singers from the court chapel ensemble performed at the Praetorius wedding and sang the six-part motet that Praetorius composed for

1. WGD, 135–36. (The author had Wolfgang Jr. "als Fuhr- und Hausmarschall," but in addition to the fact that *Fuhrmarschall* is not a German word, the source he cited only has him as *Futter-Marschall*.—Trans.)

2. Ludewig, "Genealogische Forschungen zur Familie Praetorius."

3. *See point 8 on p. 112.

the text "Ich suchte des Nachts in meinem Bette [I looked at night while in my bed]" from the Song of Solomon (3:1–4),[4] a popular text for wedding songs at the time. Duke Heinrich Julius honored Michael Praetorius with a gift "for the glorious day of his nuptials: 50 thalers."[5]

Fig. 18. Daniel Sachse's memorial slab in St. Martin's Church, photo, courtesy of Winfried Elsner.—Trans.

Their oldest son Michael was born in 1604; his exact birthdate is unknown. We can assume, however, that he was baptized by his uncle Daniel Sachse at the medieval font in St. Martin's Church.[6] Michael eventually studied in Helmstedt, was subsequently a notary in Wolfenbüttel, had a large family with ten children, and died in Wolfenbüttel on February 1, 1684, at the age of eighty.[7]

In 1605, Michael Praetorius acquired a house in the Grain Market in Wolfenbüttel and moved there with his family.[8] His and Anna's second son Ernst was born there on July 12, 1606. Unfortunately, after completing his studies in Helmstedt, Ernst died at age twenty on October 8, 1626. In 1612, Michael Praetorius was able to have a handsome house built in the Great Carpenters' Yard

---

4. GA 20:80ff.

5. "Kammerrechnungen des Herzogtums zu Braunschweig und Lüneburg," Public Archives of Lower Saxony in Wolfenbüttel, 17 III Alt Nr. 65b.

6. *See point 8 on p. 112.

7. See Deeters, "Das Lehen der Familie Praetorius," 122, for a family tree showing the male descendants of both Michael Sr. and Michael Jr.—Trans.

8. The location of this residence was somewhere between what is today Kornmarkt 7–10.—Trans.

in Wolfenbüttel, in which he was also permitted to brew beer.[9] This residence still stands today.[10]

Fig. 19. The Praetorius Residence in Wolfenbüttel, 2018, photo. The plaque on
the house (not clearly visible in the photo) reads: "From 1612 onward, [this
was the] residence and brewery of the ducal music director Michael Praetorius
(c. 1572–1621), organist and composer. From here he issued the 'syntagma
musicum' in the years 1615–1620, a comprehensive study of music and
instruments."—Trans.

9. *Deeters, "Alte und neue Aktenfunde über Michael Praetorius," 109–10. See also
p. 47 of the present work.

10. See also p. 122. The present address is Großer Zimmerhof 20.

$-4-$

Court Music Director and Composer

> The circumstances under which Heinrich Julius conferred the office of music director on Praetorius toward the end of 1604 lead us to presume that the enlargement of the chapel ensemble had provided opportunities for performing works of a new style that was still unfamiliar at the turn of the seventeenth century. These opportunities created a situation for which the old music director Mancinus was no longer competent, so that the direction of such performances had gradually devolved upon Praetorius.[1]

This "new style," Venetian polychorality, had been developed by the music directors and organists at St. Mark's Basilica in Venice—Adrian Willaert, Andrea Gabrieli, and the latter's nephew Giovanni Gabrieli. In this style the musicians were divided into different vocal and instrumental groups, and these groups were placed in separate positions in the church interior. This produced a dialogical presentation of the music that constituted a new form of textual interpretation. Heinrich Julius had become acquainted with this kind of music on his trips to diets and princes' meetings and at the imperial court in Prague, and now he wanted it at his own court too. He therefore gave Praetorius the opportunity in 1601/1602 to take a trip on which he could not only take care of some assignments for the duke but also acquaint himself with the new style. It is unknown, however, whether the plan was to extend this trip as far as Italy, the region so highly praised by many, including Praetorius, as the land of music.[2] Forchert surmises that Duke Heinrich Julius ordered his chamber

1. Forchert, "Michael Praetorius und die Musik am Hof von Wolfenbüttel," 628f.

2. *See p. 66 and n. 97.

41

organist to Dresden in September 1602, so that he could participate as a member of the Wolfenbüttel ensemble in the wedding of Christian II, elector of Saxony, to the nineteen-year-old Danish princess Hedwig, a sister of Duchess Elisabeth of Wolfenbüttel.[3] It is reported that the "distinguished potentates and noble lordships" who had been invited to the wedding were "greeted from the windows of the city by the electoral orchestra as they entered."[4] For this festival, the Elbe River was included in the setting for the festive activities for the first time (as it was in 1617 for the emperor's visit, for which Praetorius composed and directed the festival music[5]). In 1604 Heinrich Julius appointed Praetorius as his court music director, thereby apparently relieving Thomas Mancinus of his position in a sort of "power play."[6] But it may have simply been a matter of taking a situation that had already been in effect for a long time and making it official with a contract.[7]

Fig. 20. Last page of Praetorius' certificate of appointment, Public Archives of Lower Saxony, Wolfenbüttel, courtesy of Winfried Elsner. "I accordingly pledge on my honor, reliability, and faith, that I will conduct myself in keeping with the entire body of the foregoing princely appointment, in all its points, clauses, and wishes, and that I will do everything else that befits, behooves, and well becomes a diligent music director and honest and faithful servant in relation to his lord. In witness whereof I have signed myself in my own hand and imprinted my customary seal in the space below. Signed and sealed on the same date as given above. Michael Praetorius"

3. Forchert, "Musik zwischen Religion und Politik," 111.

4. Becker-Glauch, *Die Bedeutung der Musik für die Dresdner Hoffeste bis in die Zeit Augusts des Starken*, 53f.

5. See p. 96.

6. WGD, 135.

7. Forchert, "Michael Praetorius und die Musik am Hof von Wolfenbüttel," 629.

The Duties and Rights of the Court Music Director

In the certificate of appointment dated December 7, 1604, Praetorius' responsibilities read as follows:

> [He is] to retain himself, in person, here in Our customary courtly camp [in Wolfenbüttel], or wherever else We will set it up and be with it at any time; to attend diligently with vocal and instrumental music, along with his assigned associates, on Sundays and all high festivals when a church service is performed in Our palace churches or court chapels, as well as whenever We call for him at Our table, in Our chamber, or elsewhere—whether foreign lords are visiting Us or not; to employ in church fine religious motets, suited to God's honor and praise, and other Christian pieces that conform to Our church order and body of doctrine, and also to employ from time to time at Our table respectable and cheerful and lighthearted songs, arranged in figural[8] very artfully and pleasantly, all such pieces having been composed either by himself or by other excellent composers, and in so doing to direct everything so that it is all done very smoothly and decorously; to keep his associates in a sober, restrained life, also holding regular musical exercises for this purpose, and in other respects to have the utmost supervision over them; to prepare himself for festivals with new songs from time to time, as the opportunity arises—not having the compositions published publicly without Our prior consent;—
>
> also to attend in like manner when princely or other distinguished ambassadors are here in Our chambers and it should be commanded of him at Our or Our Dearly Beloved Consort's command via Our court marshal or, in Our and Her Dearness' absence, by someone else on Our behalf, or when he should also be permitted to do so at his own request; and in sum, to manage and arrange the entire musical ensemble in such a manner as to bring no reproach to Us and to redound to his own commendation;—
>
> but as he does so he is not to reveal or scatter hither and yon anything that he experiences and sees in Our affairs to Our disadvantage, but is to take everything with him quietly and silently to his grave; he is also to conduct himself in conformity with Our church-, chancery-, and court-orders, and other useful orders, so far as they concern his person and office, and to subscribe to the church order;—

8. See Glossary.

in addition he shall hereby also be appointed by Us to be of
assistance to Our already respectfully mentioned Most Dearly
Beloved Consort and Our Beloved Sons, Daughters, and Princessly Ladyships every day that he is here on location and on
Our journeys, in the forenoon and afternoon, according to the
arrangements that We or Our Very Beloved Consort's Dearness
may make, and to instruct and advise Their Dearnesses in the
playing of instruments [*Instrumenten schlagen*]; and beyond all
this, he shall be and remain appointed to Our organ at Gröningen and here [in Wolfenbüttel], and shall and will do and perform everything else that it befits, behooves, and well becomes
a faithful, diligent music director or any other pious and honest servant to do in relation to his lord, and what is honorable,
Christian, and right in itself, inasmuch as he has sworn Us his
fealty on oath and has given Us his acknowledgement letter.[9]

Thus, in addition to the palace in Gröningen, Praetorius was now
also working at the Wolfenbüttel palace, whose chapel Duke Julius had
already renovated and outfitted with an organ.

Fig. 21. *Das Fürstl. Schloss in der Vestung Wolffenbüttel* (partial, oriented
westward), engraving printed in Matthäus Merian's heirs, eds., *Topographia*
for Brunswick-Lüneburg (1654), after a drawing by Conrad Buno. Note the
beautiful palace chapel (*Schloss Capelle*) and the court print shop (*Hoff
Truckerey*). Cf. Fig. 48.—Trans.

From the text of this certificate of appointment, we can gather the
following responsibilities for Michael Praetorius:

9. Deeters, "Alte und neue Aktenfunde über Michael Praetorius," 103f. (I included
more of the original document than the author did.—Trans.)

1. Service as an organist and the direction of the chapel ensemble for the services in Gröningen and Wolfenbüttel.

2. Musical attendance at meals (table music) and in the chamber (music for entertainment and recreation).

3. Composition of music and the musical arrangement of festivals. It is unclear from the contract whether only the festivals of the church year are meant, or if weddings, baptisms, and the like are also included. Dancing music is not specially mentioned here, but it grew in importance in the years that followed.

4. Instruction of the duke's children in "the playing of instruments" (*Instrumenten-Schlagen*), as the playing of keyboard instruments was called in his day.[10] The ducal couple already had eight children in 1604, including the seventeen-year-old Dorothea Hedwig from the duke's first marriage. (Dorothea's mother had died while giving birth to her in 1587.)

Praetorius was thus expected to produce and perform not just works "suited to God's honor and praise" (sacred music), but also "respectable and cheerful and lighthearted songs" (secular music). The express mention in the contract of visits from "foreign lords" and "princely or other distinguished ambassadors" indicates, among other things, that music was also expected to benefit the prince's reputation. On top of all this, Praetorius was also responsible for the members of the chapel ensemble, whom he was supposed to keep "in a sober, restrained life, also holding regular musical exercises for this purpose."

Praetorius' salary is later specified in the contract as "a hundred thalers [and] ten thalers firewood allowance, half on the forthcoming Pentecost and the other half on the ensuing Christmas." In addition he received "free board at court [and] both a summer and winter court outfit."[11] The sum of a hundred thalers had been calculated from "three [hundred] and twelve," which presumably denoted florins or gulden; this amount was always entered in the chamber accounts as a second value next to the thalers. Praetorius had already received 270 gulden as chamber organist for the year 1603–1604, and in the roll of musicians for 1604–1605 his honorarium is specified as "307 florins, 16 groschen." Furthermore, the contract also contains a supplement in Praetorius' own hand: "As an

---

10. *See e.g. *SM* 2E1:27,66.

11. Deeters, "Alte und neue Aktenfunde über Michael Praetorius," 104.

annual bonus from Our administration here [in Wolfenbüttel], an ox, two field swine,[12] four bushels of rye, [and] four bushels of barley."[13] This bonus corresponded to that of his predecessor Thomas Mancinus. Both contracting parties had the right, among other things, to terminate the contract with a half-year advance notice.[14] Nothing, however, is to be found in the contract about fixed working hours or even vacation time.[15]

In the years that followed, Praetorius received various additional privileges from the duke, which were doubtless also rewards for his extra-musical services. He wrote in a letter dated September 26, 1608: "Our

Fig. 22. *Closter Amelunxborn,* engraving in Matthäus Merian's heirs, eds., *Topographia* for Brunswick-Lüneburg (1654).—Trans.

12. As opposed to stall swine or those kept in a smaller pen.—Trans.

13. Deeters, *op. cit.,* 104.

14. **Ibid.*

15. Following his installation ceremony on Dec. 10, 1604, Praetorius signed a copy of the church order in the princely council chamber, in the presence of seven witnesses, as follows: "Having considered this [doctrinal] position [*in hanc sententiam*] of our Most Illustrious Prince, I, Michael Praetorius, sincerely subscribe in my own hand to this body of doctrine and declaration in theses and antitheses, willingly and with premeditation. Signed in Wolfenbüttel, Dec. 10, 1604." (I created this footnote from a picture, caption, and credit in the author's original.—Trans.)

Most Illustrious Prince and Lord, gracious to us in all respects, supports me here so graciously and well that I could not desire it any better in all my life."[16] That year he became a conventual of the Amelungsborn Abbey (a voting member as an unordained clergyman) and by 1614 the prior of the Ringelheim Abbey. It is unknown, however, just how much he attended to these positions or to what extent he received a prebend for them. In 1609 the duke conferred on him the reversion of a fief in Schliestedt—also an exceptional token of the duke's favor, since a fief, strictly speaking, belonged only to a nobleman. But it then took a multi-year process for the enfeoffment to become legally valid for his sons Michael and Ernst.[17]

In 1612 Praetorius experienced two further extraordinary tokens of the duke's favor, which were both presented in Prague: In January, he received a gift of 2,000 imperial thalers "in exchange for the submissive and loyal service he has rendered to Us for some time now" and "also to alleviate the accompanying heavy expenses that have fallen upon him for the publication of his musical work, which he has prepared to God the Almighty's praise and honor for the common use and benefit of all churches and schools, having dedicated and attributed the most principal and distinguished installments to Us in submissive duty."[18] In June 1612 the duke legally transferred to him a parcel of land in the Great Carpenters' Yard in Wolfenbüttel, "fourteen spans or sixty-five feet in width and eighty-six [feet] in length," as "free, inheritable property" for the building of "a residence and brewery at his expense."[19]

16. *Ibid.*, 107.

17. Deeters, "Das Lehen der Familie Praetorius," 113ff.

18. Deeters, "Alte und neue Aktenfunde über Michael Praetorius," 108.

19. *Ibid.*, 109.

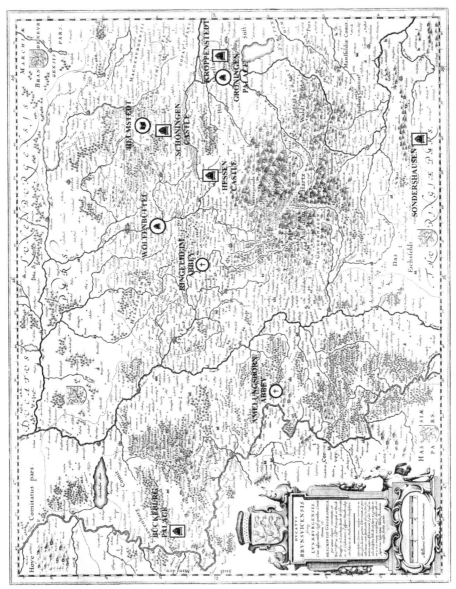

Fig. 23. Caspar Dauthendey, *Ducatus Brunsvicensis fereque Lunaeburgensis*, c. 1640, modified. The symbols represent Praetorius' activity and work in the area. Organ (circle): Service as court organist. Organ (rectangle): Service as consultant in the building of an organ. Cross: Religious position (conventual or prior). Book: Place of study.—Trans.

Musae Sioniae (The Muses of Zion)

With his appointment to the position of court music director, Praetorius began a multi-year period of intense compositional activity. The beginnings of this activity soon developed into whole series of works; Praetorius proved to be a great systematizer. The first of these series received the name *Musae Sioniae* (The Muses of Zion). With this title, Praetorius wished to convey that his muses resided on the holy Mount Zion[20] and not on the heathen Mount Parnassus. Both this title and the names he gave his later works, which combine Latin and Greek, show Praetorius' partiality for the classical languages and classical mythology.

Fig. 24. *Musarum Sioniarum Motectae et Psalmi Latini* (1607), title page. (Note the juxtaposition of the separately placed choirs answering each other on earth [with Psalm 95:1 and 9:11] and the choirs singing the *Sanctus* and *Gloria in Excelsis* to each other in heaven. On the left side of the organ is written: "The one who sighs to God finds that God saves him. M. Praetor. C." On the right side is Psalm 146:2.—Trans.)

First to be prepared for print was a collection of fifty-two compositions on religious texts in Latin, *Musarum Sioniarum Motectae et Psalmi Latini* (Latin Motets and Psalms of the Muses of Zion).[21] They are regarded as

20. See e.g. Psalms 9, 43, 132, and 137.—Trans.

21. Even though the earliest extant copies of this work were published in 1607 by Abraham Wagenmann of Nuremberg, whereas the earliest extant copies of the first installment of the German *Musae Sioniae* were published in 1605 by Bartholmäus Gräf of Regensburg (see Bibliography), a number of factors indicate that the pieces in the Latin collection were produced first, if not also published first in a now-lost edition. To name just a few: 1) Praetorius' dedication in the Latin collection dates to January 1605, just like his dedication in the first German installment. 2) The only dated poetic tribute in the front matter of the Cantus part book is dated 1603. 3) He dedicated the Latin collection to Duke Heinrich Julius, and the first German installment to the duke's wife,

experimental works, through which Praetorius cultivated the compositional craft, and they already testify to his great musical talent. It was thus
not until "quite late" in his life, at the age of nearly thirty, that he "ended
up in the practice of music,"[22] and we have yet to identify any musician
with whom Praetorius might have been apprenticed. He never made it
to Italy either, to his own great disappointment. He thus remained a self-
taught musical artist his entire life. He thereby followed in the footsteps of
many musicians, picking up the craft of composition purely by studying
the works of eminent prototypes. Praetorius dedicated the Latin Motets
and Psalms to his employer Heinrich Julius,[23] and informed him in the
dedication of his resolution "that the talent entrusted to me by God is to
be employed in the crafting and cultivation of sacred music."[24]

These compositions dedicated to the duke already exhibit the "new
style of Venetian polychorality with nearly every stroke.

> One of the pieces is arranged for sixteen voices divided into
> four choirs. This arrangement corresponds almost exactly to the
> number of musicians (not including the chapel boys) who, as the
> salary registers disclose, held steady positions of employment at
> the court since about 1602. In other pieces Praetorius divides
> the tools at his disposal into one or two solo voice choirs and a
> tutti choir in which all the remaining musicians are combined.
> In those pieces the tutti choir is not seldom used to organize
> the compositions through the use of repeating, ritornello-type
> sections that imitate each other both textually and musically.
> The individual choirs are furthermore so separated from each
> other, that even the space is incorporated in the interplay of the
> various choirs in their varied personnel.[25]

For his subsequent compositions, Praetorius initially turns to German texts, as represented in the hymns of the Reformation, "in order that
our German language may also not be completely forgotten . . . not to
mention that so many glorious Latin church songs are being produced

---

Duchess Elisabeth. It is unlikely that he would have given preference to his employer's
wife before his employer himself. See also the par. about the Diet of Regensburg in
1603 on pp. 78–79. On the possibility of an earlier edition of the Latin Motets, see
WGD, 148, n. 2.—Trans.

22. *SM 2, fol.):(11 verso (incorrectly printed) /):(13 verso (corrected).

23. *MSL, fol. (2) recto; reprinted in GA 10:vii.

24. Ibid., fol. (2) verso; GA 10:viii.

25. Forchert, "Michael Praetorius und die Musik am Hof von Wolfenbüttel," 630.

in stacks by distinguished and famous musicians and composers, more and more with every passing day."[26] Thus emerged a German collection parallel to the Latin Motets, this one containing twenty-one compositions for two choirs based on Protestant hymns, which he dedicated to Duchess Elisabeth.[27]

> Even a passing glance at the title page [of this first installment of the German *Musae Sioniae*] sheds light on [the religious context in which it was produced]. For neither the name of the composer nor the indication of the compositional genre or the manner of scoring is as conspicuously emphasized by the format of the printing as the large name of "Mr. Luther [*Herrn Lutheri*]." One cannot fail to see in this a clear expression of religious profession by the Lutheran preacher's son.[28]

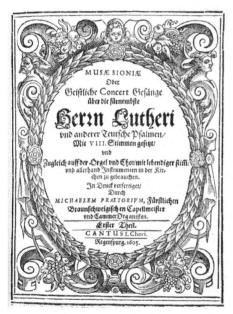

Fig. 25. *Musae Sioniae*, Installment I (1605), title page.—Trans.

Both installments—the one with the scoring of Latin texts and the other with the scoring of evangelical hymns—comprised the germ for more extensive plans: Praetorius intended to compose music for the complete repertoire of both the Latin mass and the German Lutheran mass. Both series also accounted for the different forms of worship in Gröningen and Wolfenbüttel. In Gröningen the duke, in his capacity as bishop of Halberstadt, adhered to the Latin rite, albeit with texts that had been "cleaned up" in keeping with the Reformation, while services in Wolfenbüttel were under the influence of the Lutheran-bred Duchess Elisabeth and the strict court preacher Basilius Sattler. The relatively liberal attitude of the duke

26. *MS* 4, fol. (:) ii recto; reprinted in GA 4:vii.

27. **MS* 1, fol. (*) ii recto (dated Jan. 6, 1605); reprinted in GA 1:xiv.

28. WGD, 143. (I added this quote.—Trans.)

in religious questions is probably what also prevented any destruction of images in the Halberstadt cathedral when the Reformation was introduced there in 1591.

*Praetorius now concentrated primarily on Protestant hymns; they became the chief source material for his works. Already in 1607 he published three additional installments with eight- to twelve-part choral motets for two to three choirs—together with Installment I, 121 pieces in total. He dedicated these to Electress Hedwig of Saxony in Dresden, a sister of Duchess Elisabeth (Installment II),[29] Count Ernst of Holstein-Schaumburg in Bückeburg (Installment III),[30] and Elector and Count Palatine Friedrich IV of Heidelberg (Installment IV).[31] All collections contain very revealing dedications that tell us, among other things, their author's various connections to the dedicatees.

Encircling the title plate on the title page of Installment II, we encounter these words for the first time:

> *Raptus amore chely, patiens durissima vinco.*
> *Nulla salus mundo, dulcis mihi patria coelum.*[32]

> Enraptured by love for the lute, I patiently overcome the most difficult hardships.
> There is no salvation with the world; heaven is my sweet fatherland.

The opening words, "*Raptus amore chely*," comprise an anagram of *Michael Praetorius* (the letter *y* being treated as the equivalent of two *i*'s).[33] The closing words, "*mihi patria coelum*," very nearly form a second anagram, but more importantly, they share the same first letters, in order, as Praetorius' initials—Michael Praetorius Creuzbergensis (of Creuzburg). Praetorius later modified and expanded this into two elegiac couplets and had it printed as his creed (*symbolum*):

> *RAPTUS AMORE CHELY^s sanctae, Deus, ardua vinco:*
> *Non mundana volo raptus amore tui.*
> *Nulla salus mundo, dulcis Mihi Patria Coelum,*

---

29. *MS 2, fol.)(ii recto (dated March 25, 1606); reprinted in GA 2:vii.

30. *MS 3, fol.)(ii recto (dated July 5, 1607); reprinted in GA 3:vii.

31. *MS 4, fol. (:) ii recto (dated Aug. 25, 1607); reprinted in GA 4:vii.

32. MS 2, title page; reprinted in GA 2:v.

33. He seems to have come up with this anagram himself, though in subsequent installments it is repeatedly employed by more than one poet in the tributes to Praetorius published with the installments.—Trans.

Quod mihi munde negas, hoc mihi IOVA dabis.[34]

Enraptured by love for the sacred lute, O God, I overcome difficulties;
   I do not desire worldly things, enraptured by love for you.
There is no salvation with the world; heaven is my sweet fatherland.
That which you deny me, O world, Jehovah shall give me.

He then signed this creed with the double-meaning initials "M. P. C.," which he also often used thereafter.

Praetorius adopts the Venetian polychoral form in his German compositions too. But he attempts to take the statements of faith contained in the texts and unfold them musically according to his theological understanding—by having the choirs repeat passages that he considers important in dialogue with each other, and by accentuating petitions, thanks, and praise through alternating meters and tempos, and alternating homophonic and polyphonic sections. Analyzing these compositions simply according to the rules of harmony and counterpoint will therefore not do any justice whatsoever to the intentions of their composer. Such an analysis can only provide the material to be interpreted; it cannot serve as the interpretation itself.

After the publication of Installment IV, Praetorius had Installments I–IV published together, with a new title page (1607). The artwork adorning the new title page was also used for a few subsequent installments; it will be treated at greater length later. The back side of this title page featured a woodcut portrait of Praetorius in his court music director uniform at age thirty-five. Included with the portrait is a round for five voices. The first time through, each voice sings the words of Psalm 118:17 in Latin: "I shall not die [*Non moriar*], but live, and will recount the works of the Lord." The second time through, each voice sings in Latin: "When I die [*Cum moriar*], grant that I may die a pious and peaceful death." We can therefore quite safely understand Psalm 118:17 as the motto for his work. Martin Luther was also especially fond of this psalm and a four-part composition by him on verse 17 has even come down to us.[35] Praetorius likewise prefixed Luther's *Encomion Musices*, an elaborate "praise of music," to this collection of his *Musae Sioniae*.[36]

---

34. *MS* Coll., Altus I. Chori, fol.)(2 recto; reprinted in GA 1:xii.

35. WA 35:535–38.

36. *MS* Coll., Cantus I. Chori, fols.)(2 recto—)(iii verso; reprinted in GA 1:vii–ix. Cf. *Dr. Martin Luthers Sämmtliche Schriften*, vol. 14 (St. Louis: Concordia Publishing House, 1898), 429f.

Fig. 26. *Michael Praetorius Creutzbergensis*, 1606, back side of the title page in *MS* Coll. (1607). The couplets on three sides of the portrait are in elegiac meter. Left: "I am battered all over the place, but you, O Christ, bring me help when I call, | Because in grace you humble me, but you also impart help." Right: "The Lord disciplines me, yet the shadow of death has by no means overwhelmed me; | I rejoice that Lord presses me hard but also helps me." Bottom (flipped to make sense in English): "This is Michael Praetor the musician, before whose face | The chorus of Muses and music as a whole rises out of respect." (The Latin words in the four corners of the portrait read: "Save me, O Lord, God of my salvation." Though the artist left his monogram, he has yet to be identified.—Trans.)

Also to be found in this multi-installment collection, after the general index, is a *Votum sanctum Domino*, a "holy vow to the Lord":

> Sacred Progenitor, sacred positions in wisdom creating,
>> Giving them freely to each, taking them too, as you choose,
> You who appointed my forefathers, father, and kinsmen beloved
>> Altar and gifts to approach, sacraments pure to dispense—
> Men of devotion, the gospel expounding in words and in writings
>> Ever with wholesome effect, eminent forebears indeed—
> Lo, here am I, their heir and successor, in no way inferior,
>> Though diff'rent duties than theirs I by your guidance pursue.
> One and the same is the aim (not to mention the zeal and the fervor):
>> What they endeavored with words, I seek with strings and with song.
> They served as priests, but I am a psalm-writer, singing your dogmas
>> Just as Saint David once did, using his voice and the lute.
> Lend me your aid! And if 'tis your grace has placed me in music,
>> Deeming me worthy to sound deeds of the glorious God,
> Please then increase my traces of talent, bestowed from your bounty,
>> Lest, when I put it to use, find you no pleasure therein.
> Thus shall my tinklings[37] care nothing for how proud World may esteem them—
>> Let them malign while I live, put off acclaim till I'm dead!
> Fate may decree my release when it please, whether sooner or later
>> (Oft may I these words repeat, or never pray them again);
> It will suffice if you grant me salvation the day of your judgment.
>> Add me to angel-filled throngs, choirs singing rapturous songs;
> Psalms shall I play you on strings, yea, psalms with my mouth shall I sing you—
>> Happy your psalmist to be, happy your priest to be too.
> All that I seek is this honor, O Lord: I wish to re-echo
>> Strains that I sing you on earth perfect and rich there on high.[38]

Another later text by Praetorius, on the beneficial effect of music in the hearts of men, also fits here:

---

37. Latin: *crepitacula*. In *SM 2* Praetorius uses *crepitaculum* as the Latin name for the triangle, whose appearance and use in his day was very similar to that of the modern triangle, except that it had several rings on the lower bar (p. 4; *SM 2E*, 23; and Plate XXII in the back). Here he uses *crepitacula* for the sounds produced by the triangle—a somewhat self-deprecating metaphor for the music he has composed.—Trans.

38. *MS* Coll., Cantus I. Chori, fol.)( )(iv verso; reprinted in *GA* 1:xii. (I translated this directly from the Latin original rather than from the author's German translation and included more of the original poem than he did.—Trans.)

Some are of the view that, next to theology, the highest place should rightfully be given and assigned to music,[39] since it is a beautiful and glorious gift of God and the one foreshadowing and likeness of the music in heaven, where God's holy angels, together with the entire heavenly host, continually praise and extol their Creator in a lovely harmony without interruption and sing the *Sanctus, sanctus, sanctus Dominus Deus Sabaoth* ["Holy, holy, holy is the Lord God of hosts"].[40] Perhaps not the weakest basis for this view is that, among music's many other benefits, virtues, and effects, music in itself is to be regarded more as a spiritual entity than an earthly one, and hence it awakens in human hearts an inner attention of the spirit which enables them to praise God the Almighty that much more fervently with beautiful psalms and songs of praise. This, then, is also why both King David and King Solomon, when they wished to set up the services in the temple and tabernacle in Jerusalem as gloriously and magnificently as possible, appointed so many musicians, singers, and instrumentalists at great effort and expense;[41] they wanted to make the people that much more fervent and zealous in their worship. David himself also used his harps for this purpose,[42] and he doubtless had several glorious organs prepared and installed on account of the temple's size.[43]

Still today, therefore, church music should continue to be rightfully held in esteem and celebrated with all reverence as a service to God.[44]

As the title of the 1607 multi-installment collection already makes clear, Praetorius was developing a new project for the ensuing installments of the *Musae Sioniae*. He had reflected on the fact that not all congregations and schools had choirs as well supplied as the Wolfenbüttel court chapel ensemble. He "therefore did not want to grudge the effort

39. Praetorius has Martin Luther foremost in mind; cf. n. 36 above, also WA 30/2:695f and *LW* 49:426–28.—Trans.

40. See Isaiah 6:3.

41. See 1 Chronicles 15:1—16:6; 23:1; 25; 2 Chronicles 5; 7:1–6; 8:12–15.

42. See 2 Samuel 6:5; cf. 1 Samuel 16:14–23.

43. Cf. *SM* 1:107–9; *SM* 1E:230–233. Some scholars have also inferred that organ-like instruments once existed in the temple from some obscure references in the Babylonian Talmud (*Arachin* 10b–11a). See JewishEncyclopedia.com, s. v. "Organ."—Trans.

44. *SM* 2:82; cf. *SM* 2E2, same page. (I included more of the original quote than the author did.—Trans.)

of also putting together a collection of hymns, as well as our dear God would allow, for two, three, four, five, six, and seven parts."[45]

> I have made plans to take the exact same psalms that are composed with eight or more parts divided into multiple choirs (*per choros*) in the first four installments and to score them with two, three, four, five, six, or seven parts in the following fifth, sixth, seventh, eighth, etc. installments. That way, a psalm verse that has been composed in fugal style can occasionally be sung by the [smaller] musical choir alone, and then also, as time allows and it is considered appropriate, one verse after the next can be sounded and sung together in choral and figural along with the entire congregation, both with full and unified sound and with striking and solemn harmony,[46] which is the way I think (and the Psalms themselves suggest) it was possibly done in David's time and in the years following him.[47]

His fifth installment of the *Musae Sioniae* (1608)[48] he therefore dedicated "to all godly, pious hearts at churches, schools, and congregations of the German nation, our beloved fatherland, and to admirers and patrons of the worthy art of music."[49] As an example of Praetorius' musical word-painting, in no. 52, a four-part setting of "Nun komm, der Heiden Heiland [Savior of the Nations, Come]," he has the phrase "*des sich wundert alle Welt* [At which marvels all the earth]" sung forty-two times.[50] He may have been thinking of the words in Luke's Gospel: "And *all who heard it* were amazed at what the shepherds said to them" (2:18).[51]

45. GA 5:vi.

46. Praetorius is explaining what singing "in choral and figural" means. He is talking about alternating between the choir and congregation singing the melody in unison (singing in choral or chorally) and having the choir accompany the congregation in harmonic parts (singing in figural or figurally). Also see *choral* and *figural* in the Glossary.—Trans.

47. Appendix IV, A, p. 173.

48. Even though the title page (GA 5:v) says 1607, the prefatory material contains three Latin tributes dated 1608 (GA 5:xii,xiii) and the closing page is explicitly dated 1608 (GA 5:xv, follows p. 336).—Trans.

49. Appendix IV, B, p. 176.

50. *GA 5:115.

51. In other words, Praetorius is using repetition to portray many people—"all the earth" or "all who heard it"—marveling at the Savior's birth, similar to how J. S. Bach would later have "Is it I, Lord?" (Matt 26:22) sung eleven times in his *St. Matthew Passion* to represent each disciple asking it except Judas, who would ask it separately later (26:25).—Trans.

At the end he solemnly emphasizes: "*Gott solch Geburt ihm bestellt* [God prepared him such a birth]."

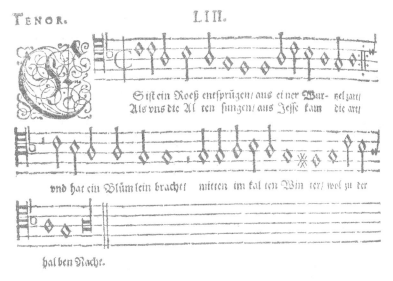

Fig. 27. Tenor part for "Es ist ein Ros entsprungen," *Musae Sioniae*, Installment VI, no. 53, courtesy of Winfried Elsner. Note the stylized late form of Renaissance mensural notation. (The soprano, alto, and tenor parts of this setting all employed a C clef, while the bass part employed an F clef [precursor of the modern bass clef].—Trans.)

For Installments VI–VIII, published in 1609 and 1610, Praetorius wrote 740 choir pieces "with only four parts in simple counterpoint,"[52] along with two in five-part settings. With settings like "Es ist ein Ros entsprungen [Behold, a Branch Is Growing *or* Lo, How a Rose E'er Blooming]" in Installment VI,[53] he proves that such restrictions do not preclude the possibility of accompanying parts that are both lovely and musical. Praetorius includes several of his own original texts in Installments VII and VIII,[54] and organ compositions on "four German psalms without text" at the end of Installment VII.[55] In addition, these collections contain detailed information on the origin of the melodies and texts. They are

52. GA 7:vii, note 3.

53. *GA 6:35–36.

54. See GA 7:viii (Index), nos. 62–66 (cf. WGD, 303, n. 2); GA 8:ix–xi (Index), nos. 29–32, 90, 251, 291, though some of these are enlargements of already existing hymns.—Trans.

55. GA 7:vii, note 2, and 263–304.

accordingly a hymnological and music-historical record of the first rank, one that also testifies to its author's scholarly methodology in thought and procedure. These numerous settings continue to be of immeasurable value for the use of music in the church's worship.

Installment IX (1610) contains "psalms and songs customarily used in churches and homes with two and three parts in motet and madrigal style, and some in another, original style invented by the author."[56] This self-invented style consisted of a melody sung by one voice at an even and unhurried pace, accompanied by other voices with distinct, more intricately structured motifs based on the melody, with the goal of emphasizing the content of the text in a particular way.[57]

In his "Author's Note to the Musical Reader" in Installment IX, Praetorius declared his plans for at least three additional collections in which he would rework the hymns he had arranged for eight parts in Installments I–IV and for two and three parts in Installment IX. He wanted, among other things, to score them "in motet style with five parts in imitation of Orlando di Lasso," "in madrigal style with five parts in imitation of Luca Marenzio and other Italians," and "with six parts in the style of [Tomás] Luis de Victoria, just as if they were scored for multiple choirs," thus in polychoral style but without being separately positioned.[58] Though these plans were unrealized,[59] he nevertheless shows here his familiarity with and fondness for the great prototypes of his time. Elsewhere he repeatedly speaks of Orlando di Lasso with high admiration.[60]

After Installment IX of the *Musae Sioniae*, Praetorius returned to the Latin compositions that he had initially shelved, publishing four collections in 1611. *Missodia Sionia* (The Missody[61] of Zion) contains 104 settings of the texts and Gregorian melodies of the Ordinary, for two to

56. *GA 9:v.

57. Thus, for example, no. 153, a setting of Martin Luther's famous hymn "Ein feste Burg [A Mighty Fortress]" in this style, generates a rich and powerful effect, despite being arranged for only three parts.—Trans.

58. *GA 9:ix.

59. *See WGD, 174, n. 1; also *SM* 3E:205–6.

60. *E.g. *SM* 3E:6,23,71.

61. That is, the singing of the Ordinary of the Mass. Note that *mass* was not a term exclusive to the Roman Catholic Church, since the Lutherans also retained most of the Ordinary in their services. The use of the word, therefore, was not in itself indicative of solidarity with, or an extending of the olive branch toward, the Roman Catholic Church, as some suppose.—Trans.

eight parts.[62] *Hymnodia Sionia* (The Hymnody of Zion) contains 145 settings of ancient hymns for two to eight parts.[63] *Eulogodia Sionia* (The Eulogody[64] of Zion) contains sixty settings of *Benedicamus* and *Deodicamus* texts (i.e. "Let us bless the Lord." "Let us give thanks to God.") for two to eight parts.[65] And *Megalynodia Sionia* (The Megalynody[66] of Zion) contains fourteen *Magnificat* scores for five to eight parts.[67]*

But musical performance *per choros*—that is, using multiple vocal and instrumental choirs variously positioned in the church interior—probably corresponded to Praetorius' musical ideas in a special way. As the artwork adorning some of his title pages shows, this arrangement portrayed for him a resounding universe, in which earthly and heavenly choirs blend their music in one magnificent song of praise. *He once wrote that admirers of singing with multiple choirs

> take special note of it not just on account of the excellence of the harmony and artistry (since oftentimes more art and industry may be found in the songs with three, four, or five parts than in others with eight, ten, or twelve parts), but on account of the singular force which emanates from the alternating or interchanging variation and which affects the souls of the listeners in the highest degree.[68]

His experience as an organ player and his fondness for that "prince of instruments"[69] also contributed to his choir performance preferences.

---

62. GA 11.

63. GA 12.

64. That is, the adoration encouraged of the people and given to God in song towards the conclusion of matins and vespers. The *eulog-* prefix stems from the Greek equivalent (εὐλογῶμεν) of the Latin *benedicamus*, the first word of the invitation chanted by the worship leader or choir toward the end of matins and vespers: *Benedicamus Domino*, "Let us bless/praise the Lord." (Praetorius says in *SM* 1:75–76, that in his time the *Benedicamus* was intoned by young boys, and the *Deo dicamus gratias* was sung in response by the entire choir.)—Trans.

65. GA 13.

66. That is, the magnifying of the Lord done by Mary in her song (Luke 1:46–55) and repeated by those who sing her song. The *megalyn-* prefix stems from the first word of Mary's song in Greek (μεγαλύνει), while the usual name for her song, *Magnificat*, is its first word in Latin. The suffix *-ody* in all four titles stems from the Greek word ᾠδή, meaning "song" or "singing" (whence also the English word *ode*).—Trans.

67. GA 14.

68. Appendix IV, A, p. 172.

69. *SM* 1:139; *SM* 1E:288.

After all, polychorality was but an imitation of the "lovely and very pleasing" alternation "between two or three [organ] manuals." Due to the strong correlation between the two, Praetorius hoped that especially the first four installments of his *Musae Sioniae* would also prove useful to and adaptable by organists.[70]*

To adapt this polychoral music to more modest circumstances, Praetorius drew on his experience from visits to the Kassel court: There the congregation sang in four parts in alternation with the court chapel ensemble, thus comprising one of the multiple choirs and taking an active singing role as such.[71] Thus in 1613 a volume of twenty-eight compositions appeared under the title *Urania oder Urano-Chorodia*, which Praetorius himself translated in one of his forewords as "heavenly music for singing by choirs, or heavenly choir music."[72] Its *cantional* settings (as they were called) were "scored very simply and plainly for use by two, three, or four choirs" singing eight to sixteen total parts, some of them accompanied by instruments, "so that the common folk can also join along in the choral singing in church."[73] Praetorius dedicated this work to Duke Johann Friedrich of Württemberg—one of his most comprehensive dedications. It contains a theological rationale for church music, with a poetic force that stems from the fourth century church father Basil of Caesarea:

> God the Lord has placed the knowledge of musical harmony in human hearts and has always had his divine doctrine and the glory of his holy name recorded in songs, thereby prompting worship to be rendered to him, primarily for these two reasons:
> First, that his holy Church might all the more joyfully and gladly proclaim his grace and truth and praise and honor him with spirit and mouth. To do so "is a precious thing" (Psalm 92:1). And secondly, that the doctrine about the true God and all divine exhortations, comfort, praise, and thanksgiving contained

---

70. Appendix IV, A, pp. 172–73.

71. *GA 16:viii. According to Moser in *Heinrich Schütz*, Praetorius visited Kassel in 1605 and 1609 (pp. 40–41). For more on Landgrave Moritz (Maurice) of Hesse-Kassel and his court, see Moser, 33–43; of particular interest is the list of instruments used in the landgrave's court orchestra on p. 41.

72. Urania (Οὐρανία; note its closeness to οὐράνια, "heavenly things") came to be known as the Muse of astronomy, but as Praetorius pointed out in one of his forewords in the work, "the ancients also attributed heavenly and angelic music" to her, "in that they painted [her] with an organ or positif" (GA 16:viii).—Trans.

73. *GA 16:v. I was rather free in my translation in these two sentences, borrowing more heavily from the title page and Praetorius' forewords than the author did.

in the psalms and in harmonious settings might be that much
more easily and deeply inculcated in hearts, so that they might be
kindled and roused to the burning zeal of true godliness.

For since the Holy Spirit has seen that the human heart is
difficult to bend toward godliness and virtue, while being all too
greatly inclined to sensuality, he has blended God's commands
with the loveliness and pleasure of melody, so that together
with its sweetness the knowledge and praise of God and of all
Christian virtues might be poured into their hearts. This is the
same practice that wise doctors have when, in order to get their
patients to take the bitter, repulsive medicine, they first mix it
with plenty of sweet and delicious juices.[74]

Thus in the eight years from 1605–1613, fifteen total installments of
the Latin and German *Musae Sioniae* (Muses of Zion) appeared in print.
These installments contained more than 1,600 compositions, along with
extensive information about their origins and performance.

When one surveys the compositions of the *Musae Sioniae*, it becomes evident that Praetorius "followed two clearly distinguishable
traditions" in producing them—

on the one hand, the tradition of arranging Protestant hymns
polyphonically, dating back to the time of the Reformation, and
on the other hand, the cultivation, in conformity with Luther's
Formula missae (Form for Mass),[75] of Gregorian hymns, with
which Praetorius had already become acquainted in the Latin
school . . . It therefore makes sense, when evaluating his music,
to separate the German choral compositions from the Latin
works that follow the pattern of the Gregorian hymn.[76]

At the same time, the fifteen installments in this series are also
aimed at different audiences. The polychoral compositions are designed
for court chapel ensembles, for use within the musical structure of court
church services, court festivities, and princely gatherings, as their dedications to princely personages show. The others are intended for the choristries in cities and villages and for the religious institutions and cloisters.

---

74. GA 16:vi. (I included more of the original quote than the author. The author
introduced the quote by saying that it "might stem from Martin Luther," but most of
these thoughts are contained in a quote from Basil's Homily on the First Psalm, which
Praetorius cites in *SM* 1:17–18. The quote can be found in PG 29:211–12.—Trans.)

75. *See *LW* 53:15ff.

76. *MGG* Personenteil, 13:887, s. v. "Praetorius, Michael."

From the start, Praetorius experienced many difficulties with the printers when having his compositions printed. He once wrote about this:

> And as rather easily and quickly as our dear God permits me, through his divine grace, to work out such admittedly modest and simple composition and to put it to paper, it is equally as difficult and unpleasant for me to get my work put into print with all the different hindrances and frustrations, so that it would be no surprise if I got so displeased and disgusted that I abandoned it all and let it lie.[77]

Granted, Praetorius was also anxious for the highest possible degree of accuracy with the prints, and would always therefore withhold them from publication initially, so that they could first be revised. As a result, he left much of his work unpublished at the end of his life, which appears to have been subsequently lost. Upon returning from a trip and reviewing the defective prints waiting for him, he would emit many sighs of frustration and break out into a cold sweat. This lasted to the end of his life, so that he once wrote that he had "sometimes thought [his] work must be repugnant to God himself, and therefore abandoning it altogether [had] frequently crossed [his] mind."[78]

But many of the problems with the printers he probably also caused himself, when he inserted new texts into the proofs because he had received new information or gained new insights in the meantime. Difficulties with the drafting and printing of his works can also be traced to "the exceedingly many demanding affairs, repeated traveling, and other notable hindrances that keep popping up, from which one cannot easily be excused at princely courts and chapels," so that Praetorius often had only "scarce and almost stolen time" for it, and even had to work late into the night to finish it. On top of all that, he also writes of "all sorts of inconveniences and physical infirmities, to which [he had] been subject for several years,"[79] so that he was "a heavily plagued man," as Pastor Tuckermann said in the graveside remarks at his funeral.[80]

Praetorius' works did not exclusively garner him approval, but also varying degrees of ill will, from people "who [were] better at criticizing

---

77. GA 9:ix. (I included more of the original quote than the author.—Trans.)

78. GA 17:xxi.

79. GA 9:viii.

80. Appendix III, p. 165.

everything than composing anything," as he once derisively remarked.[81] He self-assuredly stands up to them:

> I will accordingly use [the gifts and grace that God has bestowed upon me], modest as they may be, and whatever I have additionally learned up to this point through constant, unremitting practice and diligence (notwithstanding all those who might twist and misinterpret it on me), to the benefit of my neighbor and the most highly praiseworthy Germany, as my beloved fatherland . . . Therefore, as long any breath remains in me, I will not refrain from doing good to my neighbor and serving him with the talent God has bestowed upon me. Even if I earn only a little thanks from some people in doing so, or none at all, that does not matter enough to let me be hindered from my good, well-intentioned, Christian plans or to be dissuaded from them.[82]

Musae Aoniae (The Muses of Aonia)

Two months before penning the foreword for his general introduction to all the Latin installments of his *Musae Sioniae* on May 1, 1612,[83] Praetorius wrote the dedication for his first collection of secular music.[84] The impetus to move into this arena came from the young Duke Friedrich Ulrich, the oldest son of the ducal couple and Praetorius' eventual employer. The young duke had been on one of the grand tours through neighboring countries that were common among young noblemen at the time for educational and formative purposes, and had "brought back [the] dancing master Anthoine Emeraud of Gaul [i.e. France]" to the Wolfenbüttel court, probably in 1610.[85] Emeraud's personal effects included a large number of French dance melodies, which Praetorius now converted into full, polyphonic settings at Friedrich Ulrich's behest, so that the court chapel ensemble could perform them on appropriate occasions. The collection appeared in 1612 under the name *Terpsichore*—the Muse of dance—and comprises 312 pieces. They include "21 branles, 13 other dances with peculiar names [like 'Les Passepiedz de Bretaigne (The

81. *GA 16:vii.

82. GA 15:ix. (I included more of the original quote than the author.—Trans.)

83. *LSL*, foreword ("Lectori Salutem.").

84. GA 15:vii. (I expanded on the author's material here to make the reader aware of *LSL*, otherwise unmentioned by the author.—Trans.)

85. *Ibid.*; WGD, 200, n. 1.

Footsteps of Britannia)' and 'La Canarie (The Canary Islands)'], 162 cou-
rantes, 48 voltas, 37 ballets, 3 passamezzi, 23 galliards, and 4 reprinses."[86]
The ballets—with names like "Ballet des Coqs [The Cocks' (*or* Roosters')
Ballet]," "Ballet des sorciers [The Sorcerers' Ballet]," and "Ballet des Ama-
zones [The Amazons' Ballet]," and having as many as seventeen separate
movements[87]—are examples of the modern *ballets de cour* (French court
dances) of Praetorius' day, which were danced in elaborate, colorful cos-
tumes, with all the members of the court society participating.

The commentary accompanying the dances in *Terpsichore* is of tre-
mendous value. Praetorius explains their origins, what their names mean,
and the nature and manner of their performance, though he does not
give any dancing instructions or details about dance steps or routines.[88]
He furthermore discloses his plan "also to give the secular Muses of
Aonia their due attention, insofar as propriety and decency will allow."[89]
These Muses were to appear under the series title *Musae Aoniae* (The
Muses of Aonia) and were to consist of the following individual volumes:
English and Italian pavanes, dances, galliards, etc. under the name of Eu-
terpe; sinfonias in pavane style and ritornellos in galliard and courante
style under the name of Melpomene; toccatas and other canzonas with
colorations and diminutions, for violins and clavicymbals,[90] under the
name of Thalia (two installments); and German secular songs under the
names of Calliope (two installments) and Erato.[91] Later he writes that
they were "almost completely finished, but not yet in print"[92]—and thus
it unfortunately remained. Even so, Praetorius reports in a few places on
the performance of his madrigals and secular songs which, as he once
put it in his characteristically understated way, "a few people did not find

86. GA 15:v,x,xvi. (I added this sentence. A reprinse is a type of coda for performing at the end of a galliard.—Trans.)

87. *GA 15:x, xvii, xviii, 154–57.

88. Recently discovered authentic dancing instructions were published in *Tänze
der Renaissance*, Polyhymnia – Musik aus Wolfenbüttel 3 (Salzgitter: Kulturstadt
Wolfenbüttel e.V., 2005).

89. GA 15:viii.

90. The clavicymbal was an ancestor of the harpsichord. See Plate VI on p. 70 and
SM 2E1:66.—Trans.

91. *GA 15:viii; *SM* 3:216, 220–221; *SM* 3E:204,207. (I filled out this
sentence.—Trans.)

92. *SM* 3E:207.

so entirely unpleasant"[93]—an indication that they had belonged to the repertoire of the court chapel ensemble for a long time.[94]

The *Syntagma Musicum*: A Compendium of the Musical Knowledge of the Time

The efforts of the composer to view his work in larger contexts, as well as "the wise instigation of very good friends,"[95] caused another plan to ripen, one whereby he would provide a theoretical basis for his practical activity and describe that activity encyclopedically. To that end he began wide-ranging studies that dragged on for years, since he could only pursue them outside of his everyday responsibilities. In preparation, he conducted an extensive correspondence and had numerous prints sent to him from Venice, Florence, and Rome. He mentions in this connection more than one hundred composers whose works he has carefully scrutinized, including those of Giovanni Gabrieli and Claudio Monteverdi, whose *Vespro della Beata Vergine* (Vespers for the Blessed Virgin) he describes in fascination.[96] (He once lamented the fact that he himself had not made it to Italy to converse and form acquaintances and friendships with the many excellent musicians there, as other musicians of his time had.[97]) He gave this theoretical work the series title *Syntagma Musicum* (Musical Compendium) and planned from the start to have it appear in four volumes.[98]

Praetorius wrote the first volume in Latin and interspersed it with a plethora of Greek and Hebrew quotations. It testifies to a well-founded theological education and an encyclopedic knowledge of the Bible and the writings of antiquity. In this volume, he gives a complete overview of sacred and secular music from its beginnings on 459 pages divided into two parts. Yet his intent is not just to give a historical overview, but also to show the significance music has had in worship dating back to Old Testament times. In doing so, it is important to him that proclamation through speech (*concio*) and proclamation through music (*cantio*) stand

---

93. *SM* 3:177; cf. *SM* 3E:179.

94. Möller-Weiser, *Untersuchungen zum I. Band des Syntagma musicum*, 67.

95. *SM* 1:158. (I added this clause.—Trans.)

96. *SM* 3E:118f.

97. *SM* 3E:9.

98. *SM* 1, fol. A verso; see also the "General Register," fols. a iii recto—c 2 verso. Cf. *SM* 3E:207–9.

next to each other on equal footing.[99] In his dedication for a later musical work, he formulates this idea into his church music credo:

> For the perfection and stability of the church's administration and for full worship of God, not only is *concio*, good preaching, necessary, but also required is *cantio*, good music and singing. For Justin's opinion is right and true: . . . "It is and remains God's word whether it is pondered in the mind, sung with the voice, or struck and played on instruments."[100]

*Praetorius takes a carefully balanced position on secular music. On the one hand, he says that the Christian church "justly and piously detests" the music of the ancients used "in the worship and sacrificial rites of heathen gods," and that the church's music "outdistances [such idolatrous music] by many leagues with its excellence." Only sacred music has the power to "captivate the truly devoted mind," to "animate, comfort, and fortify the heart" with "spiritual vigor," and to stir up "affections of piety." On the other hand, he acknowledges that "most of the light of present-day music" in both the ecclesiastical and secular spheres is conveyed from the secular music of the ancients, and that secular music also has a measure of stimulative and restorative power of its own. Quoting Aristotle, he says that the entire life consists of toil and rest, and both sacred and secular music play a key role in hard work's corresponding rest.[101]

Praetorius also validates secular music's ability to arouse "the pleasurable emotions," in opposition to "certain sullen Scythians." In fact, he asserts that "human life is not possible without the pleasurable emotions.

> For what would this life be if, having been deprived of any amusement and any pleasure, it were spent in perpetual anxiety and sadness? It is precisely because we are all moved to pleasurable emotions, but few people are acquainted with decent, pure, and appropriate ones, that most people pursue unlawful, foul, and inappropriate ones and pass their entire life

99. *SM 1, fols. a 2 verso ff.; SM 1E:4ff.

100. GA 17:vii. (Cf. SM 1, fol. b 4 verso; also pp. 8, 138–39, where the quote is referenced in its broader context. The quote is taken from *Quaestiones et Responsiones ad Orthodoxos* [Questions and Answers for the Orthodox], Question 107 [see PG 6:1353–56], which Praetorius, like many before him, falsely attributed to the second century Christian apologist Justin Martyr. Scholars now generally date this work to the late fifth century.—Trans.)

101. Appendix IV, D, pp. 184,186,187.

most deplorably in shame and vice, and still never experience genuine joy all the while.[102]

With his reference to "certain sullen Scythians," he is likely taking a stance against Calvinistic tendencies. The Calvinists had reduced church music in many places to monophonic psalm singing, and they tended toward a fundamental rejection of secular music.* Thus Praetorius' statements in the first volume of the *Syntagma Musicum* serve not only to justify his musical-practical activity, but also serve as a comprehensive "foundation of music [in general] on a theological-scholarly basis."[103]

The second volume, written in German, is titled *De Organographia* (On Instrumentography) and contains on 236 pages precise descriptions "of all ancient and modern musical instruments—foreign, barbarian, unsophisticated, and unfamiliar, as well as domestic, sophisticated, lovely, and familiar ones."[104] Praetorius was also the first in Europe, since Europe's discovery of America, to provide descriptions of the "Indian" instruments "used in India and America." He included these "not for use, obviously, but for learning."[105] He then appended woodcuts "of almost all the musical instruments that are in use and available at the present time in Romance territory [*Welschland*], England, Germany, and other places,"[106] done to scale on forty-five pages—documents of incalculable worth. Praetorius devotes three of the book's five parts to the organ alone,[107] over whose "dignity and excellence" he adoringly rhapsodizes.[108] This volume, like the first, attests to the unbelievable diligence and encyclopedic expertise of the author, who also enjoyed an eminent reputation as an organ specialist.

102. *Ibid.*, 185.

103. Möller-Weiser, *Untersuchungen zum I. Band des Syntagma musicum*, 137.

104. *SM 2, title page; cf. SM 2E1:1.

105. *SM* 2, fol.):(5 verso (corrected [fol. numbering resumes incorrectly on):(7 with):(5]; dated June 19, 1619); cf. *SM* 2E1:7.

106. *SM* 2, *Theatrum Instrumentorum seu Sciagraphia*, title page (dated 1620; follows p. 236); cf. *SM* 2E1:105ff; *SM* 2E2:237. (I added this quote. By "Romance territory," both Italy and France are meant; see the reference in the previous n.—Trans.)

107. *SM 2E2:81ff.

108. *See pp. 31–32.

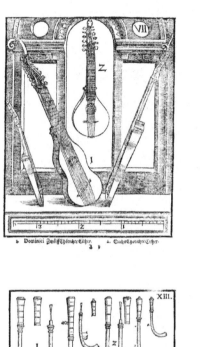
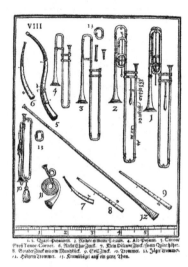
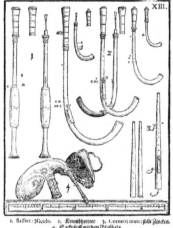
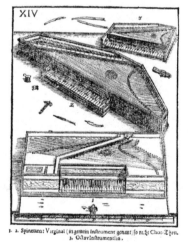

Fig. 28. Plates VII, VIII, XIII, and XIV from the *Theatrum Instrumentorum* appended to *SM* 2. Upper left: Citterns, including Dominicus' twelve-course cittern. Upper right: Sackbuts (1–4), cornetts (5–9), trumpets (10–12), and a whole tone crook (13). Lower left: Alto reed-cap shawm (1), crumhorns (2), muted cornetts (3), and bagpipe with bellows (4). Lower right: Spinets.—Trans.

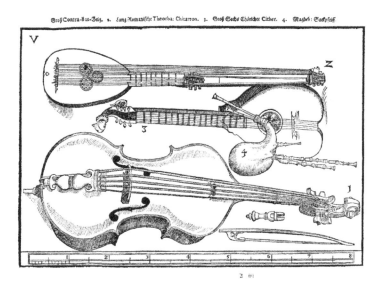

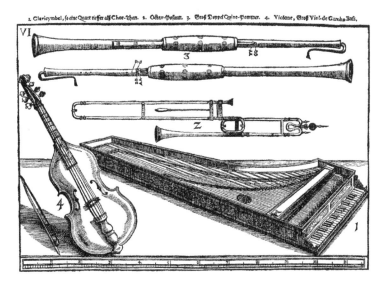

Fig. 29. Plates V and VI from the *Theatrum Instrumentorum* appended to *SM*
2. Above: Double bass (1), long Roman theorbo (2), six-course cittern (3), and a
Magdeburg bagpipe (4). Below: Clavicymbal, a fourth lower than choir pitch (1),
double bass sackbut (2), double bass bombard (3), and bass viol (4).—Trans.

The third volume, sometimes called *Termini Musici*,[109] furnishes on 260 pages explanations of musical terminology and especially disseminates information about new musical developments taking place in Italy, which were still largely unknown in Germany at the time. In providing this information, Praetorius unequivocally sides with the innovators and describes with citations from various Italian composers how, for instance, figured bass or thorough bass, newly invented around 1600, should be understood and performed.[110] With his usual thoroughness, he also systematically synthesizes the principal forms his music has taken into twelve styles, including nine methods or variations of the third style.[111] These styles comprise the theoretical-practical commentary on his own "sacred hymns and concerted songs in Latin and German,"[112] including those composed in "the current Italian manner" for concerted voices.[113]

But Praetorius did not stop there. He provides even more detailed suggestions for the performance of individual works. These suggestions mainly boil down to two concepts—adaptation (*Einrichten*) and arrangement (*Anordnen*). For the *adaptation*, the score merely provides a template that the court music director or cantor follows according to the particular resources at his disposal; no limits are placed on his creativity. The *arrangement* concerns the positioning of the different sound groups in the room, which thereby becomes more than just an acoustic space with the appeal of acoustic impressions and effects; its use should accentuate the idea of a dialogue, an artistic musical conversation in the rhetorical sense, serving the interpretation of the text.[114]

By way of example, one can see Praetorius' own abilities as an imaginative sound architect and experimenter in his adaptation of another composer's setting of the dialogue between Jesus and the Canaanite woman (Matt 15:21–28). In Praetorius' description of the performance, one can also hear the pleasure he derived from the resulting sound:

> I once had the moving, exceedingly beautiful motet "Egressus Jesus," for seven voices, by the impressive composer Giaches de

109. *See Bärenreiter's 1958 facsimile reprint, which includes this subtitle on the cover and title page.

110. *SM 3E:133ff.

111. *SM 3E:172ff. The author simply had "twelve styles and nine methods."

112. *SM 3:169; cf. SM 3E:172.

113. *SM 3:103,175; cf. SM 3E:113–14, 177.

114. The author had everything from "dialogue" to the end as a quote, but he did not cite his source.—Trans.

Wert, performed with two theorbos, three lutes, two citterns, four clavicymbals and spinets, seven violas da gamba, two transverse flutes, two boys, one alto, and a great viol (bass), without organ or regal. This produced such an impressively brilliant, glorious resonance that almost everything in the church crackled from the sound of all those strings.[115]

With all these instructions for court music directors and cantors, Praetorius nevertheless sees his function as a merely preliminary one, in terms of a facilitator. He hopes that eventually someone "who has been trained and thoroughly educated and instructed from little on in the schools of the foremost musicians (which have always been found and are still presently to be found in Italy—which is not at all meant to detract from other praiseworthy nations) might shoulder this toil himself and, with his superior understanding, treat more accurately and extensively the subjects that have been touched on but briefly and inadequately here."[116] But none of his musical contemporaries did submit themselves to "this toil." Praetorius' instructions thus occupy a unique place in music history and still serve as indispensable interpretational aids for the performance of his own music and related music, like the *Psalmen Davids* (Psalms of David, 1619) of Heinrich Schütz.

The three volumes of the *Syntagma Musicum* appeared between 1614 and 1620,[117] with considerable delay in some cases, due in large part to Praetorius' musical attendance at the electoral court in Dresden during this time. A fourth volume was to constitute a comprehensive composition manual, compiled from the works of famous musicians of his time and furnished with his own commentary and notes. Although Praetorius evidently completed it,[118] this volume is not extant—a tremendous loss. He also envisaged several other tractates,[119] but only the

115. *SM* 3:168; cf. *SM* 3E:171.

116. *SM* 3, fol.):(8 recto (incorrectly printed) /):(6 recto (*corrected*); cf. *SM* 3E:8; see also *SM* 2E1:10.

117. *See WGD, 260–275, esp. 272 (last par. with n.) and 274 (middle par. and n. 2). I adjusted the author's final date from 1619 to 1620 to reflect the fact that the *Theatrum Instrumentorum* (Exhibition of Instruments) was not published with volume II until 1620.

118. *SM* 3E:9f, 208f.

119. *SM* 3E:209f.

already mentioned "Organ contracting, construction, and delivery" has been preserved.[120]

Praetorius included all his works—those published, those available in manuscript, and those planned for the future—in a thirty-page "N.B." in volume III of the *Syntagma*, beginning on page 198.[121] Among them one can also find "a number of sacred works and writings" containing "select prayers, psalms, and songs," "various glorious, select, beautiful, and heart-strengthening consolations," "a very brief unfolding and beautiful exposition of Dr. Martin Luther's Small Catechism," and others, which were designed for publication in six volumes under the title *Regnum Coelorum* (The Kingdom of Heaven).[122] He probably intended this series for family devotions and meditations. Perhaps some of the material even originated in his parental home as he was growing up, or with his brother Andreas and Andreas' father-in-law Andreas Musculus.[123]

Michael Praetorius and Prague

As already mentioned on page 41, Praetorius undertook a trip from 1601–1602. Forchert sees the reason for it in the fact that in 1601 the council of Frankfurt an der Oder, during a vacancy at the University Church of St. Mary, attempted to regain their former organist. That could have prompted the duke to give Praetorius the opportunity to further his musical studies at qualified locations—something Praetorius had apparently been unable to do before then.[124]

Regarding this trip, an entry in the chamber accounts from 1602 says that Praetorius had "expenses from staying in Regensburg" and was "also abroad on his own business."[125] He set out on this trip toward the end of 1601 and returned to Wolfenbüttel toward the end of 1602 at the latest.[126] He was thus on the road for roughly a year. One must immediately observe that the note in the chamber accounts has two different aspects to it. The first concerns activity in Regensburg, for which Praetorius

120. *See p. 36. This work is reprinted in WGD, 307ff.
121. *SM* 3E:194ff.
122. *SM* 3:225ff; cf. *SM* 3E:210ff.
123. *See Appendix IV, E, esp. the accompanying source notes.
124. Forchert, "Musik zwischen Religion und Politik," 110.
125. Cited in WGD, 131, n. 3.
126. Forchert, *op. cit.*, 110f.

was reimbursed his living expenses. The second concerns Praetorius' own business, which did not necessarily have anything to do with Regensburg.

Praetorius' primary task on this trip was to make arrangements on behalf of the duke for the diet that was set to begin in Regensburg in the spring of 1603. We can gather this from Praetorius' dedication to Elector Friedrich IV of the Palatinate in Installment IV of the *Musae Sioniae*, in which Praetorius writes that he had met with the elector's "deputy ministers and councilors" in Regensburg in 1602[127]—meetings that doubtless had nothing to do with musical activities. Besides, at the time there were no prominent musicians in Regensburg who could have attracted Praetorius' interest.

Fig. 30. Dominicus Custos, *Hans Leo Hassler*, 1593, engraving.

After completing the duke's tasks, Praetorius might then have first traveled to Nuremberg, in order to meet the Hassler brothers there, whose acquaintance he had already made in 1596 on the occasion of the Gröningen organ dedication.[128] They could better acquaint him with "the new style" of music in which he was keenly interested, since Hans Leo Hassler had been a student of Andrea Gabrieli in Venice. Afterward Praetorius might have traveled to Prague, the capital city of the Kingdom of Bohemia and the residence of Holy Roman Emperor Rudolf II.[129] Duke Heinrich Julius was also staying there in June and July of 1602, though it remains an open question whether the two intended to meet up there. The duke may have even ordered his chamber organist Praetorius to extend his trip to Prague, since it was there that the duke himself had already gotten acquainted with "the new style" during his stay there from July to August 1598.

Praetorius' stay in Prague in 1602 is authenticated by a document in the Herzog August Library in Wolfenbüttel.[130] *It is connected with

127. *MS* 4, fol. (:) ii verso; reprinted in GA 4:vii.

128. *See p. 29.

129. I added this description of Prague.—Trans.

130. Niemöller, "Die musikalische Festschrift für den Direktor der Prager Hofkapelle Kaiser Rudolf II. 1602.," 521.

the tenor part book from a congratulatory collection of compositions for Jacob Chimarrhaeus, the grand almoner and head of the imperial court chapel, on the occasion of his sixtieth birthday in 1602. Edited by Philipp Schöndorff, a trumpeter and composer in the imperial court chapel ensemble, the contributions were composed not just by prominent members of the ensemble (Philippe de Monte, Jacob Regnart, Carolus Luython, Jacob Handl, and Alessandro Orologio) but also by outside musicians like Orlando di Lasso and Hans Leo Hassler.*

This tenor part book contains a personal inscription for Praetorius on its title page. A Wolfenbüttel bookbinder later bound it together with other documents, but in the process he unfortunately cut off the bottom part of the inscription. Consequently, the author of the fragment can only be inferred. The text reads in translation: "To his dear friend and brother Michael Praetorius, the much loved and highly esteemed organist and music connoisseur, as a perpetual remembrance."

This raises the question: Which of the Prague musicians was so well acquainted with Praetorius that he could call him "friend and brother"? The only candidate seems to be Alessandro Orologio. He had been a member of Duke Heinrich Julius' ensemble alongside the chamber organist Praetorius from about 1597–1601,[131] and they had become friends

Fig. 31. Raphael Sadeler, *Philippus de Monte*, 1594, engraving.

there. Orologio also explicitly calls Praetorius an "organist" and not "court music director"; Praetorius did not become court music director until 1604. That still leaves the question of how the tenor part book found its way into the Herzog August Library in Wolfenbüttel.

What acquaintances might Praetorius have made and what experiences might he have had during his stay in Prague in 1602? *In volumes II and III of the *Syntagma Musicum*, he mentions Philippe de Monte (1521–1603), the imperial court

131. Ruhnke, *Beiträge zu einer Geschichte der deutschen Hofmusikkollegien im 16. Jahrhundert*, 71.

music director,[132] and Carolus Luython (1557–1620), the imperial court organist.[133] He may also have become better acquainted with the music of Lambert de Sayve (1548/49–1614) through his brother Mathias de Sayve, de Monte's assistant.[134*] Praetorius apparently got to know these men personally and had professional conversations with them. He also names several instrumentalists and instrument makers from Prague. He took a keen interest in their instruments and later included some images of them in the illustrative plates in volume II of the *Syntagma Musicum*:

- *Plate V, no. 2: A Roman-style theorbo made by a certain Martin Schott of Prague[135]

- Plate VII, no. 1: A twelve-course cittern belonging to an eminent imperial instrumentalist named Dominicus, whose home Praetorius may have visited[136]

- Plate XXXVIII, no. 21: A unique reed stop invented by a Father Andreas that Praetorius saw in an organ in "the Jesuit church at Prague" (not St. Ignatius, which was built later)[137]

He also mentions an unnamed musician in Prague who designed a bass viol with the six strings decreasing in length from the bottom one up and with a diagonal bridge and nut, "pointing up and down respectively,"[138] and he describes in detail the "universal or perfect" clavi-cymbal that he studied in the home of Carolus Luython.[139]

Praetorius furthermore says that there are "outstanding examples" of eunuch singers in the imperial chapel,[140*] and he informed himself about the distinction observed in Prague between chamber pitch and choir pitch. He laments that the German organs could not be tuned to the lower Prague choir pitch, which would have been easier on the singers and more pleasant for the listeners.[141*]

132. *SM* 3E:20,50.

133. *SM* 2:63f; *SM* 2E1:67.

134. *MGG* Personenteil, 14:1052, s. v. "Sayve, Mathias (I) de."

135. See p. 70 and *SM* 2E1:59.

136. See p. 69 and *SM* 2:55; *SM* 2E1:61.

137. See *SM* 2E2:147.

138. *SM* 2E1:53f; *SM* 2:45.

139. *SM* 2E1:66ff; *SM* 2:63ff. The clavicymbal was a precursor of the harpsichord.

140. *SM* 2E1:33.

141. *SM* 2:15f; *SM* 2E1:31f.

Especially important to Praetorius was the opportunity he had in Prague to acquaint himself with the compositions of eminent musicians. In volume III of the *Syntagma Musicum* he mentions Prague composers Jacob de Kerle (1531/32–1591),[142] Jacob Regnart (1540s–1599),[143] and Jacob Handl (Gallus; 1550–1591).[144] Praetorius even provides a thirteen-page excerpt from Handl's motet "Subsannatores subsannabit Deus [God will ridicule the ridiculers]" to demonstrate the time signatures Handl employed.[145] Praetorius familiarized himself with the secular works of the court music director Philippe de Monte, which were sung and performed throughout Europe, and with the religious compositions of Lambert de Sayve of Vienna, in which de Sayve had already employed the new, grandiose style of the early Baroque (*frühbarocken Monumentalstil*). "It seems that [Praetorius] rated Lambert de Sayve especially highly; he mentions him with praise several times in his writings, one time even in the same breath with G[iovanni] Gabrieli."[146] In 1602 Sayve also published *Teutsche Liedlein zu vier Stimmen* (Short German Songs for Four Voices), which Praetorius later had reprinted in Wolfenbüttel in 1611. He writes in the foreword to the reprint:

Fig. 32. Lambert de Sayve, from his *Sacrae Symphoniae* (1612).

142. *SM* 3E:20.

143. *SM* 3E:104f.

144. I added this sentence.—Trans.

145. *SM* 3:48,56ff; cf. *SM* 3E:67,75ff.

146. Blume, "Lambert de Sayve und Michael Praetorius, " foreword; see also *SM* 3E:23,101. (I transplanted this sentence here from a subsequent paragraph in the author's original.—Trans.)

> A few years ago, the excellent musician, Mr. Lambert de Sayve, court music director for His Princely Highness, Archduke Matthias of Austria, etc., issued in print several German songs with tasteful texts having to do with civil affairs, in four parts, at Vienna in Austria. But since very few copies were published at that time, and since they are wished for and desired by everybody on account of their very artful, lovely harmony and short, charming texts, I have decided to have them issued in print a second time, both in honor of their author and in service to friends of the arts. I do so in the hope that this undertaking of mine will not displease those on either side, but that instead they always remain attached to me with good and favorable affection. Farewell.[147]

Forchert assumes that Duke Heinrich Julius occasioned and financed this reprint through Praetorius because he was thereby hoping to ingratiate himself with Archduke Matthias, de Sayve's employer and the soon-to-be Holy Roman Emperor. That would be an indication that the duke also utilized his court music director for his own political purposes. The duke did subsequently recognize de Sayve with a golden chain.[148]

Praetorius "owed endless thanks" to his connections with the Prague musicians "for the foundations of his own activity."[149] These contacts made Prague for Praetorius what Venice, the birthplace of Venetian polychorality or "the new style," was for others of his trade at the time. Prague became his Venice.

Praetorius could already let others enjoy the first compositional fruits of this stay in Prague at the Diet of Regensburg in 1603. He traveled there with a delegation led by Chancellor Werner König, the deputy for Duke Heinrich Julius, who absented himself for political reasons.[150] On this occasion Praetorius functioned once as a clerk and once as a witness in a notarial capacity.[151] But apart from that, he also got the opportunity to represent the duke with his own compositions "at an official ceremony held at the instigation of the diet, in the presence of the princes and ambassadors assembled there."[152] The soul-stirring power Praetorius'

---

147. Sayve, *Teutsche Liedlein mit Vier Stimmen componiret*, "Typographus Musophilis [Typographer's Note to Friends of the Arts]," signed "M. P. C." (I included the entire foreword.—Trans.)

148. Forchert, "Musik als Auftragskunst," 45.

149. Blume, "Lambert de Sayve und Michael Praetorius, " foreword.

150. Forchert, *op. cit.*, 39f.

151. Deeters, "Alte und neue Aktenfunde über Michael Praetorius," 120.

152. Forchert, "Musik zwischen Religion und Politik," 111.

music exerted there is attested in two poems. In the first, authored by Chancellor König, he calls upon the Danube River, Emperor Rudolf II, and Prince-Archbishop Wolf Dietrich of Salzburg as witnesses.[153] The other, authored by Christoph Donauer, a pastor in Regensburg, specifically refers to Praetorius' *Nunc Dimittis* ("Lord, You Now Dismiss"—the Song of Simeon).[154] Praetorius later included this two-choir setting in the already-mentioned *Motectae et Psalmi Latini* (Latin Motets and Psalms) that he dedicated to the duke.[155] It stands to reason that these new works were performed by musicians of the Wolfenbüttel court chapel ensemble, who were presumably already familiar with them. This performance makes it clear that Praetorius had grown out of his role as chamber organist by then, even though he was not officially appointed court music director until the following year.[156]

But Praetorius' documented presence in Prague in 1602 still does not prove that all the contacts with Prague musicians that he mentions in volumes II and III of the *Syntagma Musicum* had to have been made that year. Another stay can be connected with Praetorius' lengthy absence from Wolfenbüttel from the fall of 1607 to the summer of 1608, during which he "had to go on frequent journeys on [his] Gracious Lordship's business, as well as on [his] own."[157] There is, however, no decisive proof that these travels also took him to Prague, unless one sees a connection here with Duke Heinrich Julius' stay in Prague from September to November 1607.[158]

Gurlitt also points to another stay in Prague in his Praetorius biography. He cites an entry under "Expenditures for Provisions" in the chamber accounts from the year 1612, which reads: "To the music director Michael Praetorius and all the musicians, together with carriages

---

153. *MSL*, fols. (:) 3 verso—(:) 4 recto; reprinted in GA 10:ix. See also Forchert, *op. cit.*, and endnote 44 there.

154. *MSL*, fol. (:) 4 verso; reprinted in GA 10:x. (Donauer dated his poem, "Written in Regensburg on Ephphatha Sunday [Twelfth Sunday after Trinity], 1603." This and the preceding two sentences represent an expansion of the author's original material, which mistakenly claimed that both poems referred explicitly to Praetorius' setting of the *Nunc Dimittis*.—Trans.)

155. GA 10:8off, no. 25. See also p. 49 in the present work.

156. I added the final clause for clarification.—Trans.

157. GA 5:xiv.

158. Forchert, "Musik zwischen Religion und Politik," 114f.

and carriage personnel, to travel to Prague: 471 thalers, 12 groschen."[159]
Gurlitt's assumption that this trip had to do with the election of Archduke Matthias as Holy Roman Emperor on June 13, 1612, is unlikely,
since the emperor's election and coronation (on June 24) did not take
place in Prague, but in Frankfurt am Main. Furthermore, Duke Heinrich

Julius evidently did not take part in the
festivities,[160] which then probably would
have also been true for Praetorius and the
Wolfenbüttel court chapel ensemble.

A better explanation for Praetorius' journey to Prague with the ensemble
stems from the fact that Duke Heinrich
Julius had been making repeated trips to
the imperial court in Prague since 1598,
in order to assert his rights with Emperor
Rudolf II over the defiant city of Brunswick. The city refused the duke their fealty
up until his death, and thus did not recognize him as their sovereign. During these
stays in Prague, the duke became increas-

Fig. 33. Hans von
Aachen, *Emperor Rudolf
II*, 1606/1608, oil on
canvas.—Trans.

ingly involved in imperial politics, since he was intent on a compromise
amid the escalating hostilities between Roman Catholics and Protestants.
(He did not join the Protestant Union for that reason.) According to
one document he was "Chief Director of His Roman Imperial Majesty's
Privy Council" from 1609,[161] and from then on he devoted "a considerable amount of both his energy and his revenues, or rather his territory's
revenues (far beyond the acceptable limits), to the welfare and survival of
emperor and empire."[162]

Heinrich Julius' activity as chairman of the privy council led to his
spending very little time in his own duchy anymore and the decision to
establish himself in Prague for the longer term in a way befitting his
rank. He therefore instructed his Wolfenbüttel councilors in August

159. "Kammerrechnungen des Herzogtums zu Braunschweig und Lüneburg,"
Public Archives of Lower Saxony in Wolfenbüttel, 17 III Alt Nr. 68e II; cited in WGD,
243, n. 2.

160. Lietzmann, *Herzog Heinrich Julius zu Braunschweig und Lüneburg (1564–
1613)*, 78.

161. Deeters, "Das Lehen der Familie Praetorius," 111.

162. Lietzmann, *op. cit.*, 52.

Fig. 34. Wenceslaus Hollar, *Great View of Prague* (partial, oriented northeastward), 1649, etching. The identifiers read (L to R): Castle District, Royal Castle, Lesser Quarter, and Old Town.—Trans.

1611 how they "were to administer the territories going forward" in his absence.[163] So that he could live in Prague in befitting style, he acquired the Count of Lippe's palace in the Castle District (*Hradschin*) in 1611 and had it altered and enlarged. To pay for this, in 1612, for example, he had the revenues from the fourteen cloisters in his territory sent to him in Prague—a value of 26,522 imperial thalers.[164] There he received the soon-to-be Emperor Matthias and his household for a festive banquet on February 20, 1612. (Matthias' brother, Emperor Rudolf II, had passed away on January 20.) The duke also presented costly gifts on the occasion. Matthias received two horses with fancy saddlery, his consort and her ladies-in-waiting received valuable jewelry, and more than a hundred dishes were served at the meal.[165]

Heinrich Julius intended for his consort Elisabeth and his courtiers to join him in Prague, so that he could set up a household there similar to the one he had in Wolfenbüttel.[166] We must then also think of his court chapel ensemble in this connection, since for Heinrich Julius music at meals and in his chamber belonged to the customary comforts of life, especially when he was hosting guests. It has yet to be ascertained, however, precisely when the Wolfenbüttel musicians arrived in Prague and how long they remained there.[167] But since Archduke Matthias brought along his court chapel ensemble and stayed in Prague for a time both before

163. *Ibid.*, 66.

164. "Kammerrechnungen des Herzogtums zu Braunschweig und Lüneburg," Public Archives of Lower Saxony in Wolfenbüttel, 17 III Alt Nr. 68e I, 110.

165. Lietzmann, *op. cit.*, 76. (I added the parenthetical remark about Rudolf's passing.—Trans.)

166. *Ibid.*, 71.

167. *But see the par. beginning with "In 1612" on p. 47.

and after his coronation as emperor in June 1612, Praetorius may have met Lambert de Sayve in person at this time.[168]

After Emperor Rudolf II's death in January 1612, the privy council at the imperial court initially became defunct, "so that Heinrich Julius also could no longer preside over it as its director." He continued to reside in his palace in the Prague Castle District, "but instead of hosting lavish entertainments . . . he very quickly saw himself marginalized."[169] In August 1612, however, Emperor Matthias also asked him "to be of service to him in privy and aristocratic imperial matters," and he became the emperor's "appointed privy councilor." In this capacity he was to read the official welcoming of the participants at the Diet of Regensburg in 1613, and he planned to appear there "with an impressive entourage, including fifty musketeers and fifty bodyguards, all clothed in yellow velvet."[170] This is the final instance in a series of occasions, some already described and others not mentioned, by which Heinrich Julius sought to perform official duties on behalf of his duchy in the fashion of an early absolutist prince. His duchy experienced its greatest display of power during his reign.

Apparently Praetorius was also to travel to the diet in Regensburg (with his fellow members of the Wolfenbüttel court chapel ensemble?), as can be gathered from a letter written by Count Ernst III of Bückeburg to Praetorius, dated March 4, 1613: "We have received your various documents . . . We wish you success and safety on your planned trip to Regensburg for the diet."[171] But neither the duke nor Praetorius ended up in Regensburg, since Heinrich Julius died in Prague on July 20, 1613, "from a violent fever," after the doctors had even prescribed him "music to combat his melancholy."[172] We may therefore conclude that some musicians from his chapel ensemble were still staying with the duke at the time; a Halberstadt chronicle reports that "as he had always thought much of music, so he also gave up his spirit amid the songs and sounds of his musicians."[173] After the duke's death, significant doubts arose as to whether he had died of natural causes.[174] His corpse was transported to Wolfen-

168. I added this sentence.—Trans.

169. Lietzmann, 77f.

170. *Ibid.*, 81.

171. Cited in Laakmann, ". . . *nur allein aus Liebe der Musica*," 110.

172. Lietzmann, *op. cit.*, 82.

173. Abel, *Stiffts- Stadt- und Land-Chronick / Des jetzigen Fürstenthums Halberstadt*, 513.

174. Lietzmann, *op. cit.*, 83.

büttel on a multi-day journey and he was entombed in the princes' vault beneath the Church of the Blessed Virgin Mary (the *Hauptkirche*).

Still today, one can find an altar in the church that owes its existence to an initiative of the duke. He had commissioned it from the sculptor Bernhard Ditterich of Freiberg in Saxony for a newly constructed Protestant church in Prague during his final stay in the city. The job was delayed by the duke's death, however, and the Prague congregation

Fig. 35. Elias Holwein, *Der Leichenzug von Heinrich Julius* (partial), 1613, woodcut. (This is only part of one of the eighty-three total woodcuts that Holwein produced to portray the duke's funeral procession to his final resting place, the Church of the Blessed Virgin Mary. Esaias Korner was a member of the chapel ensemble.—Trans.)

procured themselves a different altar. The sculptor subsequently contacted the Wolfenbüttel congregation and offered the altar for their nearly completed church building. In 1623, an agreement for the altar was reached between Ditterich on the one side and Duke Friedrich Ulrich and his building directors on the other. The widowed Duchess Elisabeth assumed the cost for the altar in the amount of 2,200 thalers, having already expressed her intention "to found a princely memorial for the church."[175] The altar was then installed shortly before the completion of the church in 1624 (see Fig. 17). Duke Heinrich Julius had commissioned his architect Paul Francke with the church's construction. Its cornerstone could not be laid until 1608, after a grillage of oak timbers had been installed in the marshy subsoil. It was the first large-scale Protestant church building constructed after the Reformation, a "preaching church [*Predigtkirche*]" with galleries encircling the interior on all sides—ideal for the

175. Lietzmann, "Der Altar der Marienkirche zu Wolfenbüttel," 202.

performance of Praetorius' works in concerted style. The church's architecture is a successful synthesis of Gothic, Renaissance, and Baroque, and

**Fig. 36. Conrad Buno (?), exterior of the Church of the Blessed Virgin Mary,
before 1650, engraving printed in Martin Gosky, _Arbustum vel Arboretum
Augustaeum_ (1650). See also Fig. 17.—Trans.**

the figures mounted on the stones, with their tendency toward the gro-
tesque and bizarre, call to mind the ornamentation on the façade of the
chapel organ built in 1596 in the Gröningen palace.

Michael Praetorius' ties to Prague appear to have persisted even after the duke's death. We can gather this from a "Memorial" Praetorius
submitted in 1614. In it he makes proposals for the restructuring of the
Wolfenbüttel court chapel ensemble, which had declined considerably in
size and ability during the final years of the duke's reign due to his frequent absence. Praetorius accordingly made contact with various musicians to attempt to get them employed in Wolfenbüttel. Concerning the
ensemble's bass section he wrote: "I have already written to Prague that I
am greatly hoping to take over the imperial bass Friederich [_Fridericum_],
since this foundation needs to be steady and good, otherwise no matter
what we stack on top, it will collapse."[176]

176. Deeters, "Alte und Neue Aktenfunde über Michael Praetorius," 111f; also

But his efforts did not succeed. Heinrich Julius had lived a lavish lifestyle in carrying out his responsibilities in his territories and at the imperial court in Prague. As a result, his son Friedrich Ulrich inherited many debts. Praetorius therefore had to content himself with very modest musical assets in Wolfenbüttel, and he became a sought-after traveling music director. During the final years of his life, he primarily sought active employment at princely courts elsewhere.

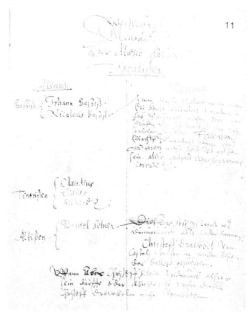

Fig. 37. First page of Praetorius' Oct. 23, 1614 "Memorial" to Duke Friedrich Ulrich, Public Archives of Lower Saxony, Wolfenbüttel, courtesy of Winfried Elsner. Praetorius composed this immediately after his return from a baptismal celebration in Dresden. In the left column he lists the available vocalists (*Adsunt*), in the right column the areas where he feels the ensemble is vocally lacking (*Desunt*).

---

cited in WGD, 243. (There are deficiencies in both transcriptions. I included more of the original quote than the author did. Praetorius switches to Latin from "otherwise" to the end, and seems to be alluding to Quintilian's *Institutes of Oratory* 1.4.5.—Trans.)

— 5 —

Nonresident Music Director[1] at the Electoral Court in Dresden and Musical Consultant at Other Princely Courts

THE DEATH OF PRAETORIUS' generous patron took his life in a completely new and unexpected direction yet again. The determining factor for this vocational shift was a letter from Elector Johann Georg I of Saxony who,

Fig. 38. Nicolaes de Clerck (?),
*Fredericus Ulricus D. G. Dux
Brunsvicensis et Lunaeburgensis,*
c. 1613, engraving, courtesy of
Winfried Elsner.

immediately after Heinrich Julius' death, asked his successor Friedrich Ulrich to relinquish Praetorius to him for the duration of the year of mourning at the Wolfenbüttel court, so that he could serve as the music director for the Dresden court. Duke Friedrich Ulrich consented. Praetorius had been well known at the electoral court in Dresden for a long time, due to the family connections at both courts and the fact that, on several occasions, he had led the Dresden court chapel ensemble in place of its frail music director Rogier Michael.[2]

*He had also already dedicated Installment II of his *Musae Sioniae*

1. See Glossary.

2. Vogelsänger, "Michael Praetorius – „Capellmeister von Haus aus und Director der Music" am Kurfürstlichen Hof zu Dresden (1614–1621)," 103f.

to Electress Hedwig of Saxony (March 25, 1606), and Installment IX to her husband, Elector Christian II of Saxony, and to Christian's brothers Johann Georg and August (April 16, 1609). In the former he recalls the "special favor and every kindness" that the electress had "most graciously and undeservingly shown and demonstrated" to him "for several years now."[3] In the latter he mentions the "various occasions when I most submissively waited upon my gracious Lordship [Duke Heinrich Julius] in Your Electoral Grace's residence." He also thanks the elector for the "great favor shown to me" and the "considerable honor done to me," namely in the form of gifts he had received for his musical services in Dresden.[4*]

Praetorius arrived at Johann Georg's court in Dresden at the end of November 1613. We can probably assume that he immediately began preparing festive Christmas music, for which he either revised works he had composed earlier or wrote completely new pieces. In March 1614, he traveled with the elector and his court chapel ensemble to a princes' convention in Naumburg, where he had to conduct the music at three special services and a banquet.[5] For this he composed, among other works, a concerted piece on Psalm 133, "Siehe wie fein und lieblich ist [Behold, how nice and lovely it is]," for eight solo voices, four-part ensemble chorus, and four-part instrumental ensemble.[6] It was one of the first sacred works he composed that was not based on a Protestant hymn.

Fig. 39. Lucas Kilian, *Elector Johann Georg I of Saxony*, 1630, engraving.—Trans.

3. *MS* 2, fol.)(ii verso; reprinted in GA 2:vii.

4. GA 9:vi. (Christian II passed away on June 23, 1611, and was succeeded by his brother Johann Georg.—Trans.)

5. The author is assuming that Praetorius conducted music at the banquet hosted by the elector on March 30. The only non-church music explicitly mentioned in Gottfried Staffel's eyewitness account is the call to dinner by trumpeters and kettle drummers.—Trans.

6. GA 17:268ff.

*Among other things, the completely new arrangement of the vocal and instrumental groups in the parish church caused a great sensation. Two contemporary eyewitnesses report on the effect of his music on those present. One of them was Praetorius' friend, the head court preacher in Dresden, Matthias Hoë von Hoenegg. He expresses his joy over "the elector of Saxony's extremely outstanding music," and says that "everyone, whether in high station or low, was delighted with it and marveled at it."[7] The other, Gottfried Staffel, a Naumburg citizen who was appointed town warden (*Stadtvoigt*) the following year, speaks of Praetorius' music in rapturous terms. He first describes how Praetorius positioned his vocalists and instrumentalists in four different places—in the "boys' choir," in the ten-meter-high organ balcony,[8] on a specially assembled stage near the memorial slab of a certain Bastian Loth,[9] and "in the back choir by the baptismal font."[10] Staffel then reports

Fig. 40. Sebastian Furck, *Matthias Höe* [sic] *ab Hoenegg*, 1650, engraving. Furck must have imitated a previous drawing or engraving, since his subject had passed away in 1645.—Trans.

that "Praetorius could be heard with all kinds of instruments, kettle drums, and trumpets. I have not heard or experienced anything like it before or since." "O Lamm Gottes [Lamb of God, Pure and Holy]"[11] was sung after the sermon in the first special service on March 30, "with all kinds of musical instruments in such a way that a person's heart could have literally leaped for joy . . . I think there were many people there who

7. Hoë von Hoenegg, *Naumburgische Fried und Frewdenport*, 36, margin.

8. Johann Bürger tells us that this organ was in the process of being rebuilt. The dismantling of the old organ had begun in 1612, and the new organ was completed in 1616 (Bürger, *Annales Numburgenses*, 42). To what extent it was available to Praetorius is unknown; Bürger says it was "disassembled" at the time (p. 538), but it is difficult to imagine that it was completely unavailable to Praetorius for all of his music.—Trans.

9. Staffel simply says that one group was "near Loth's memorial slab" (see p. 209), but Bürger provides the detail about the specially assembled stage and the first name of Mr. Loth (Bürger, *op. cit.*, 538).

10. Bürger describes this as "the lowest choir in front of the altar" (*ibid.*)

11. GA 17:154ff.

had not heard such music in their lifetime." The music for the closing service on April 3 was "once again performed and executed with all dignity by Praetorius just like before—with magnificent singing and playing on all sorts of instruments."[12]* With these performances, Praetorius "gave the signal, as it were, for the start of a new period in the music life of Middle Germany."[13]

The great success of his chapel ensemble strengthened the elector's intention to take Praetorius into his service completely as Rogier Michael's successor. But in spite of the great pains he took to do so, he did not succeed. Duke Friedrich Ulrich would only agree to Praetorius being named the nonresident music director in Dresden, thus officially remaining in his Wolfenbüttel appointment.[14] He could only travel to Dresden for special occasions, in order to conduct festival music that he had composed. These stints added up to twenty months in the years leading up to 1617, though time and again they were interrupted by other responsibilities.

For instance, Praetorius was also active as nonresident music director at the Magdeburg court in Halle, and he functioned as a consultant for the appointment of musicians, for the design and inspection of organ building projects, etc., at the courts in Bayreuth, Bückeburg, Darmstadt, Rotenburg, Sondershausen, and even in Copenhagen. The distance traveled on these trips from 1613–1620 adds up to approximately 10,000 kilometers (6,000 miles)—under conditions that we can hardly begin to imagine today.[15]

Praetorius' collaboration with the Dresden court chapel ensemble starting in 1613 represents a stroke of good fortune for his musical development. The ensemble had just been restructured shortly before that at the initiative of the privy councilor Christoph von Loss[16] and now provided for "a chapel ensemble fixed at twenty-seven budgeted persons"—sixteen singers and eleven instrumentalists.[17] This kind of personnel

---

12. See Appendix V for Staffel's full account of the convention.

13. Gurlitt, "Heinrich Schütz," 68.

14. *WGD, 235f.

15. Vogelsänger, *Michael Praetorius*, *"Diener vieler Herren."*

16. Gurlitt insists on the spelling vom Loss (WGD, 230, n. 1). Other sources spell it von Lohs or von Lohss; the author spells it vom Loos.—Trans.

17. Schäfer, "Einige Beiträge zur Geschichte der Kurfürstlichen musikalischen Capelle oder Cantorei unter den Kurfürsten August, Christian I. u. II. u. Johann Georg I.," 431f. (Schäfer says that the content of this article was "based on documentary communications kindly transmitted by the chamber musician, Mr. Moritz Fürstenau." The

made it possible to perform music in grand style in Dresden, in a way
Praetorius had so far only experienced at court festivities in Wolfenbüttel, when the visiting princes brought along their chapel ensembles. These

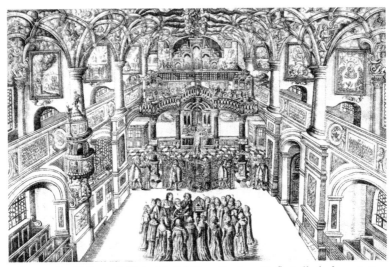

Fig. 41. David Conrad, *Heinrich Schütz mit seiner Hofkapelle*, before 1676,
engraving. (Heinrich Schütz [1585–1672] directs his ensemble in the Dresden
palace chapel.—Trans.)

existing conditions in Dresden were very accommodating to Praetorius,
for in the meantime he had begun to compose "in the modern Italian
manner of singing and playing."[18] He could now immediately test and
implement it with the Dresden musicians.

This concerted or concerto manner or style consists of taking the
musicians from what had been the different part-choirs in the polychoral performances and newly forming them into concerted voices and an
ensemble chorus, according to their various qualifications. Praetorius
describes the concerted voices thus:

> The *Parti Concertate, voci Concertate,* or *Concertat-Stimmen*
> . . . are the parts of a concerto that are expressly arranged and
> composed for singing and not for instruments . . . I call them
> concerted, or even better, concerting voices [*Voces Concertatas,*

author did not include this quote or source, but I found it in his article, "Michael
Praetorius – „Capellmeister von Haus aus und Director der Music" am Kurfürstlichen Hof zu Dresden (1614–1621)," from which he clearly borrowed heavily for this
chapter.—Trans.)

18. *As he calls it, e.g., in *SM* 3:199; cf. *SM* 3E:195.

vel potius Concertantes] who, so to speak, answer and musically compete with each other to see which of them can do it best. One must therefore select, appoint, and arrange the best *cantores* and singers for such voices, who are not only perfect and confident, but who also possess a good disposition for singing in the modern and new style and manner, so that the words are pronounced correctly and clearly, as if an oration were being intelligibly recited the whole way through. This is why the Italians also sometimes call it the *chorum recitativum* [recitative choir].[19]

But the other musicians, who are not suited for such demanding soloistic work, are all put into the ensemble chorus (*Chorus pro Capella*).[20] They come in all at once with the concerted or solo choirs at textual high points, or divide a piece into distinct parts via ritornellos, and do so "like in an organ piece when the full organ joins in. This has an excellent embellishing and impressive effect on such music and really makes it sparkle."[21]

The thorough bass (*Generalbass*) or basso continuo steps forward as a new musical-stylistic element that incorporates the harmonies of the entire concerto on a chordal instrument or "foundation instrument," such as the organ, regal, clavicymbal, harp, theorbo, or lute.[22] The bass part of these harmonies is then further strengthened by an additional wind or stringed instrument, such as a dulcian, sackbut, or bass viol.[23]

With this orientation towards concerto style, Michael Praetorius effected the transition in his work from Renaissance music to that of Early

19. *SM* 3:126 (incorrectly printed) / 106 (corrected); cf. *SM* 3E:115–16. (I included a little more of the original quote than the author did.—Trans.)

20. Praetorius explains how this separate choir or chorus got its name: "[The term *Capella*], as far as I can tell, was at first only understood by the Italians this way: In the sizable imperial, Austrian, and other Catholic chapel ensembles or music groups, several choirs with all kinds of instruments and human voices were variously positioned. When that was the case, another special chorus was then culled from all of these and called the *Chorus pro Capella* [ensemble chorus]. The idea was that this entire vocal choir, or entire *Capella*, would sing the same music in their choir [*denselben im Chor . . . musiciret*], while completely separated from the other choirs, like in an organ piece when the full organ joins in" (see next footnote). *SM* 3E translates *Chorus pro Capella* as "a large choir."—Trans.

21. *SM* 3:133 (incorrectly printed) / 113 (corrected); cf. *SM* 3E:124.

22. *SM* 3:144ff (incorrectly printed) / 124ff (corrected); cf. *SM* 3E:133ff.

23. *SM* 3:145; *SM* 3E:150–51. (The author distinguished between *Generalbass* and *Basso continuo* in the original, which Praetorius really does not do. I therefore reworded this paragraph somewhat, with the gracious assistance of Dr. Margaret Boudreaux.—Trans.)

Baroque. His remark that his early works in the *Musae Sioniae*, in the Venetian polychoral style, were "not altogether satisfactory to [him] at this time [in 1615]"[24] also shows an internal change in his thinking and stylistic tastes. As with his earlier work, in this new style he is guided by the great prototypes of his time, and not just Giovanni Gabrieli and Claudio Monteverdi, but also and above all by the very recent compositions of Agostino Agazzari, Gabriele Fattorini, and Lodovica Viadana.[25] Praetorius never tires of describing this versatile performance style with soloists and ensemble choirs, and he loves to provide all sorts of different modifications, as proven by his explanations of the twelve styles and nine methods in the third volume of his *Syntagma Musicum*.[26] The division of duties into soli and tutti also then finds its special expression in this style in the separate positioning of the musicians in the performance space. Praetorius always comes up with different possibilities for such positioning depending on the facilities available in each case, "which allows us to view Praetorius still today as one of the 'most daring sound architects of all time.'"[27] Considering this evidence from Praetorius' works, it is incomprehensible how a person can claim that his distinction between concerted voices and ensemble choirs is "a peculiarity of musical scoring apparently invented by Schütz."[28]

In his final works, Praetorius particularly favors the use of ritornellos. Among the styles and methods in volume III of his *Syntagma Musicum*, he lists this usage as the Fifth Style, which he describes thus: "Here the entire choir sings and repeats a Hallelujah or Gloria, or another beautiful thought that is worthy of attention, at the beginning, middle, and end, or beforehand and afterward, and it is not unpleasant to listen to."[29] In support of this style, he appeals on the one hand to the Bible's example and enumerates nine psalms of David (8, 24, 42, 103, 107, 118, 136, 148, and 150) in which he sees this style on display.[30] *But he also finds it in the Latin chants of the ancients[31] and in Claudio Monteverdi's

24. *SM* 1E:20; *SM* 1, fol. b 4 verso.

25. Forchert, *Das Spätwerk des Michael Praetorius*, Chapter 4.

26. *SM* 3E:172–92.

27. Forchert, *op. cit.*, 179, quoting Gurlitt, afterword to *De Organographia* (1929), 2.

28. *MGG* Personenteil, 15:396, s. v. "Schütz, Heinrich."

29. *SM* 3:184; cf. *SM* 3E:184.

30. *SM* 3E:184. (I added the specific psalms cited by Praetorius.—Trans.)

31. *Ibid.*, 184f.

Vespro della Beata Vergine (Vespers for the Blessed Virgin)—in both his eight-part setting of the hymn "Ave maris stella [Hail, star of the sea]" and his six-part setting of Psalm 110, "Dixit Dominus Domino meo [The Lord said to my Lord]."[32] Praetorius notes that in several places in Monteverdi's setting of Psalm 110, Monteverdi omits the text and simply puts *ritornello* below the notes "to indicate that there only the instruments should be employed and used, without any voices." Praetorius then continues: "And in my opinion, this is the proper way to understand the term under discussion, *ritornello*."[33]* Praetorius also lists a large number of works that he has composed in this Fifth Style, though only a minority of them are preserved.[34]

In those works he once again expresses his theological ideas and their intended effect. For instance, in his choral concerto "Vater unser im Himmelreich [Our Father, Who from Heaven Above]," based on Martin Luther's rhyming paraphrase of the Lord's Prayer, he sets Luther's final stanza ("*Amen, das ist, es werde wahr* [Amen, that is, let it prove true]") to a ritornello and inserts it after every two to three stanzas as a way of affirming the petitions that have just been prayed.[35] Or in the Christmas concerto "Gelobet seist du, Jesu Christ [O Jesus Christ, all praise to you]," also based on a Luther hymn, Praetorius again turns the final stanza ("*Das hat er alles uns getan* [All this for us God's Son has done]") into the ritornello and sticks this repeatedly between the other stanzas.[36] Sometimes his vocal concertos are introduced with instrumental sinfonias and subdivided with instrumental ritornellos. He also selects the specially gifted players from the instrumentalists and provides them with virtuoso parts.

Praetorius also writes that he has taken a number of songs by Italian composers, which he had sent for from Italy, and has "corrected and

32. *Ibid.*, 118,119.

33. *SM* 3:129 (incorrectly printed) / 109 (corrected); cf. *SM* 3E:119. (However, Praetorius later writes: "Although (as cited earlier) the word *ritornello* should be understood to mean the repetitions that are played only with instruments, without any voices, it would still not displease me if the term *ritornello* were also used to designate the repetitions that are scored for both voices and instruments" [*SM* 3:184; cf. *SM* 3E:184].—Trans.)

34. *SM* 3E:185–87.

35. *GA* 17:433ff. (I added the short descriptive clause, "based on . . . the Lord's Prayer."—Trans.)

36. *GA* 17:505ff. (I added some further descriptors in this sentence too.—Trans.)

purified the texts and added a second choir with the ripienos,[37] so that here in Germany we too may make use of this beautiful and glorious style, in order thereby to arouse our devotion in the Church of our dear, faithful God, to his praise and glory."[38] This edition of Italian songs with the ritornellos or ripienos inserted by Praetorius has unfortunately not been passed down to us, just like so much else.

An especially impressive example of the new concerto style is Praetorius' six-choir setting of "Wachet auf, ruft uns die Stimme [Wake, Awake, for Night Is Flying]."[39] In order to do musical justice to the text of this hymn, Praetorius summons all his skill, utilizing eight soloists, a four-part ensemble chorus, four violins, and four sackbuts, plus two solo violins and two cornetts that each concertize together and whose parts give us some indication of the great virtuosity of the musicians at his disposal.

The unbelievable workload that Praetorius had to manage during these years is shown by a selection of works that he performed during the years 1613–1617 on the occasion of various court festivities. They force us to ask where he ever found the time and repose for these compositions and arrangements, on top of all his other responsibilities:

- For a hunting party in July 1614 in Wolfenbüttel, a work titled *Diana Teutonica: Teutsche Jäger Lieder und Jäger Geschrey* (The German Diana [*or* Artemis]: German Hunting Songs and Hunting Cries; not preserved)[40]

---

37. According to Praetorius, ripienos and ritornellos are similar, sometimes synonymous. He writes: "The Italians use this term [ripieno] when they wish to indicate that the voices and instruments in all choirs should all enter together at once . . . The ripienos are nothing but certain sections or clauses from a concerto that are sung and played with the principal choirs by the other choirs at certain times, in order to produce a full-sounding music. Therefore ripieno actually does not simply mean 'full chorus,' but repeated full sections—the sections that are taken from the principal parts of the concerto and composed for other different, separate choirs, in order to produce a full and full-sounding concerted performance . . . I therefore like to think of ripieno as a compound term, as if it were *ritornello pieno* [full ritornello], a ritornello or repetition whereby the full choir performs together and the instrumental parts are combined with the vocal parts" (*SM* 3:131,132 [incorrectly printed] / 111,112 [corrected]; cf *SM* 3E:120,121,122).—Trans.

38. *SM* 3:188; cf. *SM* 3E:187.

39. GA 17:192ff.

40. *Mentioned on *SM* 3:221 (cf. *SM* 3E:207); see also Vogelsänger, "Michael Praetorius – „Capellmeister von Haus aus und Director der Music" am Kurfürstlichen Hof zu Dresden (1614–1621)," 108.

- For a wedding the subsequent September, a four-choir concerto, "Nun lob mein Seel den Herren [My Soul, Now Bless Your Maker]"[41]

- *For a baptism that same month (September 1614) in Dresden, two six-choir concertos,[42] probably "Gelobet seist du, Jesu Christ [O Jesus Christ, all praise to you]"[43] and "Jubiliret fröhlich und mit Schall [Make a joyful sound and ring out]"[44]

- For the wedding of Margrave Christian Wilhelm of Magdeburg and Princess Dorothea of Wolfenbüttel in January 1615 in Wolfenbüttel, a five-choir concerto, "In dulci jubilo [Now Sing We, Now Rejoice]"[45]

- After this wedding, he accompanied the young couple to Halle. There, on January 21, he positioned two choirs in the rooms of two opposing buildings, "who gave a very lovely and beautiful performance,"[46] most likely of the New Year hymn, "Das alte Jahr ist nun vergahn [The recent year is now complete],"[47] singing to each other across the street as the couple entered—an original arrangement that could probably only occur to someone like Michael Praetorius!

- For a ballet in November 1615 following a baptism in Dresden, dances from *Terpsichore*[48]

- For the city of Brunswick's oath of fealty to Duke Friedrich Ulrich in February 1616, a multi-choir setting of the *Te Deum Laudamus* ("We

41. GA 20:40ff; see also Vogelsänger, *op. cit.*, 108. (The author originally included this bullet with the previous.—Trans.)

42. Pezold, *Beschreibung Der Churfürstlichen Kindtauff / und Frewdenfests zu Dreßden*, fols. B iv verso, C recto & verso, C ii recto.

43. GA 17:505ff.

44. GA 17:253ff; see Vogelsänger, "Michael Praetorius – „Capellmeister von Haus aus und Director der Music" am Kurfürstlichen Hof zu Dresden (1614–1621)," 109. (Vogelsänger seems to have better supporting reasons for the second piece than the first, which he himself questions in a footnote. It is possible that the first piece was "Christ unser Herr zum Jordan kam [To Jordan Came the Christ Our Lord]" [GA 17:229ff]. Even though this concerto is only written for five choirs, not six, it is possible that Praetorius divided his performers into six positions in preparation for the second concerto following the sermon, or that, as with "Gelobet seist du," it was originally written for six choirs and subsequently pared down to five.—Trans.)

45. GA 17:566ff; see also Vogelsänger, *op. cit.*, 109–10.

46. Cited in Serauky, *Musikgeschichte der Stadt Halle: Von Samuel Scheidt bis in die Zeit Georg Friedrich Händels und Johann Sebastian Bachs*, 14f.

47. GA 17:23ff; see Vogelsänger, *op. cit.*, 110.

48. GA 15; see Vogelsänger, *op. cit.*, 111.

Praise You, O God"; not preserved)[49] and another concerto,[50] perhaps the aforementioned setting of "Wachet auf, ruft uns die Stimme"[51]

• For a baptism not long after Easter 1616 in Halle, probably his five-choir concerto "Hallelujah: Christ ist erstanden [Hallelujah: Christ Is Arisen],"[52] which he had likely already composed for the celebration of Easter in Dresden in 1614[53]

• For the installation of Duke Christian (Friedrich Ulrich's only surviving brother) as bishop of Halberstadt on May 1, 1617, a three-choir concerto "Veni Sancte Spiritus: Hallelujah, Komm heiliger Geist [Come, Holy Spirit (both Latin antiphon and German hymn)]"[54]

• For Emperor Matthias' visit to Dresden in July and August 1617, five concertos in representational style for as many as seven separate choirs and as many as twenty-three parts, with timpani and trumpets—a collection Praetorius titled *Polyhymnia Heroica augusta Caesarea* (The Heroic, August, Imperial Polyhymnia[55]; not preserved)[56]

• For the services celebrating the centennial of the Reformation in October and November 1617 in Dresden and Wolfenbüttel, Praetorius evidently composed the majority of the music, listed with a proposed *Polyhymnia Jubilaea* (The Jubilee Polyhymnia; not preserved).[57] In Dresden, however, the music was directed by Heinrich Schütz,[58] who had also been serving the Dresden elector since 1615, initially as court organist. Praetorius could not direct the

49. See Praetorius' letter to Duke Friedrich Ulrich, dated Jan. 29, 1616, in WGD, 253. Vogelsänger (*op. cit.*, 112) surmises that Praetorius may have had plans to include this setting in his *Polyhymnia X* (see SM 3E:203).

50. See Praetorius' drafted title page for *Polyhymnia Panegyrica & Caduceatrix* in SM 3:202 (cf. SM 3E:196); also GA 17:x–xi.

51. See p. 94 and Vogelsänger, *op. cit.*, 112.

52. GA 17:599ff; see Vogelsänger, *op. cit.*, 112–13; also WGD, 254–56.

53. Vogelsänger, *op. cit.*, 106–7.

54. GA 17:74ff; see Vogelsänger, *op. cit.*, 114; also Praetorius' drafted title page for *Polyhymnia Panegyrica & Caduceatrix* in SM 3:202 (cf. SM 3E:196); also GA 17:x–xi.

55. Polyhymnia, a Greek word meaning "she of many hymns," was the Muse of sacred poetry in classical literature. Praetorius' planned *Polyhymnia* series will be discussed in greater detail in the next section.—Trans.

56. SM 3:201; cf. SM 3E:196; see Vogelsänger, *op. cit.*, 115.

57. SM 3:210–212; cf. SM 3E:200–201 and Hoë von Hoenegg, *Chur Sächsische Evangelische JubelFrewde*, fols. b ii verso—b iii verso.

58. Hoë von Hoenegg, *op. cit.*, fol. b iii verso.

performances himself, since he had to be at the Wolfenbüttel court for their centennial celebration on November 2.[59]*

On these occasions, Praetorius acquainted himself with numerous musicians from other court chapel ensembles and was also a friend of some of them, such as the Halle organist Samuel Scheidt.[60] With others he carried on an active correspondence on technical musical questions, as with the cantor of St. Thomas in Leipzig, Sethus Calvisius, and he was likewise acquainted with Calvisius' successor Johann Hermann Schein.[61] Prae-

Fig. 42. Joachim Caesar, *Samuel Scheidt*, 1624.

torius collaborated with Heinrich Schütz for several months in Dresden and initiated him into the office of music director, since Praetorius was Schütz's superior there.[62] In volume II of his *Syntagma Musicum*, Praetorius mentions that he has "recently conferred with a number of prominent musicians";[63] the just-mentioned men should be thought of here.

59. Vogelsänger, *op. cit.*, 115–16; see also Vogelsänger, "Michael Praetorius: Festmusiken zu zwei Ereignissen des Jahres 1617," 101ff.

60. *See e.g. Israël, *Programm des städtischen Gymnasiums zu Frankfurt a. M.*, 72–73.

61. *See e.g. SM 2, fol.):(6 recto (corrected); SM 2E1:7.

62. *Vogelsänger, "Michael Praetorius – „Capellmeister von Haus aus und Director der Music" am Kurfürstlichen Hof zu Dresden (1614–1621)," 119–20. (I highly recommend this short "Addendum [*Nachtrag*]" to anyone interested in the relationship between Praetorius and Schütz. Vogelsänger takes an even-keeled approach to the topic, demonstrating that while the two were probably not the closest friends, there was probably also no "deep-seated, personal antipathy towards each other," as e.g. Gurlitt suggests [WGD, 251].—Trans.)

63. SM 2, fol.):(11 verso (incorrectly printed) /):(13 verso (corrected); cf. SM 2E1:18.

Fig. 43. Anonymous, *Hermanus Schein*, 1620, oil on canvas.

Fig. 44. Melchior Haffner, *Sethus Calvisius*, before 1673, engraving printed in Gottlieb Spitzel, *Templum honoris reseratum* (1673). Haffner must have imitated a previous drawing or engraving, since his subject had passed away in 1615.

The *Polyhymniae*[64]

Already with the publication of the choral concerto "Nun lob mein Seel den Herren [My Soul, Now Bless Your Maker]" in 1614, which had been composed that year for the occasion of the aforementioned wedding in Wolfenbüttel, Praetorius announces a new "great musical opus"[65]—what became his *Polyhymnia Caduceatrix & Panegyrica* (The Peacemaking and Celebratory Polyhymnia).[66] These initial plans for one publication would very soon ripen into something on a much grander scale—the publishing of a large collection of sacred concertos "in a number of different new styles and methods invented by the author [Praetorius] himself, and in the modern Italian manner of singing and playing," including the sacred concertos previously mentioned in the bulleted list.[67] He dedicated this series to Polyhymnia, the Muse of hymns and sacred poetry, from

64. Plural form of Polyhymnia; see n. 55 above.—Trans.

65. *GA 20:xx.

66. I added this explanatory clause.—Trans.

67. *SM* 3:199; cf. *SM* 3E:195. (I included more of Praetorius' description than the author did.—Trans.)

which the general title *Polyhymniae Ecclesiasticae* (The Ecclesiastical Polyhymniae) was developed. Praetorius planned fifteen (!) installments for this series, each with its own title and contents arranged for as many as thirty-four parts in as many as nine choirs.[68] For a long time the opinion prevailed among musicologists that this truly gigantic undertaking was infeasible. But we must keep in mind that between 1605 and 1611 Praetorius had already published a similarly comprehensive collection of compositions (the *Musae Sioniae*) and had also worked on the volumes of the *Syntagma Musicum* besides. Now in his mid-forties, he was by no means too old to contemplate a similar project.[69]

By studying these concertos more closely, we can discern that some of them were developed from earlier works; Praetorius reworked them into concertos and cantata-like forms by adding sinfonias, ritornellos, etc. This is attested, for example, by a choral concerto based on an earlier *tricinium* (composition for three vocal parts) on the hymn "Christ ist erstanden [Christ Is Arisen]."[70] By adding a thorough bass, two four-part instrumental choirs, two four-part vocal choirs, and a Hallelujah ritornello, he turned it into a festive, five-choir Easter concerto.[71]

As we can gather from the general index of his works in volume III of his *Syntagma Musicum*,[72] Praetorius planned these new works in close connection with his theoretical explanations of the styles and methods in that same volume.[73] For example, the first installment, *Polyhymnia Heroica: seu Tubicinia & Tympanistria* (The Heroic or Trumpet- and Tympani-Playing Polyhymnia; not preserved), containing works arranged for as many as twenty-seven voices in seven choirs, was designated for the First Style with trumpets and timpani.[74] Also designated for that style was the second installment, *Polyhymnia Heroica augusta Caesarea* (The Heroic, August, Imperial Polyhymnia; not preserved), which contained the works that had been performed during the emperor's visit to Dresden in the summer of 1617. It was dedicated to the four prominent participants

---

68. **SM* 3:199–217; cf. *SM* 3E:195–205.

69. Vogelsänger, *Michael Praetorius beim Wort genommen*, 96ff.

70. **GA* 9:55.

71. **GA* 17:599ff; cp. esp. pp. 602ff to previous n.; see also Vogelsänger, "Michael Praetorius – „Capellmeister von Haus aus und Director der Music" am Kurfürstlichen Hof zu Dresden (1614–1621)," 107.

72. *SM* 3:199–217; *SM* 3E:195–205.

73. *SM* 3:169–97; *SM* 3E:172–94.

74. *SM* 3:169; cf. pp. 199f; *SM* 3E:172; cf. p. 195.

of that meeting—Emperor Matthias, King Ferdinand II of Bohemia,
Duke Maximilian I of Bavaria, and the host Elector Johann Georg I of
Saxony.[75] Matthias Hoë von Hoenegg, the Dresden head court preacher,
described the impression that these compositions left on the participants
in an epigram of nine elegiac couplets:

> Are you at last, Praetorius, bringing it out in the daylight—
>   work of exceptional faith, work of dexterity broad,
> what we have all been fervently waiting for, knowing its merits—
>   worth all preservative means, coating of cedar[76] and more?
> Good! Now the virtue inspired from heaven will draw more attention,
>   through ev'ry region and clime soaring and beating its wings.
> Emp'ror and king have already heard; both one and the other
>   hearkened with thunderstruck ears while you directed the choirs.
> They with the other great men of the Empire goggled and marveled,
>   and they declared you to be organ of God Most High.
> So carry on, Praetorius. Yours is a virtue undying,
>   Nor shall envious darts have the potential to harm.
> Archers may let loose a torrent of arrows, yet none has the power
>   one so blessed to assail, breeze of the Lord at his back.
> Let the intestines of Momus[77] erupt; your harmonies holy
>   honored and lasting will be, long as the Elbe rolls on.
> Someday united with leaders of choirs and psalmists angelic,
>   you will eternally sing beautiful songs mid the stars.[78]

The "great musical opus" Praetorius originally planned became the
third installment, *Polyhymnia Caduceatrix & Panegyrica*.[79] *Darinnen
Solennische Friedt—und Frewden-Concert* (The Peacemaking and Celebratory Polyhymnia, Containing Solemn Concertos of Peace and Joy;

75. *SM* 3:172,201; *SM* 3E:175,196. (The author had Elector Maximilian I, but
Maximilian did not become an elector until 1623.—Trans.)

76. The backs of books were rubbed with cedar oil to preserve them from moths
and decay. As a result, cedar could be used as a metaphor for immortalization.—Trans.

77. Momus in Greek mythology was the personification of satire, mockery, and
fault-finding.—Trans.

78. *Pol. Cad.*, Primus [Vox], p. iv (numbering includes title page); reprinted in GA
17:xxi. (The author only included the fourth and fifth couplets. Hoë von Hoenegg
wrote this epigram to commemorate the four volumes of Praetorius' *Syntagma Musicum* and his *Polyhymniae*.—Trans.)

79. This is how it was titled in the thorough bass volume. In the other part books,
it was simply titled *Polyhymnia Panegyrica* (see *Pol. Cad.* in Annotated Abbreviations,
p. xxx). On the page advertising this work in *SM* 3, it was titled *Polyhymnia Panegyrica
& Caduceatrix* (p. 202; cf. *SM* 3E:196).

Fig. 45. *III. Polyhymnia Panegyrica* (1619), title page. The inscription to the left of Praetorius kneeling at the cross reads: "Give your servant the ability to die well if I am unable to live well, O Christ, you who are able to give both." The inscription to the right reads: "Come to my aid, O Christ, in the throes of death." The inscription above him reads: "My love is the Crucified." (The inscription on the organ at the lower right reads: "They were singing a song to the Lamb" [cf. Rev 5:9,12; 14:3]. The inscription at the bottom of the page reads: "Let us rejoice and be glad, for the wedding of the Lamb has come" [Rev 19:7].—Trans.)

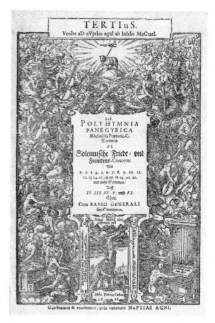

1619[80]). For this work, Praetorius "compiled an initial selection of [his] new compositions, which [he had] composed within the last five years by the grace God [had] bestowed upon [him]."[81] Some of these were already mentioned earlier with the festival performances during the years 1613–1617. Praetorius dedicated "this Muse" (that is, the compositions under the title of this Muse) to Elector Johann Georg I of Saxony, Margrave Christian Wilhelm of Magdeburg, and Duke Fredrich Ulrich of Brunswick and Lüneburg, "in whose chapels she was mostly born, and whose ears and hearts gave her their sincere attention with

---

80. A cursory glance could yield an erroneous date. At the top of the title page for all of the part books except the thorough bass, Praetorius has: "VenIte aD nVptIas agnI ab InItIo MaCtatI [Come to the wedding of the Lamb who was slain from the beginning—a combination of Matthew 22:4; Revelation 13:8; and 19:9]," which, when the Roman numerals are extracted, comes out to MDCVVIIIIIII or 1617. At the bottom of the title page "1618" is printed beneath an image of Praetorius kneeling at the foot of the cross. However, the date on the title page of the thorough bass part book, the date of Praetorius' dedicatory epistle (Jan. 4, 1619), and the date of Hoë von Hoenegg's epigram in the Primus part book all bear out the ultimate year of publication. The presence of the other years do bespeak Praetorius' usual publishing troubles.—Trans.

81. GA 17:x.

singular grace and benevolence, when she was heard for the first time as she tested out her style."[82]

In this *Polyhymnia*, Praetorius establishes the already-mentioned connection with his styles and methods by noting "that at least one or more examples of each style and method will be found" in it.[83] In the thorough bass part book he also provides an index of the compositions in this installment according to the different styles and methods.[84] Thus he correlates the third *Polyhymnia* with the third volume of the *Syntagma Musicum* in such a way that the practical musical work illustrates the theoretical musical work, while the theoretical explains the practical. Praetorius also provides additional, detailed performance instructions for these compositions in an Ordinance consisting of thirty-three points.[85] With forty compositions on 766 pages, this installment is the most comprehensive one in the *Gesamtausgabe* (Complete Edition) of Praetorius' works.

The Third Style, which he subdivides into nine methods, is the most modern one for Praetorius. He describes it thus:

> The concerted songs and psalms adapted to this Third Style are for the most part arranged in the modern Italian manner for a few concerted voices (*Voces Concertatas*). Here a person has one, two, or more vocalists sing along to an organ or regal. These vocalists should not only be composed and confident and have a beautiful, natural, pure voice, but they should also know how to control it in a very attractive and lovely way and how to sing with charm (*gratiamente*).[86]

For these works he refers in particular to the very modern Italian composers Lodovico Viadana, Giovanni Damasceni Uffererii, Antonio Cifra, Giacomo Finetti, and others.[87]

These styles and methods reveal the full breadth of his imagination by showcasing his continuous devising of new scoring possibilities. He writes: "Now although many more styles and methods could be adduced

82. GA 17:xi.

83. *SM* 3:192; cf. *SM* 3E:191.

84. *Pol. Cad.*, Bassus-Generalis, fol. A iv verso; reprinted in GA 17:xvii. (I added this sentence.—Trans.)

85. **Ibid.*, fols. A ii recto—A iv recto; reprinted in GA 17:xii–xvi. (For "Ordinance," see Glossary.)

86. *SM* 3:175; cf. *SM* 3E:177.

87. **E.g. SM* 3:176; *SM* 3E:178.

and identified beyond the twelve kinds identified here, I have contented myself with these for now. But God willing, more of them will be enumerated and specified in my *Polyhymniae.*"[88]

For the concerted or solo singers, this new concerto style meant, more than anything else, transitioning to a new way of singing. To prepare them for this, Praetorius composed his fifth installment, *Polyhymnia Exercitatrix* (The Exercising Polyhymnia; 1620[89]). He explains that he composed these songs "to exercise my chapel boys and to accustom them to a disposition and style of singing."[90] He arranged these compositions of Latin psalms and German hymns for two to four singing voices and added four instruments to them, which are actually nothing but a thorough bass distributed among several parts, "so that the organists who are not yet used to playing from the thorough bass and do not understand composition could have the middle parts when playing, and could thereby have that much more success." He also suggests that the Latin Hallelujah settings in this installment can be "mixed in with some old, familiar motets at one or two places in the middle, and inserted as an interlude, etc."[91]

The fourth installment of the *Polyhymnia* appeared last—*Puericinium*[92] . . . *Darinnen XIV. Deutsche Kirchenlieder: und Andere Concert-Gesänge: Uff die Festtage fast durchs gantze Jahr / auch sonsten: mit 4. Knaben Discantisten / neben andern Menschen Stimmen und Musicalischen Instrumenten anzuordnen und zu gebrauchen* (The Boy Singer Collection . . . Containing Fourteen German Hymns and Other Concerted Songs, To Be Arranged and Used on Nearly All the [Christian] Feast Days Throughout the Year and on Other Occasions, With Four Boy Sopranos Along with Other Adult Voices and Musical Instruments; 1621).[93] This is

---

88. *SM* 3:195; cf. *SM* 3E:192.

89. His dedicatory epistle for this collection is dated March 4, 1619.—Trans.

90. GA 18:viii.

91. *Ibid.*

92. This word, which does not appear in Latin lexicons, is a substantive compound adjective formed from *puer*, "boy," and *canere*, "to sing"—lit. "the boy-singing thing" or "the thing for boy singers" (cf. my translation in the subsequent parentheses). Praetorius' originally proposed title was *Polyhmnia παιδόφωνος seu Puericinia* (The Boy-Sounding or Boy-Singing Polyhymnia) (*SM* 3:205; cf. *SM* 3E:198).—Trans.

93. GA 19:v. (There is no dedicatory epistle in this collection, and his Ordinance is undated.—Trans.)

in the Second Style of the concerto, which Praetorius refined from the old custom of Quempas singing.[94] He describes it thus:

> In this Second Style, four boys must be positioned in four sepa-
> rate places in the church, either opposite each other or wherever
> it will conveniently work. The first one, who is stationed by the
> organ, begins all by himself; the second immediately after him;
> then the third; and finally the fourth (who must be positioned
> by the full musical choir, the ensemble chorus). Each one sings
> what is found in his part in a nice and pure, lively, distinct, and
> easily intelligible manner, articulating his notes likewise.[95]

As alluded to in these remarks, a male choir with alto, tenor, and bass voices and a four-part *Capella Fidicina*, an instrumental ensemble, is added to these four boys. This "full musical choir" and the boy voices take turns concertizing. For this installment, too, Praetorius included an *Ordinantz: oder Admonitio Generalis: wie man in Anordnung dieser ConcertGesäng / verfahren könne* (Ordinance or General Admonition: How one might proceed in arranging these concerted songs), containing thirteen comprehensive points.[96]

For the celebration of the aforementioned centennial of the Refor-mation in 1617 in Dresden, the consistory there had prescribed a number of hymns that were to be played and sung in each of the three services on October 31 and November 1. Praetorius wrote large-scale compositions in concerto style based on these hymns, and composed additional set-tings of Psalms 23, "Der Herr ist mein Hirt [The Lord is my shepherd]"; 98, "Singet dem Herrn ein newes Lied [Sing to the Lord a new song]"; and 24, "Machet die Thore weit [Make wide the gates]."[97] These works were to be published in a sixth installment titled *Polyhymnia Jubilaea* (The Jubilee Polyhymnia); he had its title printed in the third volume of his *Syntagma Musicum*.[98] He even indicates elsewhere that this work was actually printed,[99] though unfortunately it has yet to be discovered. Par-ticularly the free compositions of this Reformation music—those not tied

---

94. *See Glossary; also Forchert, *Das Spätwerk des Michael Praetorius*, 152–53.

95. *SM* 3:172; cf. *SM* 3E:175. (I included more of the original quote than the author did.—Trans.)

96. *GA* 19:vi–viii. (The first point is basically a repetition of the Second Style, as it appears in *SM* 3:172–75; *SM* 3E:175–77.—Trans.)

97. *SM* 3:210–211; *SM* 3E:200–201; see also the last bullet on p. 96.

98. *SM* 3:210.

99. Vogelsänger, *Michael Praetorius beim Wort genommen*, 72f.

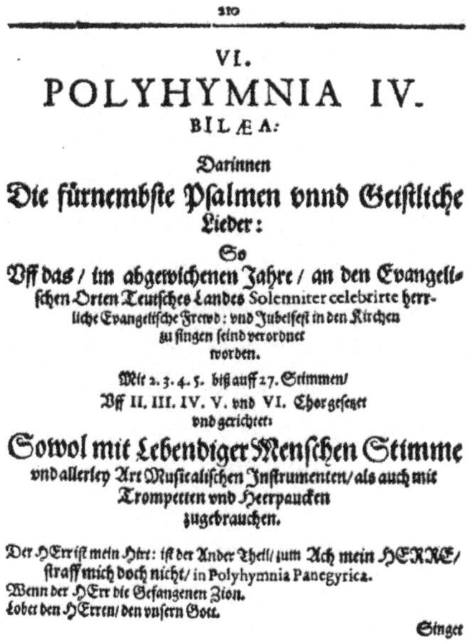

210

VI.

POLYHYMNIA IV.

BILÆA:

Darinnen

Die fürnembste Psalmen vnnd Geistliche Lieder:

So

Vff das / im abgewichenen Jahre / an den Evangelischen Orten Teutsches Landes Solenniter celebrirte herrliche Evangelische Frewd: vnd Jubelfest in den Kirchen zu singen seind verordnet worden.

Mit 2. 3. 4. 5. biß auff 27. Stimmen/ Vff II. III. IV. V. vnd VI. Chor gesetzet vnd gerichtet:

Sowol mit Lebendiger Menschen Stimme vnd allerley Art Musicalischen Instrumenten/ als auch mit Trompetten vnd Heerpaucken zugebrauchen.

Der HErr ist mein Hirt: ist der Ander Theil/ zum Ach mein HERRE/ straff mich doch nicht/ in Polyhymnia Panegyrica.
Wenn der HErr die Gefangenen Zion.
Lobet den HErren/ den vnsern Gott.

Singet

Fig. 46. Draft of the title page for *Polyhymnia Jubilaea*, printed in *SM* 3. (It was to contain settings of "the principal psalms and hymns that were prescribed for singing in the churches for the glorious evangelical festival and jubilee that was solemnly celebrated this past year [1617] in the evangelical localities of German territory."—Trans.)

to a hymn melody, like his settings of Psalm 6, "Ach mein Herre / straf mich doch nicht [O my Lord, please do not punish me]," and Psalm 133, "Siehe wie fein und lieblich ist [Behold, how nice and lovely it is]"[100]—might have shown that he was striving to achieve the ideal of monody (more on this later).

As we can gather from volume III of the *Syntagma Musicum*, Praetorius also already had very detailed ideas for the contents of additional installments of the *Polyhymniae*. The seventh installment was to contain at least nine compositions for five to twelve parts in the Ninth Style of the

100. GA 17:644ff and 268ff, respectively.

concerto,[101] organized according to the church year.[102] The ninth installment, *Polyhymnia Leiturgica* (The Liturgical Polyhymnia), was to contain
five masses and two Magnificats for eight to twenty-four parts distributed among two to six choirs.[103] In the tenth and eleventh *Polyhymniae*,
we even find twenty-two compositions that are identical to his earlier
motets, until we get to the scoring details.[104] Perhaps the earlier motets
would have undergone a remake here. Praetorius labels the fourteenth
installment *Polyhymnia Instrumentalis seu Musa Aonia Melpomene* (The
Instrumental Polyhymnia, or Aonian Muse Melpomene[105]), containing
works "in all keys and musical modes," which were to be employed as
sinfonias and ritornellos in other works.[106] But none of these installments
were apparently published.

   With his settings in the published *Polyhymniae*, Praetorius left behind yet another work of exceptional grandeur and originality after the
Musae Sioniae and the *Musae Aoniae*. Its inestimable value can be seen
when placed side by side with the compositions of his musical contemporaries. But the realization of his plans—not to mention the conditions
under which he took his many trips in the final years of his life—is probably what also robbed him of the remainder of his strength. He could
justifiably say of himself that he had often "been deprived of [his] sleep,
eating and drinking, etc., and dealt with more headaches [*mit meinem
Haupt so viel laboriret*] than perhaps anyone would be too eager to get
involved in."[107]

---

101. Praetorius describes the Ninth Style in *SM* 3:191–92; *SM* 3E:190–91.—Trans.

102. **SM* 3:212–13; *SM* 3E:202.

103. **SM* 3:214; *SM* 3E:202.

104. **SM* 3:214–15; *SM* 3E:203–4.

105. Greek: Μελπομένη, lit. "she who celebrates with song and dance." Initially the
Muse of chorus, she came to be known as the Muse of tragedy.—Trans.

106. **SM* 3:216–17; cf. *SM* 3E:204.

107. Written on Nov. 29, 1617; cited in Deeters, "Das Lehen der Familie Praetorius," 119. (This letter to Vice Chancellor Friedrich von Uder actually pertains to Praetorius' struggle to keep the fief Duke Heinrich Julius had conferred on him, mentioned
on p. 47. The entire sentence may be of interest: "Otherwise I do not know how I
should understand that such a young servant should be preferred to me (I who have
now served into my twenty-fifth year with such faithfulness, and at risk to body and
life—to the utmost of my integrity—so that I have been deprived of my sleep, eating
and drinking, etc., and have dealt with more headaches than perhaps anyone would be
too eager to get involved in)."—Trans.)

Monody, mentioned on page 105, originated in Italy around 1600 and was a completely new style of composition. It was called *stile moderno* or *seconda pratica* in contrast to traditional counterpoint, the *stile antico* or *prima pratica*. In this style, music is supposed to be the servant of the text rather than its master.[108] It required of the performers a new manner of presentation oriented towards expressive speaking. Leaning on the preface in the collection *Le nuove Musiche*, by the Italian composer and singer Guilio Caccini, Praetorius describes this style as follows:

> It is an orator's job not only to adorn an oration with beautiful, charming, and vivid words and splendid figures of speech, but also to articulate clearly and to stir the emotions by raising his voice here and lowering it there, sometimes speaking with a steady and gentle voice, at other times with a full and loud voice. In the same way it is a musician's job not just to sing, but to sing artfully and charmingly, in order that the heart of the listeners may be touched and their emotions stirred. Thus the song will achieve the goal for which it was created and at which it is aimed.[109]

"Swan Song" and Death

Leaning on the monodic style, Praetorius composed his final work, a setting of Psalm 116, "Das ist mir lieb / daß der Herr meine Stimme und mein Flehen höret [I love that the Lord hears my voice and my pleading]."[110] *The work was commissioned by Burckhard Grossman, "a court official at Jena in Thuringia and a wealthy man of letters and musical interests."[111] In 1616 he had been delivered from a threat to his life "in exactly the way David describes in Psalm 116,"[112] and therefore decided to commission sixteen different composers, including Praetorius, Schein, and Schütz, to compose a five-part setting of that psalm. Grossman writes that Praetorius "also [sent] a most moving and spiritually enriching letter," in which he wrote that that he had "composed this psalm . . . to bid farewell to himself, and with it he intended to take his leave. Shortly after [he sent

---

108. *See Forchert, *Das Spätwerk des Michael Praetorius*, 158–59.

109. *SM* 3:229; cf. *SM* 3E:214 (Caccini is mentioned on pp. 230 and 215, respectively).

110. GA 20:117ff; Wolff, *Anguish of Hell and Peace of Soul*, 39ff.

111. Wolff, *op. cit.*, ix.

112. Appendix VI, p. 218.

the composition and letter,] he died a blessed death and was transferred
to the heavenly ensemble."[113] Praetorius also sent along "an excellent Ordinance" with his "swan song" (as Grossman called it), "indicating how
he want[ed his setting] performed."[114*] The fifth point of the Ordinance
reads: "Above all, one must make sure to keep and observe a slow and
dignified tempo, so that the decorum of the text and stirring of the emotions can be respected and elicited that much better"[115]—a performance
instruction in imitation of Caccini.

The style of this composition must be "based on a knowledge of the
madrigal craft of Monteverdi and, with its markedly affective character
inclining toward monody[, it occupies] an utterly unique place in Praetorius' oeuvre—psychologically astonishing and, in its historical setting,
an almost incomprehensible phenomenon."[116] Attesting to this are not
just the five vocal parts, but also the three instrumental sinfonias, also
arranged for five parts in an altogether other-worldly harmony.

It seems that Praetorius' appointment was no longer being renewed
by Trinity Sunday of 1620.[117] By that point he was probably already lying
sick in bed. Master Peter Tuckermann, who preached the sermon and
spoke the graveside remarks at his funeral, reports:

> For after God had attacked him with illness[118] and he had recon-
> ciled with God, received the Holy Supper, and entrusted himself
> to the Lord Jesus Christ, God graciously called him away and
> delivered him from every evil and brought him safely to his
> heavenly kingdom [cf. 2 Timothy 4:18]. There his soul has now
> truly escaped intact, for blessed are the dead who die in the Lord
> from now on, as Revelation 14[:13] says.[119]

Praetorius died on February 15, 1621, in Wolfenbüttel, "after he had
already turned forty-nine."[120] He was buried on February 23 in the un-
der-construction Church of the Blessed Virgin Mary (the *Hauptkirche*),

113. Appendix VI, p. 220.

114. *Ibid.*

115. Reprinted in Wolff, *op. cit.*, 19; cf. p. 257.

116. Friedrich Blume in GA 20:xxxvi.

117. **MGG* Personenteil, 13:886, s. v. "Praetorius, Michael." (I added the "It seems
that" on the basis of this source.—Trans.)

118. One needs to read Tuckermann's entire funeral sermon to understand this
phraseology. See Appendix III.—Trans.

119. Appendix III, p. 165.

120. *Ibid.*, p. 169.

beneath the organ balcony,[121] "at its right hand."[122] Thus Duke Heinrich Julius and his court music director were also united in death, being buried in the same area.

*In his graveside remarks, Pastor Tuckermann compared Praetorius to the biblical Jacob:

> Jacob was . . . very faithful and diligent in his office and vocation . . . So too the Honorable Music Director was very diligent in his office and did not let heat or cold or sleep hinder him. Instead he strove to elevate music and to accomplish much within that field, and the work itself proves the craftsman in that regard. He accordingly enjoyed special favor not just at court here, but also with kings, electors, and lords elsewhere, as is known to everyone.
>
> Jacob had to undergo this tough struggle and affliction [as described in Genesis 32]. The Honorable Music Director often had great and difficult afflictions too, and on multiple occasions he lamented and wept that things had caught up with him and that he well deserved it, since he had misspent his youth and still possessed great failings and deficiencies. And indeed he was a sinful man and no angel, though his sins caused him remorse from the bottom of his heart. He was also visited by many crosses and misfortunes, so that he was a heavily plagued man.
>
> Jacob overcame everything through persistent faith, prayer, and patience. So the Honorable Music Director also let these spiritual shields and weapons be entrusted to him, and I must give him this testimonial: If ever there was a house in this area in which prayers were diligently said, truly it was his.[123]*

121. *WBB, 89.

122. *Appendix III, p. 169. ("At its right hand" refers to the left side of the balcony as one faces it.—Trans.)

123. *Ibid.*, pp. 164–65.

– 6 –

Postscript

The Bequest (Will)

IN MAY 1619, PRAETORIUS left behind a bequest with the ducal treasury in Wolfenbüttel, which was attested by Duke Friedrich Ulrich and three other witnesses.[1] In the opening and closing statements of the bequest, the duke pledges to keep the proper implementation of Praetorius' will "rigidly firm and inviolable."[2] With this bequest, Praetorius deposited 3,000 Marian gulden in Wolfenbüttel on six percent interest,[3] "each [gulden] valued at twenty Marian groschen"[4]—a considerable sum, and one he never had in hand. He could only make this deposit as a result of salary payments in arrears. He divided this amount among nine cities that had been of significance in his own life and in the lives of his relatives. The bequest thus takes on research significance as a biographical source.

The interest accrued on each city's amount was all to be brought to the St. Michael's Trade Fair (at the end of September) in Leipzig each year. There merchants visiting from the respective cities were to collect it and bring it back with them.[5] These earnings were to be distributed

---

1. Printed in Deeters, "Alte und neue Aktenfunde über Michael Praetorius," 114ff.

2. *Ibid.*, 114, 117–18.

3. *Zimmermann, "Zur Biographie des Kapellmeisters Michael Praetorius," 92. (I added the specific interest percentage.—Trans.)

4. Deeters, *op. cit.*, 115; cf. WGD, 291. (I added this quote from the bequest.—Trans.)

5. This peculiar procedure should have been documented, but unfortunately the author did not cite any source, and it is not mentioned by either Deeters or Zimmermann.—Trans.

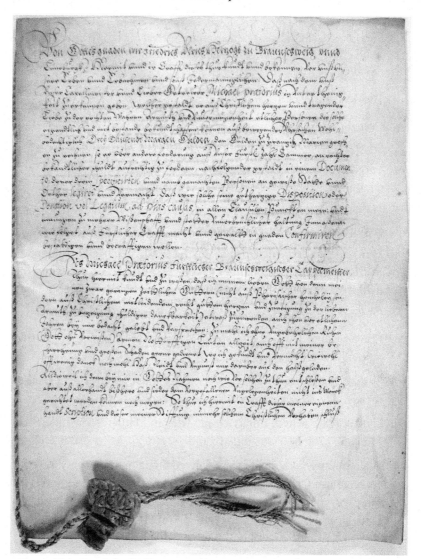

Fig. 47. First page (of six) of Praetorius' bequest, Public Archives of Lower Saxony, Wolfenbüttel, courtesy of Winfried Elsner.

not among the beggars, who run around from door to door and on the street, but among truly poor residents, widows, and orphans, who are ashamed to beg and have nowhere else they can easily go; among banished preachers and exiles; among poor students, but those who can provide good, accurate, unimpeachable proofs they they are not rovers and drifters; or, when a poor, disadvantaged child with a studious character is examined by the duly appointed assistant teachers [*Provisorn*] and they deem it advisable, the annual interest can be prescribed and given as a stipend to that child for the continuation of his studies, according to the circumstances of each place.[6]

The designated cities were as follows:

1. Creuzburg, "where I was born and my father was in the preaching ministry for many years" (300 Marian gulden);

2. Torgau, "where I was raised and my mother was born" (300 Marian gulden);

3. Treuenbrietzen, "where my parents lived in their old age, died, and are buried" (450 Marian gulden);

4. Frankfurt an der Oder, "where my blessedly departed brothers Dr. Andreas and Master Johannes Praetorius and I also served, and the two of them died and are buried there" (450 Marian gulden);

5. Dresden and

6. Halle, "where I was the recipient of many blessings" (200 Marian gulden each);

7. Zerbst, "where two of my sisters lived, and I attended the school there thirty-five years ago" (200 Marian gulden);

8. Halberstadt, "where I married my wife and fathered my oldest son Michael" (200 Marian gulden); and

9. Wolfenbüttel, "where I have now lived going on the twenty-seventh year,[7] praise God" (700 Marian gulden, "beyond the previous two hundred gulden—a hundred for the appointment of the pastor in Gottslager [*sic*] and a hundred gulden for Heinrichtown's [*Heinrichstädtischen*] new church building").[8]

6. *Ibid.* (I included more of the original quote than the author did.—Trans.)

7. German: *in das 27. Jahr.* The phrase seems to mean that he has lived there more than twenty-six years, but not yet a full twenty-seven years.—Trans.

8. *Deeters, *op. cit.*, 115–16; cf. WGD, 292. (The author's original ends at "700 Marian gulden." Gottslager [God's Encampment] was the name of the eastern suburb of Wolfenbüttel. Duke Julius intended to establish it as a great trade city, but his successor Heinrich Julius let this plan die out. In 1612 Gottslager had 130 heads of household and sixty-five renters [*Häuslinge*]. It burned down in 1617. Gurlitt says it was leveled [*niedergelegt*] in 1632 [WGD, 292, n. 1]; Zimmermann says that the church there was demolished [*abgebrochen*] in 1655 [*op. cit.*, 92, n. 2]. Heinrichtown was the name of Wolfenbüttel's central sector, named after Duke Heinrich the Admirable. Its "new

Fig. 48. Elias Holwein, *Warhafftige Contrafactur der weitberumbten Vestung unndt Stadt Wulffenbuttell*, 1620, woodcut. Though the location of the *Hauptkirche* initially gives the impression of a northward view (like Fig. 12), Holwein actually portrays the city from the east. He deliberately relocated the *Hauptkirche* so that it would not obstruct the view of the palace and palace chapel. He also portrayed the church a) from the south so that the viewer would have a full profile view of it, and b) with the steeple as designed by the church's architect Paul Francke a decade earlier—a steeple it never actually had. (The church's modern steeple was not built until the eighteenth century and did not follow Francke's design.) The *Hauptkirche* was under construction at the time, but Holwein wanted to include a finished version of it to augment the city's reputation and grandeur. Pictured in the foreground is Gotteslager (God's Encampment). Praetorius gave a hundred gulden toward the appointment of a pastor for the church there (also pictured) not long before he drew up his will. The K Tor (Kaisertor or Imperial Gate) pictured in the front (eastern) wall is the site of Trinity Church today. Note also the beautiful palace chapel where Praetorius played organ and directed many of his works.—Trans.

The actual payout of the interest earnings took place just once, in 1620, probably because Praetorius was still alive to oversee it.[9] After that it was discontinued and ultimately fell completely into oblivion. His grandchildren were the first to take up the matter again at the beginning of the eighteenth century. But they seem to have been unaware of the specifics of the bequest's provisions. They urgently requested "that, from the bequeathed 3,000 Marian gulden of their blessedly departed grandfather, 1,500 Marian gulden be left to Heinrichtown's church [the *Hauptkirche*] and the same amount to the orphanage in Augusttown [*August-Stadt*]." But the money had so depreciated by then, that each place only received 370 thalers.[10]

church building" was the Church of the Blessed Virgin Mary or *Hauptkirche*, treated toward the end of Chapter 4.—Trans.)

9. Zimmermann says that "neither the lump sums nor the interest on them were paid out" (*op. cit.*, 95), but Winfried Elsner shared with me that there is "original proof" in Frankfurt an der Oder that that city did receive money from Praetorius' bequest once (email message to translator, Jan. 20, 2020).—Trans.

10. Zimmermann, *op. cit.*, 95f. (Augusttown was the name of the western sector of

*Praetorius' last written, dated words may have been those in the margin at the end of a second copy of his bequest:

> N. B. I hereby acknowledge in my own hand and with my own signature that everything contained in this bequest of mine, including everything written on the preceding sheet, completely matches the authentic original and represents my, the testator's, actual and genuine wishes. September 29, 1620. Michael Praetorius of C[reuzburg].[11]*

The Memorial Slab

The Burial Book for the Church of the Blessed Virgin Mary in Wolfenbüttel[12] informs us that a plate in Praetorius' memory was installed "above the balcony on the north side." The plate has since disappeared.[13] It contained a portrait of Praetorius, with "the ascension of Christ ornately carved in alabaster above it." To the left of the portrait were inscribed Christ's words in John 20:17 in Latin: "I am ascending to my Father and your Father, to my God and your God." To the right, the words of Ephesians 4:10 in Latin: "Christ ascended far above all the heavens, in order that he might fill all things." *Beneath the portrait was inscribed a Latin epitaph composed by Friedrich Hildebrand, poet laureate and rector of the Wolfenbüttel school:

> Dedicated to God, the Best and Greatest [Latin: *D. O. M. S.*]
> Michael Praetorius, Prior of the Ringelheim Abbey, Master of Choir Music in the court of the Duke of Brunswick and Lüneburg located in Wolfenbüttel, yea, also Director and Overseer of Electoral and Ducal Chapel Ensembles elsewhere, advocate, ornament, and pillar of sacred music, after he had already turned forty-nine, that is, the seventh seven,

---

Wolfenbüttel.—Trans.)

11. Deeters, *op. cit.*, 118, n. p)–p). The date, St. Michael's Day, is certainly no coincidence. See Appendix II.

12. See WBB in the Annotated Abbreviations.

13. Its disappearance remains a mystery.—Trans.

the climacteric septenary, on February XV[14] in the year 1621 closed a pious life with a pious death.[15]

Though the memorial slab no longer exists, the square holes by which it was mounted to the wall were discovered during a restoration project from 1969–1985, so the location of the slab and its general shape and dimensions are known.*

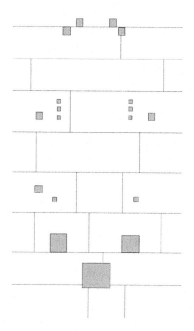

Fig. 49. Dieter Menzel, copy of the location of Praetorius' memorial slab, courtesy of Winfried Elsner. Elsner explains that, when the *Hauptkirche* was being painstakingly restored, "the walls were also cleaned with sandblasters and old paint was removed. Then Dieter Menzel, the sexton at the time, saw the plastered spots on the raw, bare wall, where the memorial slab had been . . . He made an exact copy of everything" (personal email). This is not Menzel's original. Elsner had made a graphic reconstruction of the memorial slab, using Menzel's drawing as a base. He shared the reconstruction with me and I digitally removed his text fields and the image of Praetorius.—Trans.

Estate

When we survey Praetorius' many references to his correspondence with fellow musical colleagues, with parishes, burgomasters, and councilmen of German cities, his contacts with an array of musicians, including those at the imperial court in Prague, and with printers and publishers as far away as Venice, Florence, and Rome, we must naturally conclude that he left behind an estate of considerable scope. Then there are the collections of manuscripts, half-finished printings, etc., and the no longer extant

14. WBB has an incorrect death date (February IV instead of XV), but the mistake likely lies with Woltereck the original author or Nolte the editor, not with the epitaph itself.—Trans.

15. WBB, 89–90. See also Appendix III, p. 169, n. 46.

volumes—of the *Musae Aoniae*, the *Polyhymniae*, and the fourth volume of the *Syntagma Musicum*—which evidently existed at one time.[16]

When we furthermore consider the meticulously precise measures that Praetorius took in the exact execution of his printings, it is amazing that there seem to be no references to the allocation of his estate. This astounds us all the more when we remember that his end did not take him by surprise. He prepared for it very consciously, as evidenced by his bequest of 1619, his "swan song" of 1620—"with it he intended to take his leave"[17]—and the report of Master Peter Tuckermann, who visited him on his sickbed in his final days and prepared him for death.[18]

Andreas Werckmeister is the only one to report the following in 1705 (!):

> I hold [Praetorius'] writings and memory in very high regard, and I am also the one best acquainted with his activity (*Actiones*), since all his manuscripts and hidden[19] music (*Arcana Musica*), indeed, even his calls (*Vocationes*) and many letters have come into my possession. From these I can tell and can still show anyone how much he furthered [the art of composition], for he was not just court music director for the duke of Brunswick-Lüneburg in Wolfenbüttel, but was also appointed to the service of His Electoral Illustriousness of Saxony, and in the practice of music (*Musicâ practicâ*) at the time he basically had no equal. One can also get some sense of his erudition from the first volume of his *Syntagma*.[20]

This indicates that at least a portion of Praetorius' estate managed to survive the Thirty Years' War. The question is: How did it arrive in Werckmeister's hands? There are different hypotheses on that, which will not be pursued in detail here. It would be pointless to do so anyway, since the estate has yet to be discovered in spite of every effort to track it down. In the course of Wilibald Gurlitt's research for his Praetorius biography prior to World War I (more on this in the next section), he inquired into Werckmeister's estate in the cities of Halberstadt and Quedlinburg,

---

16. Vogelsänger, *Michael Praetorius beim Wort genommen*, 27f, 72ff. See also Chapter 4, n. 118.

17. *See p. 107.

18. See p. 108.

19. That is, unpublished or extremely rare.—Trans.

20. Werckmeister, *Organum Gruningense redivivum*, 22–23, § 54. (I included more of the original quote than the author did.—Trans.)

"where Werckmeister was raised and later was court and town organist," but "unfortunately . . . entirely in vain."[21] There is also nothing about it in a biography on Werckmeister.[22]

We should also briefly cover the situation which Praetorius' widow faced after her husband's death. As the Wolfenbüttel chamber accounts for the year 1622/23 reveal, outstanding salary payments and unreimbursed boarding and clothing expenses still existed for him totaling 4,668 gulden after adjustments.[23] His widow was paid partial amounts of this several times each year through 1625.[24]

A financial matter involving the organ builder Gottfried Fritzsche proved especially unpleasant for her. Michael Praetorius had been in contact with Fritzsche multiple times since 1614, when Fritzsche built the organ for the Dresden palace chapel, which Praetorius examined. This collaboration continued up to the building of the organ for the Church of the Blessed Virgin Mary in Wolfenbüttel. Between 1619 and 1620 Praetorius had lent money to the organ builder on various occasions, totaling 270 thalers.[25] In 1620, after Praetorius had already fallen seriously ill and was "apprehensive of his impending death," he had requested of Fritzsche "a receipt and plain acknowledgment of the money I [Fritzsche] had received, which I also gladly delivered to him without any reservation on my part," as Fritzsche confirmed in 1623.[26]

When the widow fell into financial straits and demanded of the organ builder that he pay back this money, he reacted negatively and even maintained that he had "never borrowed a single groschen from the late Mr. Michael Praetorius," but that Praetorius had "voluntarily" given him the money "for work." He further asserted that it was Praetorius' fault for bringing him "to this strange place [Wolfenbüttel], with the result that he [Fritzsche] was still on the brink of destitution."[27] So it came down to a lawsuit between him and the widow, which dragged on until 1626.

---

21. WGD, 127, n. 2.

22. Ursula Herrmann, "Andreas Werckmeister (1645–1706)" (PhD diss., Martin-Luther-Universität Halle an der Saale, 1950).

23. WGD, 297f. (I corrected this from the author's figure of 5,321 thalers.—Trans.)

24. *WGD, 298f.

25. WGD, 296. (I transplanted this sentence here from the next paragraph in the author's original.—Trans.)

26. Cited in WGD, 295–96.

27. Cited in WGD, 295.

Ultimately, though, the case was decided in Anna Praetorius' favor.[28] The amount Fritzsche owed was deducted from his organ building expenses (which totaled 1,374 thalers) and paid to the widow.

*Even before the case was decided, Fritzsche himself, no doubt unintentionally, attested to Anna Praetorius' unimpeachable character. In a November 1623 statement, he said that after her husband died, she

> very insistently prevailed on me for the payment [of what her husband had given me].[29] And since I was not ready with it right away, she obtained from Your Venerable and Formidable Excellencies [the councilors], as the Ducal Administration, a mandate to the Honorable Directors of the church building, who thereupon paid the widow this money, according to her pleasure and desire, from the outstanding wages I had earned, to all satisfaction. They retrieved my obligation from her and delivered it back to me settled. The widow was not only pacified by this, but she even sent her relative, named Franz N[aumann][30] (who has now taken over a pastorate), to find me in the church and to deliver several thalers back to me that she had been overpaid by the Honorable Directors, so that there would be no need to publicly disturb her deceased husband—that good, honorable, pious man—in his blessed rest.[31]*

Anna Praetorius passed away in Wolfenbüttel in October 1632, and was buried there on October 11.[32]

28. *WGD, 295,296. (The author mistakenly said that it dragged on until 1624.—Trans.)

29. Fritzsche told this story to convince the ducal councilors that, if he did owe anything to Michael Praetorius (and now, his widow), he had already paid back it in full. But if this story is true, what he paid was doubtless not the full amount he owed, but a very small percentage thereof requested by Anna Praetorius to meet her immediate needs at the time. See e.g. Anna's July 4, 1621 letter to the councilors over a matter of thirty thalers in WGD, 295. Also compare the total amount owed by Fritzsche that she gives there, 240 thalers, to the total amount Fritzsche later confessed to receiving, 270 thalers. Perhaps then the events of Fritzsche's account here took place prior to July 4, 1621.—Trans.

30. According to Gurlitt, Anna's nephew, a son of one of Michael Praetorius' sisters

31. Cited in WGD, 296. If Anna was only requesting thirty thalers at the time (see n. 29 above), she may have received thirty-five and returned the extra five via her nephew. As the author said in his original: What a noble gesture!

32. *WBB, 101. (The author mistakenly had October 11 as her death date; the date in WBB is her burial date.—Trans.)

Praetorius' Tracks in 400 Years of Music History

In the roughly 400 years after his death, Michael Praetorius did not disappear from the consciousness of the musical community. But it was chiefly Praetorius the author of the *Syntagma Musicum* who was accorded respect and admiration. His musical works, on the other hand, and those in the concerto style above all, fell very quickly into oblivion. The devastation of the Thirty Years' War and the attendant cultural decline in Germany no longer permitted any possibility of their performance, and by the time it was all over, musical styles had already moved on.

Not until the beginning of the nineteenth century, when attention turned back to the time of the Reformation, did interest in Praetorius' musical works also kindle. His chorale settings received the most attention; they were highlighted as models of evangelical church music. These then were also his first musical works to be reprinted. His choir settings, like that of the Christmas hymn "Es ist ein Ros entsprungen [Behold, a Branch Is Growing *or* Lo, How a Rose E'er Blooming]," were regarded as the ultimate examples of such music on account of their ready singability in all parts. With such settings Praetorius was stylized as the Lutheran arch-cantor. (The melody of the hymn "Es ist ein Ros" does not originate with Praetorius. Its earliest source is a Marian hymn in a manuscript from St. Albans Carthusian monastery in Trier. Its text was altered to have a Christological focus; Jesus, not Mary, was now the "little flower," which she bore "in midst of coldest winter, at deepest midnight hour."[33]) Such choir settings, along with folk songs, comprised a major portion of the music cultivated in the German Youth Music Movement (*Jugendmusikbewegung*) at the beginning the twentieth century. This movement also incorporated the dance settings of Praetorius' *Terpsichore*—a previously unfamiliar aspect of Praetorius' work. Yet even then only a fraction of his creative work was known to the musical public.[34]

Within the emergent field of musicology, people now became interested in exploring Praetorius in his total personality, including his ancestry and self-understanding. After several years of study, the Leipzig music student and pupil of Hugo Riemann, Wilibald Gurlitt (1889–1963), presented his dissertation, "Michael Praetorius (Creuzbergensis): Sein Leben und seine Werke [Michael Praetorius (of Creuzburg): His Life and

---

33. *See Aufdemberge, *Christian Worship: Handbook*, 67–68. (I used this source to expand a little on the author's material.—Trans.)

34. Forchert, "Michael Praetorius: Werk und Wirkung," 102.

His Works]," to the University of Leipzig in 1914. The Leipzig publisher
Breitkopf and Härtel assumed the publication of this comprehensive
work. But in the meantime, World War I began and Gurlitt became a soldier. He was wounded and taken captive by the French that same year. He
was not released until 1918. Consequently, only the first two chapters of
his four-chapter dissertation appeared in print in 1915, without foreword
or table of contents.

In 1920, Gurlitt was called to fill the newly established chair of
musicology at the Albert Ludwig University of Freiburg, and the many
attendant responsibilities left him no time to continue his work on the
proofs of the remaining chapters. They therefore remained unpublished,
and his dissertation continued to be regarded as a fragment in the musicological field. Not until 1991[35] did the present author, thanks to contact
with Gurlitt's widow, succeed in locating the remaining two chapters
in Gurlitt's estate in the Department of Musicology at the University of
Freiburg. Copies of this part of the dissertation can now also be found in
the Herzog August Library and in the Public Archives of Lower Saxony
in Wolfenbüttel.

We can gather from the foreword of Gurlitt's dissertation[36] that he
also had plans for a second volume beyond these four chapters. But neither notes nor drafts for this could be found in his estate. The many tasks
that Gurlitt undertook in Freiburg also included the building of a Praetorius Organ, following a disposition drafted by Praetorius in volume II of
the *Syntagma Musicum*.[37] The organ was built by Walcker of Ludwigsburg
and was dedicated on December 4, 1921, by the famous cantor of St.
Thomas in Leipzig, Karl Straube.[38] This work helped pioneer the Organ
Movement (*Orgelbewegung*) with its attempt to orient the building of organs towards the Baroque sound ideal. In connection with the efforts to
perform early music as correctly as possible, the second and third volumes
of Praetorius' *Syntagma Musicum* with their information and illustrations,

35. In his appendix to WGD titled, "Zur Geschichte der Dissertation von Wilibald
Gurlitt," Vogelsänger gives the year 1990.—Trans.

36. The author said that the foreword was "only preserved in manuscript," but the
same year his book was published (2008), Dr. Josef Floßdorf published a complete
edition of Gurlitt's dissertation, which included his foreword on pp. vi–ix. See WGD
in Annotated Abbreviations.—Trans.

37. *SM* 2:191f (no. 2); *SM* 2E2, same pages.

38. Unfortunately this organ was destroyed in 1944 in a World War II bombing
raid.—Trans.

not to mention Praetorius' numerous instructions in his individual works, also played an important role in period-correct performance practice.

Fig. 50. Concert invitation, 1922, courtesy of Winfried Elsner. After the completion of the Praetorius Organ in the University of Freiburg, a number of concerts were given on it. This invitation attests to one of them, given by the famous "organist maker" Karl Straube, cantor of St. Thomas in Leipzig.

At the 1927 Freiburg Organ Conference, plans finally emerged to issue Praetorius' musical works in a new edition, which was to benefit both research and practice. Friedrich Blume (1893–1975) assumed the leadership of this project. Seven other musicologists worked with him to publish the twenty total volumes. They appeared from 1928 to 1956 and were completed in 1960 with a comprehensive *Generalregister* (General

Index) volume. Initially the Wolfenbüttel publisher Georg Kallmeyer assumed the printing of this edition. In 1929 he had purchased the house at Großer Zimmerhof 20, without knowing that Praetorius was the one who had it built in 1612.[39] When he learned of this, he took it as a good omen. From 1947 onwards, the Möseler Verlag carried the edition through to its conclusion.

The ensuing period saw the appearance of more musicological works in the field of Praetorius research. First, Friedrich Blume published a comprehensive article in 1935, in conjunction with his work on the complete edition of Praetorius' musical works. In it he traced the historical development of Praetorius' works and highlighted his systematizing method.[40] In 1959, Arno Forchert's (1925–2011) dissertation appeared in print—*Das Spätwerk des Michael Praetorius: Italienische und deutsche Stilbegegnung* (The Later Work of Michael Praetorius: A Convergence of Italian and German Styles).[41] With its numerous detailed investigations, it is a standard reference, alongside the works of Gurlitt and Blume, for understanding Praetorius the composer. Forchert continued to contribute much to the field of Praetorius' biography and work, thereby keeping Praetorius research alive. The works of Kurt Gudewill, Hans Haase, Martin Ruhnke, and Siegfried Vogelsänger likewise brought many particulars of Praetorius' life and work to light. Yet all these investigations, inclusive of the present work, show in detail that a comprehensive presentation and evaluation of Praetorius' person and work is still lacking.

In 1994, the Michael-Praetorius-Gesellschaft (Michael Praetorius Society) was founded in Creuzburg an der Werra, the city of Praetorius' birth. They made their goal the cultivation and promotion of his works, and since then have held annual Praetorius conferences with lectures and concerts. An exhibition with documents carefully selected and arranged in a room of the Creuzburg Castle conveys to visitors a vivid impression of the life and work of this distinguished Protestant court music director.

For some time the Michael Praetorius Collegium, founded in Wolfenbüttel in 1971, has also been striving to make their namesake

39. See the end of Chapter 3.

40. *Blume, "Das Werk des Michael Praetorius."

41. 244 pages, including foreword, introduction, and indexes; see Bibliography.—Trans.

more widely known.[42] For the historically significant year 2005,[43] Winfried Elsner prepared an exhibition under the theme "Michael Praetorius in Wolfenbüttel" with the subtitle, "Residenz und Renaissance," and made it available in the Wolfenbüttel Palace to the interested public. Divided into twelve parts, this exhibition provided an extremely informative look into Praetorius' life and work with the aid of select textual and pictorial artifacts, three listening stations with sound samples of his works, and an accompanying booklet. This exhibition was also displayed in Halberstadt and Torgau, and each time it was supplemented with a lecture by the present author.[44]

Praetorius in the Assessment of Posterity

Wilibald Gurlitt:

> Michael Praetorius, the widely renowned, accomplished, and outstanding musician highly gifted by God (may God be pleased to preserve him in long life to his glory and as an adornment to his Church!) was once allegedly asked whether the beloved art of music, having reached such a high level at the present time, would be able to advance even farther. In response, his excellency allegedly gave this Christian answer: Yes, it would improve even more and reach a very high level, until finally the joyous Last Day drew near, when it would then be equal to the music of heaven and the angels . . . The fact that the beloved art of music has indeed reached a very high level is attested not only by a consideration of the outstanding and magnificent music that has been composed, but also by a consideration of the places where music is prevalent. For I do not wish to talk about the music at princely and electoral courts right now, since it is obvious that music at those places is always improving by the day. This is sufficiently attested by the magnificent

42. The website jointly run by the Michael-Praetorius-Gesellschaft and the Michael Praetorius Collegium can be found at http://www.michael-praetorius.de.—Trans.

43. This was the year Wolfenbüttel celebrated the four hundredth anniversary of Praetorius' appointment as Duke Heinrich Julius' court music director, which was certified on December 7, 1604.—Trans.

44. Since September 2008, the exhibition has been on permanent display in the Church of the Blessed Virgin Mary (*Hauptkirche*) in Wolfenbüttel, though there are tentative plans to revise it for 2021.—Trans.

works of the outstanding and highly gifted musicians
Praetorius, Schütz, and others, so that a person might
easily end up questioning whether the beloved art of
music can advance any farther at those places too. But
just consider how music is completely prevalent in every
place. There is hardly even a small village, especially in
Thuringia, in which one cannot expect to find both vocal
and instrumental music well supplied and flourishing in
a splendid and aesthetic manner—place after place. Even
when there is no organ, the vocal music is enhanced and
adorned with at least five or six violins, which previously
could hardly be had in the cities.[45]

These progress-infused words [of Michael Altenburg in 1620[46]]
transport us right into the middle of the active and lively musical activity of Middle Germany at the beginning of the seventeenth century. They likewise showcase the towering reputation
that Michael Praetorius enjoyed in the music life of his time.
This artist stood at the head of the party of musical progress—
admired and revered on many sides, but hated and feared even
more—during the second decade of the seventeenth century,
right in the heart of Germany's musical interest. In this position, he very distinctly felt himself to be the reformer of German
music "following the example of the Italians,"[47] considering that
two years before his death he expressly acknowledged that he
was "perhaps the first one to have broken the ice and paved the
way," "so that in Germany, the fatherland we all share, the noble
art of music might flourish more and more and be brought to a
perfect condition and ideal."[48] For the execution of his music-
reforming plans, he put his greatest hopes in the "genuine and
ardent lovers of noble music . . . who will emerge in the dear
future generations."[49] All of his life and activity was driven by
this impassioned confidence in a bright and better future for
German music. This ability to get excited about everything truly

45. *Gurlitt was probably quoting an original copy, but this quote can also be
found in Mönkemeyer, *Michael Altenburg (1584–1640): Intraden*, vol. 1, p. 2; cf. Walter
Bergmann's translation there on p. 3.

46. The original work cited by Gurlitt is: Michael Altenburg, *Erster Theil. Newer
Lieblicher und Zierlicher Intraden, mit sechs Stimmen* (Erfurt: Johann Röhbock,
1620).—Trans.

47. *SM 3, fol.):(7 recto; SM 3E:10.

48. *SM 3, fol.):(8 recto (incorrectly printed) /):(6 recto (corrected); cf. SM 3E:8.

49. *SM 3, fol.):(2 recto; cf. SM 3E:4.

progressive and innovative (*Zukunftsmächtige*) in the music of his era is alive in every pen-stroke of this artist.[50]

Hans Haase:

Michael Praetorius . . . is the most significant personality of music history that has lived and worked within the walls of Wolfenbüttel. [Here] is the place at which the premier maestro in Protestant North Germany at the turn of the seventeenth century spent the decades critical to his occupation and his creative work . . . This was the cultural environment for the chamber organist, court music director, composer, and music theorist in the time of the stylistic transition from the so-called Renaissance to the age of the Baroque—if one is permitted to regard these terms as valid for music history too. Here, then, the young organist subsequently evolved into the guardian of the heritage of Reformation hymnody, into the transmitter of comprehensive music knowledge, and into the transmitter of the innovative style and composition that had quickly also begun to spread north of the Alps, especially from Italy.[51]

Friedrich Blume:

German erudition and precision; the German penchant for contemplation and speculation; German pedagogism and pedantry; at the same time inexhaustible creative energy; truly comprehensive knowledge and ability; conservative stubbornness and an obsession with systematization taken to the point of fussiness, but also passionate devotion to new convictions; the most pretentious parading of the beloved self, but also the once again genuinely German readiness to employ all of one's own person and one's entire life for a great purpose—all of these traits combine in the person of Michael Praetorius. If we just take a cursory glance at his works that have been passed down to posterity, they appear seemingly randomly thrown together, like tatters that have been arbitrarily torn out from a great abundance of material possibilities. But we will not fulfill the master's wishes and we will not understand the work passed down to us until we see it for what it really is—the torso of an enormous project whose purpose was nothing less than encompassing the total field of music in all its parts and mastering it in a

50. WGD, vi–vii. (I included more of the original quote than the author did.—Trans.).

51. Gudewill and Haase, "Zur Einführung," in *Michael Praetorius Creutzbergensis (1571[?]–1621)*, 5.

distinctively creative and comprehensive system . . . A genuinely Baroque and genuinely German enterprise, with its penchant for self-forgetting devotion, the absence of boundaries or limits, the exhilaration of power, and self-promotion.[52]

Arno Forchert:

[The later works of Praetorius] are evidence of a completely new attitude of the composer toward his work . . . The desire for presentation, for action—the most common mark of the new era—is now already noticeable in the concept stage, and more than that, in individual cases it even becomes the *primum agens* [primary agent] of his artistic activity as a whole. This is where we find the common denominator of all the characteristics that could be recorded as essential features of Praetorius' later work. It is the knowledge of the form that the sound of the music will take and the increasing awareness of that form's possibilities. For the musicians of the new century—and Praetorius belongs to their number wholeheartedly—music has gained the ability to make ideas and feelings tangible to the senses through the medium of speech (the treatment of speech in madrigals and monody). She has been ushered into a world where musicians can use her to physicalize time and space acoustically by means of repetition (correspondence and analogies, or echo) and structure (contrasting scoring or choir division). Finally, music has now been given the chance to express herself purely in the sound of the instruments, apart from any spoken words.[53]

Kurt Gudewill:

In our days there is an increasing tendency to explain creative achievements exclusively or primarily in terms of their societal conditioning. But the lifework of Michael Praetorius is so highly characterized by an unusually strong and unconventional personality, that the preexisting societal conditions in which his work emerged seem to be of secondary importance. Even with the character of his compositional work we are hard-pressed to find an analogy. Added to that is the fact that, besides Johann Mattheson, there has also not been any composer to leave behind such a significant work of music theory as Praetorius. And in spite of all this, every attempt to find a parallel in music history to what Praetorius planned to produce but was unable

---

52. Blume, "Das Werk des Michael Praetorius," 322.
53. Forchert, *Das Spätwerk des Michael Praetorius*, 189.

to realize—over and above what he actually did produce—is doomed to failure from the start . . . But Praetorius was even more than a musician, composer, and music theorist. He also enjoyed an outstanding reputation as an organizer, who advised the Middle German princes on the structure and enlargement of their chapel ensembles, so that they could meet the requirements imposed on them by the new, personnel-heavy music of the Italian style. This activity occurred in the time between 1613 and 1619 . . . It was the time when he was the *de facto* musical teacher of the [German] nation.[54]

54. Gudewill and Haase, *op. cit.*, 7,11.

– Appendix I –

Remarks on Praetorius' Ancestry

WILIBALD GURLITT ASSUMED THAT Michael Schulteis, Michael Praetorius' father, only had one wife. He wrote:

> The ancestry and name of [Michael Schulteis'] wife, who herself was born in Torgau, is unknown. His marriage with her, which lasted upwards of fifty years, produced several daughters and three sons, two of which, Andreas and Johannes, followed in their father's footsteps and became respected theologians.[1]

He then affirmed in a footnote: "According to the information in their son's [Michael's] testament, we have little reason to suspect a potential second marriage."[2]

Vogelsänger, apparently leaning on the genealogical information he received from Randolf Ludewig, says that Praetorius "was the youngest child of the Lutheran pastor Michael Schulteis and his second (or third) wife Magdalena, the daughter of the Torgau patrician Andreas Leicher." He thereby indicates that, by 2008, there was indeed "reason to suspect a . . . second marriage," and possibly even a third.

To my knowledge, Praetorius only gives two explicit hints as to the identity of his mother. In his bequest, he says that his mother was born in Torgau and that she passed away in Treuenbrietzen. But these facts do not offer us much help, since primary source evidence cited by Gurlitt indicates that Schulteis' first wife also lived (and presumably was born) in

---

1. WGD, 18.
2. *Ibid.*, n. 6.

Torgau, and that, as of February 1538, he and his first wife were already expecting a child "any day,"[3] though what became of that child is unknown.

Praetorius also does give us a hint that his father remarried at some point. In his dedicatory epistle for *Missodia Sionia*, he refers to *"fratrem meum germanum p.m. Doct. Andream Praetorium"*—"my brother-german of pious memory, Dr. Andreas Praetorius."[4] Some scholars have misinterpreted this, claiming that this must mean that Andreas and Michael shared the same father and mother. However, while the Oxford Latin Dictionary defines *germanus* as an adjective meaning "having the same father and mother," Lewis and Short's dictionary qualifies this meaning: "of brothers and sisters who have the same parents, *or at least the same father*" (emphasis mine). Thus this phrase all by itself does not tell us anything about Michael Praetorius' mother in relation to his brother Andreas'. It is also interesting that in the very next paragraph of the aforementioned dedicatory epistle, he goes on to mention *"ecclesiasten quoque alterum, fratrem Iohannem p.m."*—"my other brother Johannes, of pious memory, who was also a churchman."[5] Notable by its absence is the word *germanus*, which might initially lead us to suspect that Johannes might have been a stepbrother with a different father. Speaking against this, however—especially in light of what follows—is that Johannes is always listed in matriculation and promotion entries as "Cruciburgensis," born in Creuzburg. Having said all of this, Praetorius' phraseology is still worth noting, because his use of *germanus* does imply that he did have at least one stepbrother having a different father, that is, that Michael Schulteis had at some point married a widow with children.

Another detail adds interest: In Praetorius' "holy vow to the Lord" (see page 55), Praetorius says that his "forefathers"[6] had been clergymen, in addition to his father. In his graveside remarks at Praetorius' funeral (see Appendix III), Pastor Tuckermann also said that Praetorius' "father and grandfather were preachers and served God and his church for a long time." It is virtually impossible that Praetorius' paternal grandfather is under discussion. First, from the best evidence we have, Michael Schulteis came from a line of furriers and cloth-workers.[7] Second, Schulteis was

---

3. *Ibid.*, 16–18.

4. *Miss.*, fol.)(4 verso.

5. *Ibid.* This could also be translated: "also another churchman, my brother Johannes, of pious memory."

6. This may be a poetic plural.

7. WGD, 7–8.

born around 1515 and enrolled at the University of Wittenberg in 1528, just a few years after Luther's reformatory teachings had begun to inspire widespread marriages among his clergymen followers. That means that if Schulteis' father was a clergyman, he was a priest, not a Lutheran pastor. Since Roman Catholic priests were forbidden to marry,[8] that would mean that Michael Schulteis was an illegitimate child. In that case, it would be highly unlikely for Praetorius and Pastor Tuckermann to speak positively of the fact that Praetorius' grandfather had been a clergyman.

This means that Praetorius' maternal grandfather must have been a pastor, and that his mother was a pastor's daughter. Interestingly, Gurlitt already raised the remote possibility in 1914 that Gabriel Didymus/ Zwilling was Praetorius' maternal grandfather.[9]

This brings us to a blog entry written by Dr. Detlev Küttler of Burgwedel, a descendant of Michael Praetorius through marriage.[10] There he refers to marriage entries pertaining to Michael Schulteis "in the relevant parish books for the two Thuringian congregations," namely those that Schulteis served in Creuzburg and in Roben by Gera.[11] Though the entries contain some contradictory information and Dr. Küttler seems to make some questionable deductions, the entries do permit us to infer that Schulteis did in fact marry three times:

1. He married a daughter of Georg Brückner, a court chef in Torgau, in 1537. As mentioned above, she apparently gave birth to at least one child in February or March 1538.

2. He married Magdalena Leicher, the daughter of Andreas Leicher, a (the?) municipal judge in Torgau sometime before 1554. (Apparently this date is given because Maria Schulteis, who was born in 1554, is known to be a daughter from this marriage.)

---

8. The only exception was the very rare circumstance where the man had already married and subsequently decided to enter the priesthood, in which case he still had to obtain a special dispensation for his marriage.

9. WGD, 76, n. 6.

10. "Recherche: Wer ist die Mutter von Michael Praetorius?", *Familiengeschichte Küttler* (blog), Nov. 28, 2009, http://kuettler.net/recherche-wer-ist-die-mutter-von-michael-praetorius/.

11. Note that, when he cites Book IV as "Die reußischen Herrschaften," *reußisch* does not refer to the Russians, but to Heinrich Reuß XV "the Middle" of Plauen and Greiz (r. 1564–1578).

3. Finally, in 1567 he married "Gertrud Leicher gen. Didymus aus Torgau, To. v. Gabriel Sup. Torgau." As best I can tell—and this also seems to be the way Dr. Küttler takes it—the abbreviation "gen." stands for "geboren" (née) rather than "genannt" (called *or* named).[12] In that case, Schulteis' third wife was "Gertrud Leicher née Didymus of Torgau, a daughter of Gabriel [Didymus/Zwilling], Superintendent of Torgau." The fact that she is called "Leicher née Didymus" means that she had already married a Mr. Leicher and he had presumably died.

Didymus was Schulteis' superior when Schulteis was a deacon in Torgau. (Didymus was also a close associate of Luther.) Since Schulteis' second wife had been a Leicher, we can guess at a possible scenario: Schulteis was already familiar with Gertrud twice over, so to speak, since she was both his former superior's daughter and had married a relative (brother?) of Schulteis' second wife. When Schulteis' second wife died and Gertrud's husband died, he took her as his third wife in a manner similar to that of the biblical kinsman redeemer (Deut 25:5,6; Ruth 3–4), also taking in the children she already had.

One of those children appears to have been Michael Praetorius' (step-)sister, Sabine/Sabina, whose death entry, from August 1633, Dr. Küttler also records in his blog post: "Mrs. Sabina Lussovius, born a Leger [Leicher],[13] the late Mr. Superintendent Master Christopher Jordan's mother-in-law, who passed away on Monday night between ten and eleven o'clock, at age seventy-five and a half, is being buried on August 21." This puts her birth year in the early part of 1558 and makes her about nine years old by the time Michael Schulteis became her stepfather.[14]

All of this seems to confirm that Michael Praetorius was in fact born from Michael Schulteis' third marriage, and that his mother was a daughter of Gabriel Didymus, the firebrand preacher and associate of Martin

12. It is also possibly a misprint for the original "geb." My efforts to follow up on this with Dr. Küttler were in vain.

13. Leicher could also be spelled Lecher, and from there it is but a small step to the spelling Leger since, depending on the region, the pronunciation of "ch" and "g" could be very similar.

14. Dr. Küttler also confirms that this Sabine née Leicher is in fact the same as the Sabine known as Praetorius' sister. He cites the entry for her marriage to Andreas Lussovius in the parish book of the Margraviate of Brandenburg, in which she is called "Sabine Prätorius, daughter of the Superintendent Michael P. in Creuzburg an der Werra."

Luther. At any rate, Vogelsänger's assertion that Praetorius was born to Magdalena née Leicher appears to be false, since if she were his mother, neither he nor Pastor Tuckermann could make the claim that Praetorius' grandfather was also a preacher. This could only be true if a number of considerable documentary mistakes were made elsewhere.

However, it still leaves questions unanswered, such as: Who was the mother of Andreas and Johannes?[15] Who was Praetorius' brother(s) that did not share his father? What was the relationship of Gertrud Leicher née Zwilling/Didymus and her children to Michael Schulteis and his children before the two married? When did Schulteis' wives pass away?

15. We might be tempted to assume that Schulteis had already married for the second time in Torgau before he moved to Creuzburg in 1549, since his second wife was from Torgau. But according to the parish record information, he married his third wife, who was also from Torgau, in 1567, even though he was pastor in Roben by Gera at the time. Although Roben is much closer to Torgau than is Creuzburg, it is still more than seventy miles distant.

– Appendix II –

Michael Praetorius' Birthdate

IF I AM NOT mistaken, I am the first to propose the date of September 27 or 28, 1571, for Michael Praetorius' birthdate. What follows is my attempt to defend this proposal.

Ultimately, every debate about Praetorius' birth needs to grapple with the only two contemporaneous sources:

1. The inscription surrounding the woodcut portrait of him created in 1606 and published in 1607,[1] and

2. the epitaph Friedrich Hildebrand composed for him that was published both as an addendum to Tuckermann's funeral sermon[2] and on Praetorius' memorial slab itself (in slightly abbreviated form).[3]

A superficial look at these two sources seems to reveal a contradiction and is responsible for Praetorius' birth year often being printed as "1571/72." The inscription (#1) is dated 1606 (MDCIVX) and explicitly lists Praetorius' age as thirty-five (*A[nn]o aetat[is] XXXV*). Without any further details, we would deduce that he was born in 1571 (1606 minus thirty-five equals 1571). The epitaph (#2) says that Praetorius died on February 15, 1621, "*Cum jam ageret quadragesimum nonum aetatis annum*," as printed in the addendum to Tuckermann's funeral sermon,[4] or "*cum jam ageret 49. aetatis annum*," as Woltereck prints it in his book

---

1. *MS* Coll., fol.)(1 verso; see also p. 54 of the present work.

2. FS, 47.

3. WBB, 90.

4. FS, 47.

of burials.[5] We will look at the different ways this Latin phrase can be understood later, but without any further details, we would deduce from this source that he was born in 1572 (1621 minus forty-nine equals 1572).

However, even though these two sources seem to contradict each other on the surface, I am proceeding on the assumption that both Praetorius (who was most likely responsible for the portrait inscription) and Hildebrand knew Praetorius' birthdate. Thus, if at all possible, these two sources should be harmonized and reconciled with each other.

The inscription (#1) is much more straightforward and leaves less to interpretation. The portrait it accompanies first appeared in a special collection of Praetorius' works, namely *MS* Coll.[6] This collection was already in the works in 1606, but was not published until 1607. Installments II, III, and IV of the *Musae Sioniae* were all first published separately in 1607,[7] and then *MS* Coll. quickly followed on their heels. The preface Praetorius wrote for the special collection was dated October 16, 1606,[8] and, as already mentioned, the inscription circling the portrait on the back side of the special title page for this edition expressly pairs Praetorius' thirty-fifth year with 1606 AD. This information gives us two possibilities:

a. Praetorius was thirty-five when the portrait was done, but would turn thirty-six later that year, which would put his birth in 1570. This option, however, is impossible, since his sister Magdalena was born in Creuzburg either after August in 1569 or sometime in 1570,[9] and no amount of wrangling with Hildebrand's epitaph for Praetorius (#2) can produce a birth year that early.

b. Praetorius had been thirty-four earlier in 1606, but had turned thirty-five by the time the portrait was done, which would put his birth in 1571. This is the option with which we must proceed. We should also note here that it would make sense for Praetorius to have his portrait done and to write the preface for the special collection at roughly the same time. Plus, if his birthdate occurred in the general neighborhood of October 16, 1571 (exactly thirty-five years from

5. WBB, 90.

6. See Annotated Abbreviations.

7. See the reprinted title pages in GA 2–4.

8. See p. 174.

9. WGD, 56f; Vogelsänger, *Michael Praetorius, Hofkapellmeister und Komponist zwischen Renaissance und Barock*, 9, probably leaning on Ludewig, "Genealogische Forschungen zur Familie Praetorius."

the date of his preface for *MS* Coll.), that would fit with the possible birthdate range for his sister Magdalena.

In the epitaph (#2) that "Master Friedrich Hildebrand of Blankenburg, Poet Laureate, Rector of the Wolfenbüttel School" composed for Praetorius after his death, he says that Praetorius, "*Cum jam ageret quadragesimum nonum aetatis annum, hoc est, septimum septenarium Climactericum: A.D. XV. FEBR. ANNO XPI. M. DC. XXI. Pia Vitam Pia Morte Terminavit.*" He is noting the date of Praetorius' death (February 15, 1621 AD) and the age he was when he died.

This phrase—"*Cum jam ageret quadragesimum nonum aetatis annum,*" or "*cum jam ageret 49. aetatis annum,*" as Woltereck says it appeared on Praetorius' memorial slab—is the nub. In this phrase, Hildebrand is saying something about Praetorius' forty-ninth year using a temporal conjunction (*cum*, "when"), a temporal adverb (*jam/iam*, "now, at this time, just now; a little while ago, just; by this time, already"), and a third person imperfect subjunctive form (subjunctive used with *cum*) of the verb *ago* ("drive, do, pursue"), with the object of *ago* being "the forty-ninth year of age." Lewis and Short's Latin dictionary says that *ago*, when used of time, means "to pass, spend," and when used "with *annus* ['year'] and an ordinal [i.e, 'first,' 'second,' etc.], means 'to be of a certain age, to be [so many years] old.'"[10]

However, it seems that there was not uniformity in how this idiom was employed or understood. For instance, in Philipp Melanchthon's biography of Martin Luther (the first Luther biography ever published), he uses "*cum iam ageret*" twice. Once he says that Johann von Staupitz transferred Luther to Wittenberg in 1508 (we know it took place late in the year, for the winter semester)[11] "*cum iam [Lutherus] ageret*" his twenty-sixth year.[12] Since Melanchthon earlier identified Luther's birthdate as November 10, 1483, either Melanchthon got one year off in his math or he is using *ago* plus *annum* differently than Lewis and Short's interpretation and our usual way of identifying age today. Accordingly to our way of reckoning, Luther could, at the oldest, only be twenty-five years old (1508 minus 1483

10. Lewis and Short, *A Latin Dictionary* (Oxford University Press, 1879), 75.2.

11. Martin Brecht, *Martin Luther: His Road to Reformation* (Minneapolis: Fortress, 1985), 92.

12. "Philippus Melanthon [*sic*] Pio Lectori S. D." (*Praefatio*) in *Tomvs Secvndvs Omnivm Opervm Reverendi Domini Martini Lutheri* etc. (Wittenberg: Hans Lufft, 1546), fol. iii verso (http://digitale.bibliothek.uni-halle.de/vd16/content/pageview/4385076; accessed Apr. 13, 2019).

equals twenty-five), not twenty-six. So, unless Melanchthon is off on his math, he must mean that this happened after November 10, 1508, "when Luther was now [*iam*] living out [*ageret*] his twenty-sixth year"—looking forward to the upcoming birthday instead of looking back at the one already passed. Melanchthon does similarly at the end of Luther's life, saying that his soul departed from his body "*cum iam ageret*" his sixty-third year.[13] Again, since Luther was born on November 10, 1483, and died on February 18, 1546, we would think of him being sixty-two (1545 minus 1483 equals sixty-two). Thus, unless Melanchthon is continuing to perpetuate a simple math mistake, he must mean that Luther died "when he was now [*iam*] living out [*ageret*] his sixty-third year" (having completed his sixty-second year on November 10, 1545).

But another writing by the Jesuit Diego Granado (1571–1632, thus a contemporary of Praetorius), commenting on the works of Thomas Aquinas, shows that this expression can be used in another way, a way more in line with Lewis and Short's interpretation and the way we think and speak today. In talking about the incarnation of Jesus, he writes (excerpted): "*& propterea sancti . . . dicunt, unctum fuisse Christum Dominum in Iordane, cum iam ageret trigesimum annum, ac proinde perventum esse ad hebdomadam septuagesimam, in cuius dimidio, id est, post tres annos mortuus est Christus Dominus, cum iam 33. explesset, & 34. inchoasset*" (emphasis mine).[14] That is, "and therefore the saints say that Christ the Lord was anointed in the Jordan after he had turned thirty [*or* when he was already (*iam*) of the thirtieth year of age] and accordingly reached the seventieth seven, in its half [*or* in the middle of it],[15] that is, after three years Christ the Lord died, when he had already [*iam*] completed his thirty-third year and had begun his thirty-fourth." Regardless of whether or not Granado's content is accurate, he is matching Jesus' death to age thirty-three (using a reckoning identical to our own), saying that it happened "after three years" in relation to his baptism in the Jordan, which forces us to translate "*cum iam ageret trigesimum annum*" as "[he was baptized] after he [had] turned thirty." If we translated it in Melanchthon's sense, "when he was

---

13. *Ibid.*, fol. vii verso (http://digitale.bibliothek.uni-halle.de/vd16/content/pageview/4385084).

14. Tractatus 1, Disputatio 5, Sectio 3, par. 21 in *R. P. Iacobi Granado Gaditani e Societate Iesv in Tertiam Partem S. Thomae Aqvinatis Commentarii: In Dvos Tomos Distincti, quartum, scilicet, & quintum* (Granada: Antonio René de Lazcano, 1633; https://books.google.com/books?id=osNefKgopooC&printsec=frontcover), 21.

15. In reference to Daniel 9:24–27.

now living out his thirtieth year," that would make him twenty-nine at his baptism, which would not fit with his dying "after three years" and having completed his thirty-third year and begun his thirty-fourth.

This second usage is thus more in line with Lewis and Short's definition of the idiom and our own modern usage.

We now return to Hildebrand's epitaph for Praetorius (#2). Recall that Praetorius died on February 15, 1621. If we take *"cum jam ageret quadragesimum nonum aetatis annum"* in Melanchthon's sense, then Praetorius died "when he was now [*iam*] living out [*ageret*] his forty-ninth year," after he had turned forty-eight according to our way of thinking. If, say, Praetorius' birthday was in January, that would put his birth year in 1573, which does not fit with the inscription (#1) or with the fact that Praetorius enrolled in the Torgau Latin School in 1576. But if his birthday fell between March and December, that would put his birth year in 1572, which also does not fit with the inscription (#1); the inscription yielded a birth year of 1571 at the latest. If we are going to assume that the two sources do not contradict each other and can be reconciled, we cannot take *"cum jam ageret quadragesimum nonum aetatis annum"* in Melanchthon's sense.

Before seeing if we can take this phrase in Diego Granado's sense, let us look at one other way the Latin phrase can be understood—an understanding that Johann Caspar Wetzel apparently had when he had part 2 of his *Historische Lebens-Beschreibung Der berühmtesten Lieder-Dichter* published in 1721.[16] As already mentioned, *iam/jam* can also be used and understood in the sense of "just (now)." It would therefore not be impossible to render *"cum jam ageret quadragesimum nonum aetatis annum"* thus: "when he was just turning forty-nine," or "right when he turned forty-nine." The fact that J. C. Wetzel provides February 15 not just as Praetorius' death date (which is well established),[17] but also as his birth date[18] (he appears to be the first person to do so) must trace back to this translational possibility. No other explanation presents itself. Interestingly, however, Wetzel still gives Praetorius' birth year as 1571,[19] in harmony with the inscription (#1), but not in harmony with the epitaph

16. Johann Gottfried Walther appears to have copied Wetzel's information for his *Musicalisches Lexicon* of 1732.

17. *Johann Caspar Wetzels Historische Lebens-Beschreibung Der berühmtesten Lieder-Dichter*, 316; cf. Walther, *Musicalisches Lexicon*, 494.2.

18. Wetzel, *op. cit.*, 315; cf. Walther, *op. cit.*, 491.1.

19. *Ibid.*

(#2) from which he apparently derived the February 15 birthday. For if Praetorius did die on his birthday, "right when he turned forty-nine," that would make his birth year 1572 (1621 minus forty-nine equals 1572), which does not fit with the inscription (#1).

What then if we take the phrase in Diego Granado's sense? That would lead us to conclude that Praetorius died "after he had already turned forty-nine [*or* when he was already (*jam*) of the forty-ninth year of age]." If, say, Praetorius' birthday was in January, that would put his birth year in 1572, which still would not fit with the inscription (#1). But if his birthday fell between March and December and he had already turned forty-nine, that would make his birth year 1571, which would agree perfectly with the inscription.

Therefore, regardless of whether my proposed birthday of September 27 or 28 is correct, we can establish with reasonable certainty that Praetorius' birth year should not be listed as "1571/72," but should in fact be firmly recognized as 1571, between February 16 and December 31.

From where, then, do I get the proposed birthday of September 27 or 28?

First, consider that this date fits into the time slot we just established.

Second, consider that a birthday in the early part of 1571 does not fit well with the already mentioned birth of his sister Magdalena either after August in 1569 or in (early) 1570 and the weaning practices of the time.

Third, consider that Michael Schulteis apparently did not have a strong desire to impart his own name to one of his sons, as he had two previous chances to do so with sons that he named Andreas and Johannes, who both did him proud.[20] This suggests a special reason that coerced him, as it were, to use his own first name when his last son was born. A common practice of the day immediately presents itself as a qualifying reason. Consider that Martin Luther—Michael Schulteis' great theological hero (as well as a hero to many other Lutherans)—received his first name as a result of being baptized on November 11, the Feast of St. Martin of Tours, the day after he was born.[21] The theologian Martin Chemnitz (1522–1586), whose son Paul was acquainted with Praetorius,[22] received his first name exactly the same way, being baptized on November

---

20. WGD, 59.

21. Brecht, *op. cit.*, 1; Melanchthon, *op. cit.*, fol. ii recto–verso.

22. GA 6:vii; 8:vii; 9:x.

11, two days after he was born.[23] The birthdate of the Lutheran musicologist Lucas Lossius (1508/10–1582) is given as October 18, the Feast of St. Luke the Evangelist,[24] though this too was likely the date of his baptism. The theologian Nikolaus Selnecker (1528/30–1592) was either born or, more likely, baptized on December 6, the Feast of St. Nicholas.[25] This is just a sampling of examples.

September 29 is, as early German sources put it, "*S. Michaels tag*"[26]— St. Michael's Day, or more fully, the Feast of St. Michael and All Angels, in reference to the archangel Michael (mentioned in Daniel 10:13,21; 12:1; Jude vs. 9; and Revelation 12:7). This day has always held a special place in the hearts of Lutherans and other Christians who follow the liturgical calendar. It is reasonable that Michael Schulteis' last son was baptized on that day and thus received the name of the biblical archangel. Since even laypeople, non-clergymen, did not delay baptism, and Michael Schulteis was a pastor, the likely date of his last son's birth would then be the day before, September 28, or September 27 at the earliest.

Fourth, consider how that date fits well with the date of the preface Michael Praetorius wrote for *MS Coll.*—October 16, 1606. September 27 or 28, 1606, would have been his thirty-fifth birthday. It makes sense that he would have made his preparations for the special collection of the *Musae Sioniae* around the same time. He may have had his portrait sketched to mark the occasion of his birthday and then finished penning the preface about half a month later, perhaps around the same time the sketch portrait was finished into a woodcut. That would also explain why Installments II, III, IV, and the special collection of the *Musae Sioniae* appeared in rapid succession in 1607. In addition to other potential concerns, Praetorius was probably hoping to get the special edition published before his thirty-sixth birthday in September 1607, so that when his readers first saw his portrait and read the inscription, the given age of thirty-five would still be valid.

23. Preus, *The Second Martin*, 88.

24. Julius Bodensieck, ed., *The Encyclopedia of the Lutheran Church* (Minneapolis: Augsburg, 1965), 2:1343.

25. *Ibid.*, 3:2155; Julius August Wagenmann, "Selnecker, Nikolaus," in *Real-Encyklopädie für protestantische Theologie und Kirche*, 2nd ed., vol. 14 (Leipzig: J. C. Hinrichs'sche Buchhandlung, 1884), 76.

26. E.g. Andreas Poach, ed., *Haußpostill vber die Sontags vnd der fürnemesten Feste Euangelien / durch das gantze Jar / von D. Martino Luthero seligen gepredigt* etc. (Jena: Christian Rödingers Erben, 1559; https://reader.digitale-sammlungen.de/de/fs1/object/display/bsb11059725_00005.html; accessed Apr. 13, 2019), fols. 491ff.

It is interesting to note in this connection that the woodcut portrait for the court music director who preceded Praetorius, Thomas Mancinus (1550–1610), was also done when he was thirty-five, in 1585.[27] Could there have been some tradition behind this? Or was a thirty-fifth birthday portrait perhaps an original token of honor that Duke Heinrich Julius showed to his court music directors?

Fifth, consider the marginal note that probably represents Praetorius' last written, dated words.[28] In that note, he legitimizes a copy of his will and confirms its contents before dating it September 29, 1620. It was certainly not by coincidence that the ailing man chose this day, St. Michael's Day, to make sure that his will was executed and perhaps to pen his final words. If he himself was unsure of the day he was born and only sure of the day he was baptized and named, he likely penned these words to mark his forty-ninth birthday, "the climacteric seventh septenary," as Poet Laureate Hildebrand called it.[29]

Finally, consider how this might also help to account for Praetorius' fixation on the angels and angelic songs. Assuming that at some point his parents told him why he was named Michael, or that he himself made the connection, it would have left an impression on his active mind and would have likely enhanced his interest in the angels. Praetorius mentions singing with the angels in heaven, especially the angelic *Sanctus* and *Gloria in Excelsis*, in any number of his prefaces and other writings;[30] it is also depicted in the woodcuts appearing with several of the title pages of his works.[31] The last four pieces of Praetorius' final published collection of works, *Puericinium*, are designated for "Michaelis," the Feast of St. Michael.[32] The connection between his birthday and the feast day might also have contributed in some small way to his choice of motto—*Mihi Patria Coelum*, "Heaven is my fatherland." Granted, all Lutherans of Praetorius' stripe think about the angels in heaven and look forward to joining their number before God's throne—but again, one can tell the songs of the angels and singing with the angels are one of Praetorius' special themes.

27. See Fig. 11 on p. 25.

28. See p. 114.

29. See p. 169.

30. E.g. GA 1:xi,xii; 5:vi; 16:viii; *SM* 2E1:18f.

31. GA 1:v (same as 5:v, 10:v, and *Theatrum Instrumentorum* title page in *SM* 2, following p. 236); 17:xxii; 19:x.

32. GA 19:ix. The other pieces are designated for Advent, Christmas, New Year, Lent, Easter, Ascension, and Pentecost.

As for the lack of mention of Praetorius' birthday and its connection to his name and his subject matter in the extant writings of Praetorius and his friends, his birthday may just have been that obvious, thus requiring no special mention. Plus, the same kind of fuss over birthdays was not made back then as is done today.

In summary, a birthdate of September 27 or 28, 1571, and baptismal date of September 29, St. Michael's Day, fits the information imparted in the two contemporaneous sources having to do with Michael Praetorius' birthdate, fits chronologically with the other events in his life and his family's life, fits the naming traditions and practices of the time, and might help to explain some of Praetorius' actions and aspects of his character and interests.

– Appendix III –

Funeral Sermon and Tributes[1]

GENESIS 32[:24B–32].

> Then a man wrestled with him [Jacob] until the break of dawn, and when he saw that he was not overpowering him, he touches the joint of his hip, and the joint of his hip became dislocated from wrestling with him. And he said, "Let me go, for the day is dawning."
>
> But he replies, "I will not let you go unless you bless me."
> He said, "What is your name?"
> "Jacob," he replies.
> He said, "You shall no longer be called Jacob, but Israel, for you have contended with God and with men and have prevailed."[2]
> And Jacob asks him and said, "Tell me please, what is your name?"
> But he said, "Why do you ask for my name?" And he blesses him there.
> And Jacob called the place Peniel, "since I have seen God face to face, and my soul has escaped intact."[3] And as he crossed over by Penuel, the sun rose on him, and he is limping on his hip. That is why the children of Israel do not eat any sinew on

---

1. Source: FS. The sermon was delivered by the assistant court preacher Peter Tuckermann on February 23, 1621.

2. Tuckermann will explain the connection between Jacob's new name and his contending with God and with men.

3. Tuckermann will explain the connection between Jacob's words and the name he gave the place.

the joint of the hip up to the present day, because Jacob was touched at the sinew on the joint of his hip.[4]

Beloved in the Lord, we read in Isaiah 57[:1,2][5]: "The righteous man perishes and there is no one who takes it to heart, and holy people are snatched up and no one takes notice of it. For the righteous are snatched away before misfortune, and those who have walked a straight path for themselves attain to peace and rest in their bedchambers." These words indicate that, when a misfortune is at hand, God is accustomed to take away pious and godly people. For since they are children dear and pleasing to him, he does not wish for them to see and experience the misfortune.

We have a great example of this in Chapter 22 of 2 Kings, when God intended to bring a great misfortune on the land on account of the people's sin, but he first had it announced to the pious and godly King Josiah: "I will gather you to your fathers, so that you are gathered to your grave in peace and your eyes do not see all the misfortune that I am going to bring on this place" [22:20].

Now since God the Lord has snatched away several pious and godly court ministers over the recent stretch, and we rightly include among them the Honorable Music Director who has now passed away in God, we should thus rightly be concerned that a misfortune is at hand, even as things are already looking bad in the entire Holy Roman Empire.[6] Therefore we should not make light of this, but take notice of it and take it to heart and be sincerely admonished to repentance. For there is no better remedy to be found against such misfortune, as God himself makes clear in Amos 4[:12]: "Since this is what I will do to you, get ready, Israel, and meet the Lord your God." And in Joel 2, there too a great misfortune was at hand, and he says, "Turn yourselves to me with all your heart, with fasting, with weeping, with wailing. Rend your hearts and not your clothes, and turn yourselves to the Lord your God, for he is gracious, merciful, and filled with kindness, and he quickly relents from punishment. Who knows? He may relent again and leave behind a blessing" [2:12–14].

God also makes a glorious promise in Jeremiah 18[:7,8]: "Suddenly I speak against a people and kingdom, that I am going to eradicate, demolish, and destroy them, but if they turn themselves from their evil when I

4. The verb tenses reflect those in Luther's translation.

5. 56 was erroneously printed.

6. The Thirty Years' War would in fact reach Wolfenbüttel's doorstep just five years later, in 1626.

speak against them, then I shall repent of the misfortune that I intended to do to them." So too the example of the Ninevites is well known, who turned away their great and imminent misfortune and ruin through repentance and praying to God [Jonah 3]. God grant us grace through his Holy Spirit, that we may do the same and escape the misfortune that is at hand and stand with joy before the Son of Man on that day.

But for the funeral sermon for the Honorable Music Director who has passed away in God, I had certain reasons for wanting to use the beautiful narrative that I just read, where a man wrestled with Jacob. For one thing, since we heard this past Sunday about *the devil's* temptations,[7] I thought we could now hear something about *God's* afflictions. Next, I selected it because this history also fits nicely with this coming Sunday's Gospel about the Canaanite woman,[8] since Christ, who put the Canaanite woman to the test, also put Jacob to the test here, and just as the Canaanite woman emerged successful, so did Jacob. And finally, I selected it because the Honorable Music Director, of blessed memory,[9] also often suffered distress from such great *tentationibus* [afflictions] and trials, and each one of us who intends to be saved must expect the same for himself, so that we know the right way to reconcile ourselves to such afflictions.

We now wish to speak in God's name, first, about the man who wrestled with Jacob and what Jacob had to suffer and endure; second, how Jacob conducted and acquitted himself; and third, how it turned out in the end and what benefit Jacob took away from it. To this end may God bestow on us the grace of his Holy Spirit for the sake of Jesus Christ. Amen.

1.

Concerning the first point, it is indicated in the beginning that the time when this event took place was not during the day, but at night. That made this contest that much more dangerous and difficult for Jacob, for

7. The Gospel appointed for the preceding Sunday, Invocavit (today also known as the First Sunday in Lent), was Matthew 4:1–11, the account of the devil tempting Jesus in the wilderness.

8. The Gospel appointed for the approaching Sunday, Reminiscere (today also known as the Second Sunday in Lent), was Matthew 15:21–28, the account of Jesus healing the demon-possessed daughter of a Canaanite woman from the region of Tyre and Sidon.

9. German: *der Herr Capellmeister S.* I have taken "S." to be an abbreviation for *Selig(er)*, which means "deceased, late, of blessed memory."

when someone is attacked by someone else during the day, he can see him that much better and can also counter him that much better. But at night he'll have his hands full. No doubt Jacob was sure it was a ghost or a murderer who wanted to bring him down life and limb, for it is said, as the poet writes, *surgunt de nocte latrones*, that is, such brigands usually creep about and can be found at night.[10]

Next it is indicated that "a man" came to Jacob at night, but the man later betrays himself and says, "You have contended with God and with men." It was therefore not God the Father, for he is certainly God, but not human. It was not the Holy Spirit either, for he is also true God, but not human. Much less was it a good or evil angel, for they are neither God nor human. No, it could only and exclusively be the Son of God, our Lord and Savior Jesus Christ, who is God and human in one undivided person, θεάνθρωπος [the-AHN-throw-pus—God-man], "Champion man and God's own Son"[11]—God, begotten of the Father in eternity, and human, born from the virgin Mary in time, as we confess in the Second Article of our Christian creed.[12] Here, however, he is called a man because he appeared to Jacob in the form of a man. He would also actually become a man and genuinely assume man's or human nature, and Eve, the mother of us all, had also called him a man in Genesis 4[:1]: "I have the man, the Lord."[13]

It is furthermore made clear what this God-and-human man did— he wrestled with Jacob. As wrestlers and fighters positively attack one another, grab each other's arms, and crash about all over the place, so this man, the Son of God, grabbed Jacob's arms, attacked him violently, and presented himself as his enemy. In Jacob's language *wrestle* is derived from the word *dust*, as Luther also testifies in the margin of his translation, like

10. Horace, *Epistles*, Book I, Epistle II, line 32; cf. H. R. Fairclough, tr., *Horace: Satires, Epistles, and Ars Poetica* (Cambridge: Harvard University Press, 1929), 264,265.

11. Third line from the original st. 4 of Martin Luther's hymn usually known in English as "Savior of the Nations, Come" (a translation of Ambrose's hymn "Veni Redemptor gentium"), though Luther's original st. 4 is usually omitted. The entire stanza reads:
From king's chambers he does stride
Toward a home less dignified—
Champion man and God's own Son—
Eagerly his course to run.

12. Namely, the Apostles' Creed

13. This was Luther's legitimate translation of the original Hebrew; he interpreted it as Eve erroneously thinking her firstborn son was the offspring God has promised who would crush the serpent's head (Gen 3:15). It can also be translated, "I have acquired a man *with the help of* the Lord."

when two men wrestle each other so that the dust rises and forms a thick cloud around them. So it basically reads, "A man stirs up the dust with him." It was a fierce battle.

Finally, it is reported what Jacob suffered and endured in this fight— he suffered distress in body and soul. We can tell that he suffered in his soul from the fact that he says after the fight was finished, "My soul has escaped intact." In Latin, *salva facta est anima mea*: "My soul has been delivered, rescued, or saved." Therefore during the fight he felt like it was going to cost him his soul, like he was going to sustain damage to his soul and be condemned and lost. But his body also went through a rough time. Not only was he undoubtedly attacked harshly by the man, so that Jacob was aching and was practically looking death in the face, but the man also seized the joint of his hip, which became dislocated on him as a result, so that he limped on his hip and, as a number of people suppose, had to drag himself around with the injury for the rest of his life. This man, the Son of God, made use of a strategic maneuver, just as wrestlers and swordsmen are usually accustomed to keep one trick in reserve for themselves that they can use as a last resort. And the man makes just one move and Jacob's hip is done for, to bring home to him that if it were a question of outward strength and if he were in earnest, Jacob would not be able to last. The fact that Jacob was winning he could not ascribe to the powers of his body, but to the power of the Spirit and to faith. And that is the understanding and significance of the first point.

In connection with this, we now have a necessary and beneficial doctrine to consider, namely that of God's afflictions and trials which he inflicts most severely on his dearest children. This strikes us as strange and it is hard for us to conceive that God would test his own. But in addition to the example before us, God's word affirms it in many places. Genesis 22[:1] states explicitly, "After these events God tested Abraham." And we read in Deuteronomy 8[:2] that God tested the children of Israel in the desert for forty years, and the Canaanite woman was also thoroughly tested by the Lord Christ [Matt 15:22–26]. And Sirach says in Chapter 2, "My child, if you wish to be God's servant, prepare yourself for affliction" [2:1].[14]

---

14. Ecclesiasticus, or the Wisdom of Jesus Son of Sirach, is one of the books in the Old Testament Apocrypha. Concerning the Apocrypha, Luther said in his Bible translation that those books "are not held equal to the Scriptures, but are useful and good to read." In his preface to Sirach, Luther wrote, "This is a useful book for the ordinary man." Because of his endorsement, many Lutheran preachers continued to

And in such trials and tribulations, God attacks the godly in body and soul, as happens to Jacob here—his soul suffers great distress and it seems to him that his soul will perish and be condemned. The same thing happened with Abraham in his trial from God, for since God gave him the promise of the Savior for his soul's salvation through Isaac, and now Isaac was to be slaughtered in his youth, one can easily imagine the condition of Abraham's soul during that affliction. In the same way Hannah confesses in 1 Samuel 2[:6] that God kills and brings to hell; during her affliction she felt as though God had killed her and brought her to hell. David says in Psalm 31[:22], "I said in my alarm, 'I have been cast away from your sight!'" He is suffering great affliction, feeling like he belongs to the *reprobos* [rejected] who are condemned. It is written in Psalm 77[:2], "My soul refuses to be comforted," and in Psalm 88[:15][15], "I suffer your terrors so much that I nearly despair." From Hezekiah we read in Isaiah 38[:10,17], "I said, 'Now must I go through the gates of hell.' . . . Behold, for comfort I was very anxious; you have lovingly concerned yourself with my soul so that it would not perish, for you cast all my sins behind your back." In this way he indicates that his soul suffered distress during this trial. Jonah says in Chapter 2 from the belly of the whale[16], "I cried out from the belly of hell. . . I thought I had been cast away from your sight. . . My soul was despairing with me" [2:2,4,7]. In the Passion history, we hear about Christ that in his great affliction he sweated bloody sweat, his soul was troubled to the point of death, and he cried out on the stem of the cross, "My God, my God, why have you forsaken me?" [Matt 26:38; 27:46; Luke 22:44]. This is how it goes with the soul in God's afflictions.

But it usually doesn't stop with just the soul. No, just as here the Son of God touched the joint of Jacob's hip so that he limped for a time, as some suppose, while others suppose he limped for the rest of his life, so also God is accustomed to prepare for his own not just afflictions of the soul but also a heavy physical cross, as has been demonstrated in all saints and children of God. We read about Moses in Numbers 12[:3] that he was

---

cite the Apocrypha in their sermons.

15. 87 was erroneously printed.

16. While the German *Walfisch* sometimes specifically denotes the bowhead whale, which has the largest mouth of any animal, it is generally recognized that its usage in the Bible was broader and could include other large sea creatures. Luther used it both for the Hebrew תַּנִּין (*tannin*), a term which covers not only whales but all the other large sea creatures or "sea monsters," and for the דָּג גְּדוֹל (*dag gadol*), "large fish," of Jonah 1:17.

a very plagued person, more so than all people on earth.[17] God had closed up Hannah's womb and her rival vexed her and kept provoking her, as we read in 1 Samuel 1[:6]. David had to be as elusive as a partridge and could not remain in the land on account of Saul his enemy [1 Sam 20:18ff]. Job lost his children, possessions, and health. "If someone could weigh my misery," he says in Chapter 6, "and put all my suffering together in a scale, it would be heavier than the sand along the sea" [Job 6:2,3]. Asaph complains in Psalm 73[:14] that he is plagued daily and his punishment is there every morning. How things went for the prophets and apostles is also known; they were like a curse of the world and a scum-offering of all people, according to 1 Corinthians 4[:13]. Paul drew up a whole list of his sufferings in 2 Corinthians 11 and 12.

And in summary, "a righteous person must suffer much," as Psalm 34[:19] says. "We must enter the kingdom of God through much tribulation," as Acts 14[:22] says. "All who want to live a godly life in Christ Jesus must suffer persecution," as 2 Timothy 3[:12] says. They have all taken part in discipline, as Hebrews 12[:8] says. Thus Christians truly belong to a very tough order,[18] where they must endure great afflictions and suffer much in body and soul. They must always struggle, as Job 7[:1] says, and among them one will find conflict on the outside and fear on the inside, as 2 Corinthians 7[:5] says.

But God does not have mean intentions with such trials and crosses. No, he has and retains a true father's heart with them, and like a father he plays with his children. An earthly father will occasionally pretend to be hostile towards the child he loves and will act as though he wants to kill him or wants to shun him and no longer acknowledge him as his child. He does this in order to test him and see how he will react. Then, when the child starts to get dismayed or to cry and yell, he acts that much more kind. *Sit licet in gnatos facies austera parentum, aequa tamen semper mens est et ubique voluntas.* [Even if parents' faces may be austere toward their children, even so their hearts and minds remain ever friendly.][19]

17. The Hebrew עָנָו (*'anav*) is usually translated *humble* in that verse, but it is translated *afflicted* in other verses (e.g. Psalm 10:17; 34:2).

18. Tuckermann is likening Christians as a class to an order of monks or nuns.

19. Baptista Mantuanus (1447–1516), *Adulescentia* (Youth), Eclogue I, lines 131–132. Tuckermann seems to have slightly misquoted the second line, which appears thus in Mustard's edition: *aequa tamen semper mens est et amica voluntas* (Wilfred P. Mustard, ed., *The Eclogues of Baptista Mantuanus* [Baltimore: The Johns Hopkins Press, 1911], 66; cf. also p. 7). Mantuanus' *Adulescentia* was a collection of ten Latin eclogues in dactylic hexameter and was commonly used by schoolmasters because of

So too God the heavenly Father occasionally acts rough and harsh and like an enemy. "You have turned cruel on me," Job says in Chapter 30, "and are showing your animosity towards me with the strength of your hand" [30:21]. But that isn't who he really is; God "does not plague and grieve humans eagerly," as Lamentations 3[:33] says. He puts them to the test so that they are proved genuine in faith, hope, prayer, and patience. Chapter 2 of Sirach says, "As gold is proved genuine in the fire, so those with whom God is pleased are proved genuine in the fire of tribulation" [2:5].[20] First Peter 1[:6,7] says, "You are now, for a short time, sorrowful in various afflictions, in order that your faith may be found authentic and much more precious than perishable gold (which is proved genuine in the fire)—for praise, glory, and honor when Jesus Christ is revealed." In such afflictions one also pays all the more careful attention to God's word, of which others take little notice. Isaiah 28[:19] says, "Affliction teaches attention to the Word."

But undoubtedly God especially lets pious souls suffer distress in afflictions so that they have some sense of the wrath of God and of the anguish of hell, so that they give Christ all the more heartfelt thanks into eternity for redeeming them from it. For the godless, however, it serves as a warning and shock to get them to take to heart and consider: "If this is what happens when the wood is green, what will be the case when it is dry?" as Luke 23[:31] says. And "if the judgment of the Lord has such a severe beginning for the house of the Lord, what kind of end will it have for those who do not believe the gospel? And if the righteous person is barely preserved, where will the godless and the sinner end up?" as 1 Peter 4[:17,18] says. Yes, the pious are often treated so harshly by God to keep them from exalting themselves and to preserve them in humility. Second Corinthians 12[:7] says, "To keep me from exalting myself over this sublime revelation, there was given me a thorn in the flesh, an angel of Satan, to pummel me, in order that I might not exalt myself." Indeed, sometimes they are even crippled in their hip or other bodily members so that their old Adam is debilitated, put to death, crucified, and subdued. First Peter 4[:1,2] says, "Whoever suffers in the flesh ceases from sinning, in order that from then on he may spend all of his remaining time in the flesh living not for human desires but for the will of God." Through such sufferings a person likewise becomes similar to the image of Christ. "For

its relatively easy Latin and appealing subject matter. Mantuanus' works were popular among Lutherans in general because of his willingness to criticize the papacy.

20. See n. 14.

those whom God has predestined he has also foreordained to be like the image of his Son," as Romans 8[:29] says.

The benefit, then, for pious and godly hearts in this point is that it keeps them from imagining that God is always going to smile roses at them, as the saying goes. No, just as Jacob has to go through a tough situation and has to be gravely afflicted and tested, that's the way God has always dealt with the most pious people, and how he continues to deal with them. What befalls the pious is not something strange, as 1 Peter 4[:12] says; all their brothers throughout the world have experienced the exact same sufferings, as 1 Peter 5[:9] says. And they should not consider such a struggle to be a token of wrath but of grace. Tobit 12 says, "Since you were dear to God, it could not be otherwise; you had to have affliction so that you would be proved genuine."[21] Hebrews 12[:5–8] says, "'My son, do not think little of the Lord's discipline, and do not lose courage when you are punished by him, for it is the one the Lord loves that he disciplines, and he lashes every son whom he accepts' [Prov 3:11,12]. If you endure discipline, God is presenting himself to you as his children. For where is a son whom his father does not discipline? But if you go without discipline, in which they all have taken part, then you are illegitimate and not true children." Therefore no one should wish or desire to remain unafflicted and without struggle forever.

2.

Now follows the second point about Jacob—how he acquitted and conducted himself in this wrestling match. At first the text implies that, when the man, the Son of God, attacked Jacob, his hands and feet did not go limp right away, but we read that he held out and also wrestled and fought for his own part, and he put the extreme limits of his powers and ability into it. But he not only wrestled using his hands and physical powers, but also—yes, most of all—using his faith. For he had a twofold affliction during the fight—in part over his body and possessions, since he thought he was going to die and leave everything behind, and in part over his soul, since he thought he would be condemned and lost. To combat this, he called to mind the promises God had made him in Genesis 28[:13–15]

21. Luther's translation here does not really correspond to any modern English translation; it roughly corresponds to verse 14. Tobit is another book in the Old Testament Apocrypha (see n. 14).

and 31[:3]. God promised him that through his seed all clans and thus also he himself would be blessed and that he would be saved through the promised Savior of the world. God had then commanded him to return to his fatherland and promised that he would be with him and would protect him. To these promises of God affecting body and soul Jacob clung with true faith, and he concluded from them that, since God had promised him this, there could not and would not be any risk of it failing, even if more men were to set upon him and attack him. And if he had not had faith in these promises, he would doubtless have been so startled and stunned by this unexpected attack that he would not have known what to turn to or where to start. But his faith won the day and kept him safe, so that the man, the Son of God, could not overpower him without treating him in a way contrary to his own promise and pledge, which was impossible.

Next it is reported about Jacob here that, when the morning dawned, the man who was the Son of God desired that Jacob let him go, but Jacob was not ready for that. Instead he kept his hold and said, "I will not let you go unless you bless me." Here people are rightly astonished: Why wouldn't Jacob just let the man go, when you would think that he should have rather been thanking God that he had gotten rid of him? And they especially wonder: Why does he seek a blessing from the man who makes himself out to be his worst enemy?

Some are of the opinion that during a break in the action the man, the Son of God, presented himself differently and more amicably to Jacob than he had earlier, and made it clear in his manners or words that he was not his enemy and meant no harm. This then prompted Jacob to ask him for the blessing.

Luther writes about these words that Jacob sought a retraction or recantation from the man, since he had told Jacob that he was cursed, and Jacob's soul was frightened and most violently disturbed by that. Jacob therefore wanted the man to take back his words and acknowledge that he was blessed, or else he would not let him go.[22]

Others explain it this way: Jacob was demanding an assurance and token of peace from the man when he said he should bless him. For although, strictly speaking, only God has the right to bless, it is also true that one person can bless another not just with words and well-wishes, as Jacob blessed Pharaoh in Genesis 47[:7], but also with tokens of honor, presents, and gifts, like in the next chapter, Chapter 33, where Jacob calls

---

22. See *LW* 6:139.

his present and gifts a blessing and says to Esau, "Accept the blessing from me that I have brought you" [33:11]. This is the kind of blessing Jacob also desired from this man, namely that in return for attacking him and displacing his hip, he should show him some kindness in word or deed. He has frightened and disturbed him; he should now also cheer and comfort him. He has set upon him as an enemy and has acted like he wanted to take his life; he should now assure him that he didn't mean anything by it and that Jacob doesn't have to fear any harm from him.

This request and prayer and the fact that Jacob holds on so steadfastly pleases the man, the Son of God, so much that he does what he desires and blesses him. And this was no doubt his purpose in pretending like he couldn't get away from Jacob—he wanted to draw out this kind of prayer and steadfastness and leave behind a blessing.

Finally, we can also gather from this that Jacob possessed great patience. For even though his hip was dislocated, he still did not grumble against God, but suffered and bore it with patience, and he doubtless took pride in the fact that he received such a scar from the fight.

With this second point we now have a sincere exhortation to consider, that in afflictions and trials affecting body and soul, temporal and eternal welfare, we should follow Jacob, walk in his footsteps, and study at his feet, for he can be regarded as a master according to the testimonial he is given here. He has wrestled and fought; so we too should wrestle and fight. That is what Christ himself encourages us to do in Luke 13[:24]: "Fight to get in through the narrow gates." Ἀγωνίζεσθε [ah-go-NI-dzes-the]—that is a vocable used not just to describe what fighters do, but also to describe someone in the throes of death, like when it is used of Christ's wrestling with death in Luke 22[:44][23]: "And he began to wrestle with death." That's how serious it should be for us. The holy apostle Paul also commanded it in 1 Timothy 1[:18,19]: "Pursue a noble knighthood, keep the faith and a good conscience."[24] And in 2 Timothy 2[:3–5] he says, "Endure suffering as a good soldier of Jesus Christ. No soldier gets wrapped up in affairs of subsistence, in order that he may please the man who enlisted him. And even when someone fights, he is not crowned unless he fights fairly." And in 2 Timothy 4[:7] Paul writes about himself, "I have fought a good fight; I have finished the course; I have kept faith.[25]"

23. 23 was erroneously printed.

24. Tuckermann paraphrases the passage here. His first imperative is singular, the second is plural.

25. Just like the Greek πίστιν τηρεῖν and the Latin *fidem servare*, the German

But the man who wrestled with Jacob—the Son of God, our Lord Jesus Christ—does not wrestle with us visibly like this today. Instead it takes place through great and difficult *tentationes*—trials and afflictions of the body through cross and misfortune, and of the soul through dismay, fear, and dread. We therefore also cannot depend on our arms and physical strength during the struggle, and we are also much too weak for it like Jacob. We should rather primarily use faith in this wrestling and struggling, just as Jacob's faith did more than his arms, for nothing is impossible for the one who believes, as Mark 9[:23] says. And our faith is the victory, as 1 John 5[:4] says. Therefore God is also mainly concerned that our faith is exercised. God's eyes "look for faith," as Jeremiah 5[:3] says, and "whatever does not proceed from faith is sin," as Romans 14[:23] says, and "without faith it is impossible to please God," as Hebrews 11[:6] says. Faith means making God's word and promise your own and relying on it cheerfully. Such faith can overcome great and difficult afflictions, as the examples from Scripture demonstrate.

Abraham made God's word and promise his own, namely that Sarah would give birth to a son from whose line the Savior of the world would come. He clung to that word and promise, and he trusted and believed it even when it seemed to be no good, and in so doing he overcame his great affliction, as it is written in Romans 4[:18–22]: "He believed on hope when there was nothing to hope for, in order that he might be a father of many heathens, just as was said to him, 'So shall your offspring be' [Gen 15:5]. And he did not grow weak in faith, nor did he look at his own body, which was already withered since he was almost a hundred years old, or at the withered body of Sarah. For he did not doubt the promise of God in unbelief, but grew strong in faith and gave God the glory and knew for an absolute certainty that what God had promised, he was also able to do. Therefore it was also credited to him as righteousness [Gen 15:6]."

And when he was again tested by God later and was supposed to slay and offer up this son of his, he likewise overcame that great and difficult affliction through his faith. With that faith he clung to God's word and promise, which we can read about in Hebrews 11[:17–19]: "By faith Abraham, when he was tested, offered Isaac as a sacrifice and gave away his only-begotten son, even when he had received the promise of whom it was said, 'In Isaac will your seed be named for you' [Gen 21:12]. He

---

Glauben halten (without the definite article) does not mean "to persevere in (the) faith, to keep on believing in God," but "to keep a solemn pledge of loyalty or faithfulness that one has made."

thought, 'God is certainly also able to raise from the dead,' which is also why he got him back as a foreshadowing."

In the same way David relied on God's word and promise and overcame his afflictions through faith. "Lord," he says in the twenty-seventh psalm, "my heart holds your word in front of you," and so on [27:8],[26] since I have your word and promise on which I rely. And he says in Psalm 116[:10], "I believe, therefore I speak." Thus when he was about to fight Goliath—and that fight did not take place without great affliction—he clung with his faith to the word of God he had, namely that he was going to be king, and to the promise connected to circumcision, as is recorded in 1 Samuel 17.

Similarly, Jehoshaphat was facing a powerful enemy and was just about to pay the piper. But when he received God's word and promise, he put his confidence in it and also exhorted the people to faith and said, "Believe in the Lord your God and you will be safe, and believe his prophets and you will have success" [2 Chr 20:20]. And that is what happened, as can be read in 2 Chronicles 20.

In John 4[:46–53], the royal official believed the word that Jesus said to him and went away, and immediately his child recovered.

The Canaanite woman also clung with faith to Christ's word and obtained what she desired. Christ gave her this magnificent testimonial for her faith: "O woman, your faith is great" [Matt 15:28].

For the sake of our salvation, therefore, we should rely on God's word and promise in struggle and strife, especially in great and difficult afflictions, and we should let nothing seduce or drive us away from it. "His word," we sing, "let still more certain be, And though your heart should disagree, Dismiss your fears deceiving."[27]

---

26. Tuckermann follows Luther's rather free translation here. In the clause that follows, he continues to play the part of David.

27. Lines 5–7 from the original st. 12 of Paul Speratus' esteemed hymn "Es ist das Heil uns kommen her," though Tuckermann appears to have changed one word ("flesh" to "heart"; see below). Several of the original fourteen stanzas are usually omitted from the English version, "Salvation unto Us Has Come." The entire st. 12 reads:

Though God should most unwilling seem,
Fear not nor be deluded;
It is to those he does esteem
His ways remain secluded.
His word let still more certain be,
And though your flesh should disagree,
Dismiss your fears deceiving.

Luther writes just beautifully on this text: "I will hold on to God's word and be content and satisfied with it. There shall I die; there shall I live. I have promise and protection enough in God's promise—not only against devil, world, and flesh, but also against this great affliction.[28] For if God sent an angel who said, 'You should not, or are not permitted to, believe these promises,' I would reject him and say, 'Get away from me, Satan,' etc. [Matt 4:10]. Or if God himself appeared in his majesty and glory and said, 'You are unworthy of my grace. I am going to change my mind and not keep my promise to you,' then I should not and must not waver but rather fight my fiercest against God. As Job says, 'Even if the the Lord should kill me, I will hope in him nonetheless' [13:15]. If he should throw me into the deepest hell and set me amidst the demons, I would still believe that I was going to be saved, for I am baptized, I have been absolved of sins in confession, I have received the pledge of my salvation and blessedness, the body and blood of the Lord in the Supper. I therefore do not want to see or hear anything else, but will live and die in this faith, whether God or an angel or the devil speaks to the contrary."[29]

Luther also cites the example of Mechtild the nun, who "was intensely vexed and afflicted by the devil for not having an awareness or perception of her faith. This was a temptation to dismay and uncertainty, which is an intense pain and torment of the conscience. . . [Then] the nun would oppose [him] with nothing else but this phrase: 'I am a Christian.' That is, I am baptized in the blood and merit of the Son of God; I am fed and watered with the body and blood of Christ. To these I will cling; with this comfort I will be content—even if God himself should say something different."[30]

28. In the original context, Luther is talking about apparitions and this would be better translated, "in this great temptation"—namely the temptation to believe what an apparition has said in preference to God's word. Tuckermann adapts Luther's words to apply to trials in general.

29. See *LW* 6:131. Tuckermann appears to have translated the Latin himself, since his citation does not correspond to vol. 11 of the German volumes of the Wittenberg edition of Luther's works (*Der Eilffte Teil Der Bücher des Ehrwirdigen Herrn D. Martini Lutheri / Nemlich / die herrliche Auslegung vber das Erste Buch Mosi / welches ein Quell vnd vrsprung ist / aller Prophetischen vnd Apostolischen Schrifften / Vom anfang des XXV. Capitels / bis zum ende* [Wittenberg: Thomas Klug, 1558]), translated and edited by Johannes Gudenus the Elder. (Gudenus was responsible for Luther's lectures on Genesis 25–50; Basilius Faber translated and edited vol. 10, containing Luther's lectures on Genesis 1–24.) The Gudenus edition served as the basis for the corresponding volumes of subsequent German editions of Luther's works (Altenburg edition, vol. 9 [1663]; Leipzig edition, vol. 2 [1729]; etc.).

30. See *LW* 6:132. Both the WA and *LW* assert that Luther is referring to Mechtild

Where such a faith exists, no distress prevails and God must give himself up in defeat, since he is not and cannot be against his own word and promise to which faith looks, to which it clings, and on which it relies. Therefore, in the struggle against all afflictions and temptations, faith ought to and needs to be there.

Next, just as Jacob's faith gives birth to prayer and he will not let go of the man, the Son of God, unless he blesses him, and thus he asks him and holds on to him for that blessing, so in great and difficult afflictions of body and soul we should, in addition to faith, also draw on precious prayer and diligently call on God. When it seems to us that he is cursing us, then we should pray that he would bless us instead; when he is making us sad, that he would comfort us instead; when he has struck and wounded us, that he would make us well again; when he has killed us, that he would bring us back to life; when he has brought us into hell, that he would bring us back out; when our faith has grown weak, that he would once again strengthen, increase, and preserve it in us; and so on. And Jacob isn't the only one who prayed like this in his situation; the other saints of God also did the same:

What prayers and sighs Abraham must have made and used during his great and difficult affliction when he was supposed to slay his son!

Hannah prays diligently during her afflictions, when she felt as though God had killed her and brought her to hell. She goes to Shiloh where the ark of the covenant was, pours out her heart before God, and says her prayer with ardent tears, according to 1 Samuel 1[:3–16].

In David's trembling and afflictions, he did not fail to pray. He says in Psalm 31:[22], "I said in my alarm, 'I have been cast away from your sight!' Yet you hear the sound of my pleading when I cry out to you." He says in Psalm 116[:3,4], "Cords of death had surrounded me and agonies of hell had befallen me; I encountered misery and distress. But I called on the name of the Lord, 'O Lord, deliver my soul!'"

Jonah also prayed diligently in the belly of the whale[31] during difficult afflictions. He says in Chapter 2, "When my soul was despairing

---

of Magdeburg (c. 1214–c.1277, though her death date is often given as c. 1282 and sometimes as late as c. 1294), who became a beguine in Magdeburg and finished her life in the Cistercian convent of Helfta by Eisleben. But there is also a Mechtild of Hackeborn (c. 1240–c. 1310), a Benedictine nun who also lived at the Helfta convent. The former authored *The Flowing Light of the Godhead*, while the latter was responsible for the content of the *Liber spiritualis gratiae* (Book of Spiritual Grace).

31. See n. 16.

with me, I remembered the Lord, and my prayer came to you in your holy temple" [2:7].

When Christ was in extreme distress and affliction, he did not forget to pray, but clung to prayer and went off to pray three times. And on the stem of the cross he said, "My God, my God, why have you forsaken me?"

Paul also pleaded with the Lord three times that Satan's angel might leave him, as he says in 2 Corinthians 12[:7,8].

And the more God acts like he wants to leave and forsake us or the more aggressively he assails and batters us, the more earnestly and intensely we should pray, as the example of the Canaanite woman shows, as well as Christ's own example in Luke 22[:44][32]: "And he began to wrestle with death, and he prays more intensely." With this kind of faith and zealous and earnest prayer, a person can equalize God as Jacob does here. Lot does the same in Genesis 19[:20–22] when he asks God to let him flee to a small village and save himself there. God answers him, "See, I have respected you, or granted your request, in this matter too. . . Hurry and save yourself there, for I cannot do anything until you get there." In the same way God let himself be held onto with prayer by Moses, even though he desired to break away. "Now leave me alone," he says in Exodus 32[:10], "so that my wrath may rage on them and consume them." That's how much influence a true prayer has with God. Psalm 145[:18,19] says, "The Lord is near to all who call on him, who call on him in earnestness. He does what the God-fearing desire and hears their crying and helps them." Sirach 35[:21][33] says, "The prayer of the miserable penetrates the clouds and does not cease until the Most High inspects, and does not let up until it reaches him." James 5[:16] says, "The righteous person's prayer has a lot of power when it is earnest."

Finally, just as Jacob endured the battle with patience and, even though the joint of his hip was dislocated, he did not grumble or get impatient over it but gladly bore this scar from Christ in his body and doubtless took pride and pleasure in it, so when we get something from struggling with God and sustain damage to our body or property and possessions, we should be patient and at peace with God. After all, since everything really belongs to God, he may manage it all however he pleases. He can give or take it, build or break it, weaken or strengthen it. We

32. 23 was again erroneously printed (rf. fn. 22).

33. This is the reference in the New Revised Standard Version; in the Septuagint and King James Version it is 35:17. Also see n. 14.

should say as Job does in Chapter 1, "The Lord has given it; the Lord has taken it away. May the name of the Lord be praised" [Job 1:21].

Patience like this is a precious thing to come by. Isaiah 30[:15] says, "If you keep calm"—that is, as Luther puts in the margin, if you endure, stay patient, and wait—"then you would be helped. By being calm and hoping, you will be strong." In Chapter 3 of Lamentations Jeremiah says, "It is a precious thing to be patient and to hope in the help of the Lord. It is a precious thing for a man to bear the yoke in his youth, for a forsaken person to be patient when something overtakes him, and to stick his mouth in the dust and wait for hope" [3:26–29]. Luke 21[:19] says, "Clothe your souls with patience." Romans 12[:12] says, "[Be] patient in tribulation." Second Corinthians 6[:4] encourages us to "prove ourselves as the servants of God—through great patience." Hebrews 10[:36] says, "Patience is necessary for you in order to do the will of God and to receive his promise."

Yes, you should take pride in it when you get a mark or scar from God, for it is an honor for a person to become similar to the image of Christ and to bear his scars on his body [Gal 6:17]. Romans 5[:3–5] says, "We glory in tribulation, for tribulation brings patience, patience brings experience, experience brings hope, and hope does not humiliate." Second Corinthians 7[:4] says, "I am overflowing with joy in all our tribulation." And the list could go on.

Therefore the benefit for us in this point is that it helps us to know the proper way to prepare ourselves in the struggle with God and in great and difficult afflictions affecting body and soul. And this is it: When God fights and wrestles, then we should also fight and wrestle and not give ourselves up in defeat, but cling to his unfailing word and promise with true faith, pray diligently, and patiently put up with God when our hip or other body parts or possessions get put out of joint, and speak to our soul when it wants to get impatient as David did to his in Psalm 42[:11]: "Why do you fret, O my soul, and why are you so restless within me? Wait confidently for God, for I will yet thank him for being my face's help and my God." And we should steadfastly persevere to the end, for "whoever perseveres to the end shall be saved," as Matthew 24[:13] says. And "be faithful until death and I will give you the crown of life," as Revelation 2[:10] says.

3.

For the third and final point, it remains for us to see how the fight ended and what benefit Jacob took away and received from it.

The fight did not last forever, but just until dawn, when it reached an end. And in the fighting the dawn had already broken; yes, the longer the fight lasted, the clearer and brighter it became. Once morning dawned, Jacob gained the victory. The man did not overpower him, but he overpowered the man and received a special name for doing so. Since he had been called Jacob up till then, he is given the name Israel, which means "a prince *or* contender of God," one who wrestles with God and comes away the winner, as the man himself, the Son of God, confesses, "You have contended with God and with men and have prevailed."

Now this victory did not take place without blessing either, for it says the man blessed Jacob. What kind of blessing it was Moses does not record. Luther is of the opinion that it was the blessing his fathers had received: "In your seed all peoples on earth shall be blessed" [Gen 12:3; 22:18; 26:4].[34] From the blessing, Jacob now recognizes who the man is and thinks, "Oh, my heavenly Father and Lord! I thought it was a ghost or an enemy, and now I find out that it was you, the One who blessed my father Isaac and my grandfather Abraham!" And this made him sincerely glad, which then leads him to give a special name to the site where this happened. He calls it Peniel "since," he says, "I have seen God face to face, and my soul has escaped intact." *Peniel* or *Penuel* means "God's face," for since God appeared to him there face to face, he did not want to forget that great privilege, and in order to remember it by its location, he assigned it that name. And when he says, "my soul has escaped intact," he is indicating how he felt before and how he feels now. Before his soul was distressed a thousand times over and it suffered the anguish of hell, but now it was comforted, perfectly at peace, and happy, as if it were in heaven and experiencing the joy of salvation—that's how well it felt.

And as soon as he went past this place Penuel, the sun rose on him, so that it was a special token of joy for him. For it does not read simply, "the sun rose," but it "rose on him." It seems to him that the very sun in the sky is rejoicing over his victory and smiling at him, and that this thing created without the ability to reason is just as joyful as he is and must rise and serve to his advantage.

---

34. See *LW* 6:144.

But it is added that he was limping on his hip. Even though the difficult affliction and the fight had come to an end, the precious cross still remained, and in the opinion of some, as mentioned earlier, he had to drag himself around with it the rest of his life. But it was nothing to him when compared with the great grace and kindness of God.

With this third and final point, a mighty and powerful comfort is held out to us, which we should use in the face of great and difficult afflictions and when body and soul have to suffer in the struggle against God: Just as Jacob's struggle and affliction did not last forever, but only lasted the night up until dawn, so all afflictions and crosses have their limit and come to an end. Psalm 30[:5] says, "Weeping lasts the evening long, but joy comes in the morning." Second Corinthians 4[:17] refers to "our tribulation, which is temporary and light." Christ says in John 16[:16], "A little while from now you will not see me, and after another little while you will see me." First Peter 1[:6] says, "you who are now, for a short time, sorrowful in various afflictions." For God is faithful and does not let us be tempted beyond our ability, but makes it so that the temptation reaches an end in such a way that we can bear it, as Paul writes in 1 Corinthians 10[:13].

And the longer the fight lasted, the more the light of dawn shone forth; the longer it was, the brighter it was. So too the longer the pious and godly undergo crosses and afflictions, the brighter it gets for them. The light of God's word breaks forth more the longer it lasts; it becomes that much better known to them, since "affliction teaches attention to the Word," as Isaiah 28[:19] says. The light of faith also grows greater and stronger the longer it lasts, as happened to Jacob and to the Canaanite woman; the light of comfort and joy rises on them. Psalm 18[:28] says, "You give light to my lamp; the Lord my God makes my darkness bright." Psalm 97[:11] says, "Light must rise again and again on the righteous, and joy on pious hearts." Psalm 112[:4] says, "Light rises on the pious in the darkness, from the Gracious, Merciful, and Righteous One." Second Peter 1[:19] says, "We have a sure prophetic word, and you do well to pay attention to it as to a light that shines in a dark place, until the day dawns and the morning star rises in your hearts."

As Jacob gained the victory and received the name Israel, so all believing and pious people gain the victory, and every Christian has the right to the name and honor of being called Israel, seeing as the entire church and all her members frequently wear that name. Psalm 130[:7] says, "O Israel, hope in the Lord." And other passages could also be cited.

Yes, we also gain the victory over sin, death, the devil, hell, and damnation in and through Christ. First Corinthians 15[:55–57] says, "'O death, where is your sting? O hell, where is your victory?' [Hos 13:14] Now the sting of death is sin, and the power of sin is the law. But thanks be to God, who has given us the victory through our Lord Jesus Christ!"

As Jacob is blessed, so the godly are blessed. Psalm 128[:5] says, "The Lord will bless you from Zion." And the blessing originates with this man, the Lord Christ, who is the seed in whom all peoples on earth shall be blessed. Paul writes about this in Galatians 3[:13,14]: "Christ has redeemed us from the curse of the law when he became a curse for us (for it is written, 'Cursed be everyone who hangs on wood' [Deut 21:23]), in order that the blessing of Abraham might come among the gentiles in Christ and we might thus receive the promised Spirit through faith." And on the Last Day, the blessing will do the best thing yet, when Christ will say to those on his right, according to Matthew 25[:34], "Come in, you who are blessed by my Father," and so on.

As Jacob saw God the Lord, or his face, and received joy from seeing it, so God also lets himself be seen by the pious and gladdens them with his face. Certainly he does hide himself for a while, which brings great sorrow, as one can tell from David, who whines and complains about it so much when God has hidden his face. "How long will you hide your countenance?" he asks in Psalm 13[:1]. "When you hid your countenance, I was terrified," he says in Psalm 30[:7]. Psalm 80[:19] says, "O Lord God of hosts, comfort us; let your countenance shine, so we will be delivered." Psalm 67[:1] says, "May God be gracious to us and bless us; may he let his countenance shine," and so on.

But when God has hidden his face like that for a while, he ultimately comes back out and lets it shine, though not exactly as he is in his essence—that doesn't happen here, but will first be experienced in eternal life. To that point, Exodus 33[:20] says, "No human who sees me will live." John 1[:18] says, "No one has ever seen God." And 1 Timothy 6[:16] says that God "dwells in a light that no one can approach, and no human has seen or can see him." But he does let himself or his face be seen in his Word, and there he lets us see how he has a completely fatherly mind and heart toward us. Psalm 42[:2] says, "When will I come to the place where I may see God's face?" Here it is referring to the temple, where God's word was taught. Second Corinthians 3[:18] says that God's glory "is reflected in us with an uncovered face, and we are being transfigured into the same image from one glory to another, as by the Spirit of the Lord."

First Corinthians 13[:12] says, "We are now looking through a mirror at a dark message."

Psalm 100[:1,2] says, "Shout to the Lord, all the world! Serve the Lord with joy; come before his face with rejoicing." This face of God in the Word and sacraments gives genuine joy; there one can see and taste the kindness of God, as Psalm 34[:8] says. That's why it is written in Psalm 89[:15,16]: "Blessed are the people who know how to shout for joy. O Lord, they will walk in the light of your countenance; they will rejoice over your name daily," and so on.

As Jacob's soul escaped intact and was delivered from hell and placed in heaven, so to speak, so it must ultimately turn out well for the souls of the pious. Psalm 84[:2] says, "My body and soul rejoice in the living God." Psalm 25[:13] says, "His soul will dwell in prosperity," and that is especially true after the body passes away. Wisdom of Solomon 3[:1–3][35] says, "The souls of the righteous are in God's hand and no torment touches them. To those lacking understanding they are regarded as though they died, and their departure is reckoned a misery, and their decease a ruin, but they are at peace." First Samuel 25[:29] says, "The soul of my lord[36] will be bound securely in the bundle of the living by the Lord your God, but the soul of your enemies will be slung with the sling." And when body and soul come together on the Last Day, we will see God face to face and will know him as we are known, as 1 Corinthians 13[:12] says. Then our perishable body will be glorified and will become similar to the glorified body of Christ, as Philippians 3[:21] says. And our present sufferings will not be of equal worth to the glory that will be revealed in us, as Romans 8[:18] says. And our tribulation, which is temporary and light here, will produce an eternal glory that exceeds any possible measure, as 2 Corinthians 4[:17] says. And the list could go on.

Therefore the benefit for us in this point is that it helps us not to despair over our afflictions, but to take heart and not let the difficult beginning frighten us, but instead to wait for the desired end when everything turns out well, when God brings to life those who have been killed and brings those he has brought to hell back out, in the words of 1 Samuel 2[:6], when he binds the wounded and heals the shattered, in the words of Job 5[:18]. These are the things with which the godly Sarah comforts herself in Tobit 3: "This I know for certain: Whoever serves God is comforted

35. Wisdom of Solomon is another book in the Old Testament Apocrypha (see n. 14).

36. Abigail speaks these words to David, the eventual king of Israel.

after affliction and delivered from tribulation, and after being disciplined he finds favor. For you do not take pleasure in our ruin, but after the storm you make the sun shine again, and after our wailing and weeping you cover us with joys."[37] David says in Psalm 30[:11], "You have turned my lament into a dance; you have taken off my sackcloth and girded me with joys." Malachi 4[:2] says, "On you who fear my name the sun of righteousness shall rise with salvation beneath its wings." Hebrews 12[:11] says, "No discipline at the time seems enjoyable to us, but sorrowful, but later it will produce a peaceful crop of righteousness for those who are trained by it." But what should especially cheer us up is the eternal light of eternal life in which we will rejoice with eternal joy and be released from all afflictions and crosses. May God bring us all safely there—Father, Son, and Holy Spirit, the God highly praised forever. Amen.

Graveside Remarks

So we have now accompanied the Honorable Music Director, who has passed away in God, to his final resting place. In several points he can be compared to Jacob, who went through this struggle.

Jacob sprouted from godly parents and ancestors who served God in a special way and were like preachers. In the same way the Honorable Music Director also came from such parents and ancestors, for his father and grandfather were preachers and served God and his church for a long time. Many of his brothers and relatives also administered that office well, and some of them are still administering it well to the present day. He himself also greatly desired to pursue that profession, and he often regretted the fact that he did not devote himself to the public ministry.

Jacob was also very faithful and diligent in his office and vocation. During the day he languished from the heat, and from frost at night, and no sleep came to his eyes, as is noted in Genesis 31[:40]. So too the Honorable Music Director was very diligent in his office and did not let heat or cold or sleep hinder him. Instead he strove to elevate music and to accomplish much within that field, and the work itself proves the craftsman in that regard. He accordingly enjoyed special favor not just at court here, but also with kings, electors, and lords elsewhere, as is known to everyone.

Jacob had to undergo this tough struggle and affliction and put up with the cross in his hip and many other hardships. The Honorable Music

---

37. See n. 21.

Director often had great and difficult afflictions too, and on multiple occasions he lamented and wept that things had caught up with him and
that he well deserved it, since he had misspent his youth and still possessed great failings and deficiencies. And indeed he was a sinful man
and no angel, though his sins caused him remorse from the bottom of his
heart.[38] He was also visited by many crosses and misfortunes, so that he
was a heavily plagued man.

Jacob overcame everything through persistent faith, prayer, and
patience. So the Honorable Music Director also let these spiritual shields
and weapons[39] be entrusted to him, and I must give him this testimonial:
If ever there was a house in this area in which prayers were diligently said,
truly it was his.

It turned out well with Jacob in the end, so too with the Honorable
Music Director. For after God had attacked him with illness and he had
reconciled with God, received the Holy Supper, and entrusted himself to
the Lord Jesus Christ, God graciously called him away and delivered him
from every evil and brought him safely to his heavenly kingdom [cf. 2
Tim 4:18]. There his soul has now truly escaped intact, for blessed are the
dead who die in the Lord from now on, as Revelation 14[:13] says. The
grieving widow, children, and friends who survive him should be happy
not to begrudge him this and should thank God for such a blessed departure. We should all prepare ourselves for such struggle and call upon the
Holy Spirit for help and assistance, knowing that he will always do what
is best, and we should daily pray:

> O Holy Fire, Cheer so sweet!
> Help us, with joy and cheer replete,
> To serve you steadfast, come what may,
> Nor by our trials be driven away.

---

38. These couple lines in particular led Heinrich Beyer to remark: "This music
director must have been on very bad terms with the clergy, to be sent off with an
obituary like this" ("Leichensermone auf Musiker des 17. Jahrhunderts," 178). But this
is nonsense. Anyone who has grown up in a Lutheran church that takes the Lutheran
Confessions seriously can tell you that a pastor does not shy away from talking about
the sinfulness of the deceased at a funeral, precisely so that those in attendance can
rejoice and find their comfort and hope in Christ, the savior of sinners (Luke 5:31–32;
1 Tim 1:15; 1 John 1:8—2:2). A confessional Lutheran funeral does not trumpet the
merits of the deceased, but the merits of Christ.

39. An allusion to the opening of Martin Luther's famous hymn, "A Mighty
Fortress"

O Lord, lend power for the fight,
Repress for us Old Adam's fright,
That we as knights wage battle brave,
Press on to you in heaven through grief and grave.[40]

Amen and amen.

---

40. St. 3 of Martin Luther's great Pentecost hymn, which usually appears under the title, "Come, Holy Ghost, God and Lord."

To the blessed memory of the esteemed Michael Praetorius,
a most excellent musician and most deserving of the church's thanks,
the undersigned's esteemed supporter and in-law, a man both supremely
virtuous and most sorely missed:

Others call countries and cities their home, but the creed of Praetorius?
    "Heaven is my fatherland[41]—*is*, ever *will be*, and *was*."
Is, since now he enjoys all the blessings of dwellers of heaven,
    dead to and done with the world, fellow to angels in white.
Will be forever, since units of time in that place are unheard of;
    seconds nor minutes nor hours mark off the passage of days.
He from whom "fatherland" takes its own name never tires of giving
    apples delightful and sweet, bursting with life, to his son.[42]
On his dear brother humanity's Brother, the star of the morning,
    showers his light without end—righteousness, honors, and more.[43]
Likewise the Paraclete, bringer of comfort, who taught him who labored
    next to his fellows to sing comforting strains here below—
lo, he himself makes the man now in heaven to triumph unceasing,
    shouting with thousandfold choirs, singing in thousandfold modes.
Yet understand that by faith this fatherland *was* such already
    during his sojourning life, transient span now traversed—
life to which, even as Tuckermann preached in his splendid oration,
    biblical Jacob's can be aptly and seemly compared.
Jacob the patriarch truly confesses his life is but sojourn,
    made up of pain-filled days, years all too fleeting and few;[44]
here in the world our stranger and sojourner also has suffered
    stresses aplenty in days fewer in number than his.
Jacob of old, in a nocturnal fight with the God-man contending,
    conquers, though not without cost, walking away with a limp,
limping, yet glad in the Lord he'd defeated—no rather, exultant—
    knowing that seeing His face meant his salvation ensured.
So too Praetorius knew this contestant, his Lord and his Maker,

41. Latin: *Mihi Patria Coelum.*

42. Cf. Song of Songs 2:5; Revelation 2:7; 22:2,14; John 1:12,13; Galatians 3:26. This couplet, referring to God the Father, begins a trinitarian reference that continues in the next three couplets with the Son (one couplet) and the Holy Spirit (two couplets). Note also the corresponding references to Praetorius in each of the couplets.

43. Cf. Hebrews 2:11,12; Malachi 4:2; 2 Peter 1:19; Revelation 22:16.

44. Genesis 47:9

conqu'ring when evils beset, wrestling with Him in his prayers.
'Twas through the Word that he knew him, mirror we oft look in darkly;
   now he beholds him with joy, shadows dispelled, face to face.[45]
And though it's true all humanity limps, since none knows or reaches
   heavenly joys and delights absent of all cause for blame,
these missteps were concealed in our friend by a piety truthful,
   Muses most keen to employ serving the only true God.
Hon'rable gentleman, conqu'ring emotional pleasures terrestr'al,
   seeking for heart and for mouth joys only heaven could give!
Finally, just as the biblical patriarch dreamed of a staircase
   bright with its angel-filled steps, bright with the message of God,
so for our friend was the only true staircase ascending to heaven
   confidence anchored in Christ, kept by the words of the Lord,
while, with a genius more suited to heaven, his constant endeavors
   furnished the steps for his feet wending their heavenward way.
This is the creed that the saint and his labors affirmed and intended—
   proven in all of his work publicly issued in print.
We must content ourselves duly attempting to honor his mem'ry,
   following sad and distraught him who has gone on before.

Written in a flood of emotion
in the territory of Brunswick,
while traveling through Wolfenbüttel,
by Tobias Herold of Halberstadt,
doctor and preacher in his hometown [*Patria*].

45. First Corinthians 13:12

Dedicated to the Pious Shade.[46]
Michael Praetorius of Creuzburg,
Prior of the Ringelheim Abbey,
Master of Choir Music
In the Court of the Most Serene Duke of Brunswick and Lüneburg, located in Wolfenbüttel,
yea, also Director and Overseer
of Royal, Electoral, Ducal Chapel Ensembles elsewhere,
Advocate, Ornament, Pillar
of Sacred Music,
After he had already turned forty-nine years old, that is, the Climacteric[47] seventh septenary,
On February XV in the Year of Christ MDCXXI A.D.,[48]
Closed a Pious Life with a Pious Death.[49]

Hence:
Dolefully, mournfully sounds far and wide the lament of the Muses;
    loudly does Phoebus himself wail the bright light disappeared.
Harmony sobs, torn hair in her hands, trimmed toga in tatters;
    all whom the Muses inspire bury their faces in grief.

Inside your worship house newly constructed, O sector of Heinrich,[50]
    rises a pipe organ grand, now being built as I write.
Intricate art and radiant shine and pipes in abundance
    masses indeed may astound, locals and strangers alike.
At its right hand lies Michael Praetorius deep in his slumber,

---

46. Latin: *PIIS MANIBUS S[ACRUM]*—a perceptibly more elevated expression for "to the blessed memory" (see previous tribute), borrowing from the language of Roman mythology. Since everything that follows through "Pious Death" matches, with few exceptions, Praetorius' epitaph as it appeared on his memorial slab (WBB, 90), it appears that its author, Friedrich Hildebrand, was specifically entrusted with this responsibility. For the few differences between the epitaph here and that on the memorial slab, compare the one here to that on pp. 114–15.

47. See Glossary.

48. The redundancy of having both "in the Year of Christ" and "A.D." is in the original.

49. I reflected the author's somewhat peculiar capitalization in my translation.

50. See Chapter 6, n. 8. Construction on the Church of the Blessed Virgin Mary actually continued until 1624, but services and burials were already being conducted in it.

passing the years undisturbed right up until the Last Day.
Certainly fitting, when leaving the living, that such a great maestro
have this bed for his bones, well-chosen site for their rest!

Composed by Master Friedrich Hildebrand of Blankenburg,
Poet Laureate and Rector of the Wolfenbüttel School,
filled with posthumous emotion.

– Appendix IV–

Translations of Primary Sources
by Praetorius

A. Preface to *MS* Coll. (1606)

To CHURCHMEN AND FRIENDS of the Arts,
Greetings.

At first, kind reader, when I published the first installment of my *Musae Sioniae* (Muses of Zion) at the insistence of good people, I did not have in mind to continue taking up so many German hymns. In undertaking this work, however, I have not only discovered that these hymns are heard with pleasure by many devout, God-fearing persons of both high and low station, but I have also been asked to produce more of the same. I have accordingly deemed it a necessity (since they were not originally positioned in the customary order in which they are used on Sundays and festivals throughout the year, but were indiscriminately mixed together) to preface this work with another general index covering the first four installments, following the order in which these hymns usually appear in the standard psalmbooks and hymnals. In addition, I have systematically recorded in which installment and under which number each hymn can be found. In the final installments that remain, basically the same order has been retained as in this general index, although I have included many other additional psalms and songs in the mix, as will be clearly seen from the separate index accompanying each of the installments.

Allow me also to explain what moved me to arrange the psalms and hymns customarily sung in the church of God for performance by multiple choirs (*per choros*): I had been told, and in part had seen for myself,

how in almost every locale—even in small villages, where I would not
have previously expected to find such choristries and music—people had
started singing the Latin psalms and harmony (as composed with eight or
more parts by distinguished and excellent musicians in Italy, Lower-, and
Upper Germany, as well as in the Gallic nation [i.e. France], England, and
other nations) using multiple choirs (*per choros*), thereby affecting the
listeners (since it was both still somewhat novel at the time and charming
on its own merits) and stimulating their Christian devotion in a remarkable way. This has also been rightly observed by all admirers of God's
word and of Christian songs and psalms in these more recent times, when
this heavenly and genuine art, first developed by King David, has risen
to considerable heights. And these admirers take special notice of it not
just *propter concentus & artificii praestantiam*[1] (since oftentimes more
art and industry may be found in the songs with three, four, or five parts
than in others with eight, ten, or twelve parts), but *propter singularem ex
alterna illa seu vicissitudinaria variatione promanantem, animosque au-
ditorum maxime afficientem vim*,[2] and thus on account of the charming
alternation which is also still novel among us at this time.

I therefore hope that these German psalms and songs, whose texts
and melodies are familiar even to small children, scored in this way, might
perhaps be just as agreeable to a few people as the Latin ones, especially
since the chorale melody, which is usually in the soprano part, can be
easily and intelligibly heard and detected above the other parts, and can
be imitated by each person when singing by himself after his devotion.

Such variation through multiple choirs (*per choros*) is additionally
to be found on organs (which are consequently still a special ornament
and adornment in Christian churches at the present day as they once
were in the temple of David and Solomon), since one may switch between two or three manuals in a way that is lovely and very pleasing not
just to the learned and those experienced in this most liberal art, but to
all Christian listeners in general. I would thus like to hope that not just
singers and choristries, but also organists and instrumentalists who were
perhaps not about to take up this work or any like it, will be served in
some measure by this admittedly modest work achieved by God's grace
in a short time in the midst of various occupations, and that those who

---

1. That is, on account of the excellence of the harmony and artistry.

2. That is, on account of the singular force emanating from the alternating or
interchanging variation and affecting the souls of the listeners in the highest degree.

have greater ability will be given a modest inducement to give these matters further consideration.

So that I may then also be of service to those whose schools do not always have the same number of voices or are not always sufficiently supplied with boys, I have made plans to take the exact same psalms that are composed with eight or more parts divided into multiple choirs (*per choros*) in the first four installments and to score them with two, three, four, five, six, or seven parts in the following fifth, sixth, seventh, and eighth installments, and any others that may follow. That way, a psalm verse that has been composed in fugal style can occasionally be sung by the musical choir alone, and then also, as time allows and it is considered appropriate, one verse after the next can be sounded and sung together in choral and figural along with the entire congregation *plena & unanimi voce, concinnaque & solenni harmonia*,[3] which is the way I think (and the Psalms themselves suggest) it was possibly done in David's time and in the years that followed him.

It is now up to each person's own discretion and judgment how and in what form he may wish to use this work of mine and others like it. For the circumstances and situation of each person's choir and church will dictate and determine whether he wants (as I currently observe in this princely chapel here) to take up the first verse with five, six, or eight parts in fugal style right from the start after the organ has finished playing,[4] and then to sing the second verse in simple choral style with the congregation; the third verse arranged simply with four or five parts straightforwardly without fugues, with the choir and congregation singing together; the fourth in choral style again; the fifth in figural (yet with the congregation always singing along); and so forth, one verse after the next. This is the usual procedure with German and Latin psalms in Bavarian and other Roman Catholic churches. In all of this I do not intend to presume upon anyone or to set any limits or bounds, since it is by no means shared to instruct those who know better.

Since the melodies for many psalms and songs are also sometimes dissimilar and different in different countries and cities, I have likewise not let this escape my notice entirely. Insofar as I might have been aware of them, I subjoined and added the harmony of every location, in the

3. That is, both with full and unified sound, and with striking and solemn harmony.

4. German: *alßbaldt im Anfang nach geschlagener Orgel.*

confidence that, as each location might have opportunity to use them, this will not prove disagreeable to pious Christians.

Morever, everything else that I have mentioned in notes and dictated for heeding in each installment, a musician will have to observe throughout in all the installments and obligingly adjust his practice accordingly.

And so, with that, I pass along my sincere wish that the trusting reader, after this life, will join me and all true Christians in gratefully performing in figural with perfect, unremitting voices and singing for all eternity the heavenly songs of praise *Sanctus, Sanctus, Sanctus Dominus Deus Sabbaoth* and *Gloria in excelsis Deo*, which now ring out with stammering tongues in this fleeting life, and will do so in the heavenly, immortal choirs, together with all the holy angels and archangels, to the glory, honor, and praise of the absolutely Most High Majesty and eternal, indivisible, single-essence Trinity. And I faithfully commend us all, collectively and individually, to the care and protection found in the alreadymentioned heavenly musicians and attendants and won for us by Christ.

Written in Wolfenbüttel on October 16, 1606.
Michael Praetorius C.

B. Dedicatory Epistle for Installment V
of *Musae Sioniae* (1607)

To all Christian churches of the Holy Roman Empire of the German Nation, our common fatherland, the author wishes prosperity, peace, and edification from the Most High, through Christ, in the grace of the Holy Spirit.

As the art of music is a noble and precious gift of the Most High, in which his divine wisdom and kindness shines and glows, it should therefore be employed for his praise, glory, and worship, and for the edification of his congregation, by all to whom he has granted even a single talent[5] of skill in it.

The great, honorable king and prophet David both composed songs and explained to the choir how to pray and give thanks with them, and he also did not shy away from or consider himself above all sorts of musical instruments, as can be seen in 2 Samuel 6. Theophilos, the emperor in the East around 830, likewise exercised himself in the hymns of the church, composed, and directed his choir himself, as Zonaras has left behind in writing in his third tome.[6] So too Robert the Pious, son of Hugh Capet, king in France, a patriarch of all the kings who succeeded him, composed the sequence *Sancti Spiritus adsit nobis gratia* ("The Holy Spirit's grace be near us") and the responsory *Judaea et Jerusalem* and many other songs, built churches, and died in 1030. Leo II, Bishop of Rome; Vitalian I; Gregory the Great; Gianfrancesco Pico, Lord of Mirandola and Count of Concordia, etc.; and many countless others also exercised themselves in music in a praiseworthy manner and labored only to this purpose, that this art might serve to the glory of God in his church.

Having considered all these examples, it pleased me a few years ago to imitate these Christians by employing the little talent I had received in the art of music to the same end through the grace of the Most High, in a manner according with the requirements of my office—even though I cannot be compared in the least to such excellent luminaries with regard to my insignificant person and the gifts bestowed upon me by God. Thus far I have published our usual hymns arranged with a larger number of

5. German: *ein pfündtlein*, lit. "a little pound." The reference is to the Parable of the Minas in Luke 19:11–27, which is similar to the Parable of the Talents in Matthew 25:14–30. In these parables, the minas or talents are units of weight and currency, but Praetorius understands them as representing what we call "talents" today—aptitudes or skills given to us by God.

6. *Johannis Zonarae Monachi Tomus Historiarum tertius* (Basel: Johannes Oporinus, 1557).

parts, e.g. eight, nine, and twelve, divided into multiple choirs, and I have observed that these were pleasing to Christian congregations. Yet I also weighed and considered at the same time how churches and congregations allied with the Christian religion, as much as they would have loved to, could not make headway with that many voices in all locations and at all cities, villages, and market towns. I therefore did not want to grudge the effort of also putting together a collection of hymns, as well our dear God would allow, for two, three, four, five, six, and seven parts for the choirs and churches in such places. I accordingly consecrate and dedicate this well-intentioned work of mine, which I have begun to that end, to all godly, pious hearts at churches, schools, and congregations of the German nation, our beloved fatherland, and to admirers and patrons of the worthy art of music. I do so desiring of them nothing more than that, in receiving this work favorably, they join me in calling upon the Almighty to use this medium to rouse and stir up the Christian hearts of many people to praise and honor God for the kindnesses he has rendered us in Christ, and to receive them from him with true gratitude, until we are privileged to behold him face to face and to honor, praise, and glorify him with angelic and Zionic hymns of praise in full strains of joy and rapture of heart, together with the choirs of all the saints and elect angels, when we are assembled before his throne of grace in the New Jerusalem and heavenly Zion and we all afford this indescribable and most worthy honor, praise, and glory in these choirs for all eternity. Amen.

C. Dedicatory Epistle to Duchess Elisabeth for the Reprint of Andreas Praetorius' BPABEION (1608)[7]

To the Most Serene, High-Born Princess and Lady,
Lady Elisabeth,
Born of the Royal Family in Denmark,
Duchess of Brunswick and Lüneburg, etc.,
My Most Gracious Princess and Lady.

Most Serene, High-Born Princess, let me first duly affirm that Your Princessly Grace has my humble prayers to God, in addition to all the submissive obedience that I owe. Most Gracious Princess and Lady, Your Princessly Grace must still most graciously recollect when, approximately a year ago, she found me, during my attendance at court in keeping with my responsibilities, reading a book (which my brother, Dr. Andreas Praetorius of blessed memory, issued in print twenty-four years ago, and which had recently come into my hands from my in-law [*Schwager*], Master Joachim Buchholtzer [Buchholz], Superintendent of Schöningen, who lives with my aforementioned brother's eldest daughter in Christian marriage). She caught sight of it and also began reading it herself. Your Princessly Grace, as a special admirer of the Divine Word, in reading through that book with such diligence and devotion, derived genuine pleasure from it—as from a precious, costly jewel—on account of the scripturally sound doctrine and the spiritual and powerful comfort contained in it, so that several copies of it were also kindly requested. But soon after discovering that all the copies had long ago been quickly sold off and that no more were available in the bookstores, Your Princessly Grace, as a tremendous promoter and patroness of beneficial Christian writings and books, gave the most gracious order and impetus that this book be reprinted in the ducal printing press here for the blessed edification of many pious Christians, and that it be properly produced as a small handbook.

Your Princessly Grace has now so altogether graciously concerned herself with this little book, as though with a deceased little orphan, and

---

7. Andreas Praetorius, BPABEION (1608), fols.)(ii recto—)(v recto. A βραβεῖον is a prize; Andreas Praetorius defines it as "a most precious jewel." The book includes meditations on "the fatherly heart of God the Father," "the brotherhood of Jesus Christ," and "the fellowship of the Holy Spirit," "along with a brief explanation of [Jesus'] ascension and sitting at the right hand of God, and of several other prominent articles of our Christian faith, also what our take should be on unbaptized children, who come into the world dead, for the comfort of pious parents."

has restored it and brought it into the light once again, which not only I, but also the surviving heirs of my dear, blessedly departed brother, will all know how to acknowledge most submissively, with a grateful heart, as a special princely favor, in addition to our continuous prayers of thanksgiving to God, and we will take the utmost pleasure in it. I therefore had both the obligation and the desire, out of rightful propriety and duty, to consecrate this little book most submissively, with this dedication, to Your Princessly Grace, my most gracious Princess and Lady, and thereby to devote it to her as her own, since it was promoted by her Princessly Grace. And I do so with the most humble and submissive request that Your Princessly Grace would kindly receive and accept this dedication from me as a declaration and announcement of my most submissive gratitude for all kinds of grace and kindnesses shown to my inferior person, and that she would be and remain a most gracious Princess and Lady to me, as well as to my family and personal connections. Now may the dear and faithful God and Father of our Lord Jesus Christ grant that this little book may, by the power of his Holy Spirit, work a blessed effect on all Christendom as a precious medal and most valuable jewel in the comforting assurance of our most intimate brotherhood with Christ.

I hereby commend Your Princessly Grace, together with her highly commendable and much beloved lord and consort, my gracious Prince and Lord, along with their young lordships and ladyships, to the Father of all grace and mercy for long-lasting health, successful governance, and all beneficial prosperity of body and soul in his divine protection, and at the same time commend myself to the favor of the same,[8] collectively and individually, with all due obedience. Written in Wolfenbüttel on the Holy Day of Easter, in the Year of Christ 1608.

Your Princessly Grace's
Most Obedient Servant,
Michael Praetorius,
Music Director

---

8. Namely the princess, her husband, and their children

D. Dedicatory Epistle for Volume I, Part 2 of the *Syntagma Musicum* (1615)[9]

To Magnanimous, Distinguished,
Most Noble, Most Honorable Men,
the Electoral Lord of the Saxon Court and
Ducal Lord of the Court of Brunswick,
and Other Privy Councilors,
Collectively and Individually,
Most Sincere Maecenases[10] of Music,
This Second Part of the Musical Compendium,
Succeeding the First Part,
Is Devoted,
Consecrated,
and Dedicated
with a Faithful Heart,
an Earnest Vow,
and Grateful Affection,
by Michael Praetorius C.

Magnanimous, Distinguished, Most Noble, Most Honorable Men, Maecenases Worthy of Devoted Veneration,

What that οὐρανοδίδακτος [heaven-taught] teacher of the gentiles requires of us in 1 Thessalonians 4:11 is golden and worthy of cedar oil.[11] There he instructs everyone ἡσυχάζειν καὶ πράττειν τὰ ἴδια, that is, to keep quiet and to pursue one's own affairs. He places keeping quiet and pursuing opposite each other; he wants the former to be observed with the affairs of others, the latter with one's own affairs.

---

9. Praetorius' full title for the second part reads: "The Second Part | joined | to the First Volume | of the Musical Compendium, | namely, | on Music outside the Church | Which Can Be Called | Profane, Liberal, Natural, Human, Genial, etc., | Comprising Two Sections, | the First, on Vocal Music and the Knowledge of Music in General, | Which Was Basically Common to both Vocal and Instrumental Music, | the Second, on Instrumental Music or Polyorganody." The descriptors "liberal [*liberalis*]" and "genial [*genialis*]" are both tied to Bacchus or Dionysus, the god of wine who loosens inhibitions and inspires creativity in music and poetry.

10. Gaius Maecenas was a patron of the poets Horace and Virgil. His name therefore came to be used as a synonym for *patron*.

11. That is, of careful preservation and perpetuation. Cedar oil was applied to the backs of books to preserve them from moths and decay.

He almost seems to be alluding to that πολυθρύλητον[12] [well-known saying], ἀνέχου καὶ ἀπέχου: *Bear* indeed what concerns your own affairs; *forbear* what concerns the affairs of others. With the former, he desires endurance and busyness; with the latter, avoidance and quietness.

To pursue one's own affairs belongs to justice, as the band of human society and the whole of the commonwealth learn from Plato, and it consists ἐν τῷ τὰ αὐτοῦ πράττειν, καὶ μὴ πολυπραγμονεῖν, namely in this, that everyone does what belongs to his own office and does not reach for someone else's affairs (Book IV of *The Republic*).[13] Certainly in every commonwealth, just like in any very large home, there are many affairs, and these diverse responsibilities ought not all be commended to one person, nor should anything whatsoever be commended or distributed at random to anyone whatsoever, but these responsibilities should be given and entrusted to some and those responsibilities to others based on disposition, abilities, and dedication. Once the task has been entrusted, everyone, insofar as he is able and fit, ought to discharge it with diligence and to stay within its boundaries, not at all concerned about other affairs, much less getting himself involved in them. And when this is done, in the widely separated waves of disturbance and storms of division, the state sails in safety and reaches the port as prosperously as possible.

To forbear the affairs of others belongs to wisdom. For that is what that king of all who are, who have been, and who are yet to come, that wisest of mortals Solomon, says in his book [Proverbs], which Hegesippus and Irenaeus call παναίρετον σοφίας [comprehensive wisdom], Chapter 12, verse 11:

וּמְרַדֵּף רֵיקִים חֲסַר לֵב
which the Septuagint interprets:
οἱ δὲ διώκοντες μάταια, ἐνδεεῖς φρενῶν
or as Symmachus translates the first part:
ὁ δὲ ἐπισπεύδων εἰς ἀπραγίαν
Aquila and Theodotion: εἰς κενά
Vulgate: *Qui sectatur otium, stultissimus est.*
Luther rendered with the Greek interpreters according to the Hebrew sense:
Wer unnötigen Sachen nachgehet / der ist ein Narr.

12. Praetorius' spelling: πολυθρύλλητον

13. Plato, *Republic* 4.10, or 433a. See Paul Shorey, tr., *Plato: The Republic, in Two Volumes*, vol. 1 (Cambridge, MA: Harvard University Press, 1937), 368,369.

In this proverb, the theologian not ignorant of languages will note that vacuities, רֵיקִים, or vanities (as the Greek version reads) or unnecessary affairs (German) are reprehended.

Under this label are included and reprehended:

1. ἀτεχνία, unskillfulness, when a life lacking in skill and devoid of work is spent in shameful leisure,

2. ματαιοτεχνία [vain skill], which in Quintilian "is a useless imitation of skill" (Book 2, Chapter 20[14]),

3. περιεργία [side-work *or* trivial pursuit], which carelessly and half-heartedly rushes through what ought to be treated seriously, and on the contrary lingers over that which was to be done perfunctorily. Clement of Alexandria, in Book 5, Chapter 14 of the *Stromata*, and Athenaeus in Book 5, Chapter 1 of the *Deipnosophistae*, reproach this perversity using Agathon's distich:

> Τὸ μὲν πάρεργον ἔργον ὡς ποιούμεθα,
> τὸ δ' ἔργον, ὡς πάρεργον ἐκπονούμεθα.
> [We treat side-work as though our job,
> while working at our job as though side-work.]

Nazianzen denounces this "diligence" with these verses:

> Ἔργον πάρεργον οὐδαμῶς ἔργον λέγω,
> τῶν γὰρ πάρεργον δὴ[15] καταφρονητέον.[16]
> Work that is unnecessary I by no means call work,
> for unnecessary things should be disdained.[17]

But under the name of vanity and vacuity, φρενήσεως [delirium] and senselessness, Solomon is also condemning all ἀλλοτριοπραγμοσύνην [meddlesomeness] and πολυπραγμοσύνην [busybody-ness]. Ἀλλοτριοπραγμοσύνη—getting mixed up in the affairs of others, having neglected one's own—is foolhardiness. Πολυπραγμοσύνη [Busybody-ness]

---

14. Section 3; Praetorius erroneously cites Chapter 21. Cf. H. E. Butler, tr., *Quintilian: Institutio Oratoria, Books I-III* (Cambridge, MA: Harvard University Press, 1920), 350,351. Quintilian goes on to cite the example of a man who could continuously shoot chickpeas through a needle from a distance without missing, and whom Alexander rewarded with a peck of beans, "a reward most appropriate for that feat."

15. PG (see next n.) reads: Τὸ γὰρ πάρεργον καὶ etc.

16. Gregory Nazianzen, *Verses*, Book 1 (Theological Verses), Section 2 (Ethical Verses), Poem 32 (Aphoristic Distichs), lines 139–140, in PG 37:926–27.

17. Praetorius' translation.

is the undertaking of many things and the performing of all of them; Gellius very elegantly explains the name for this most foul vice in his *Attic Nights*, Book 11, Chapter 16.[18] We can call this nosiness in affairs καινοπραγίαν from Plutarch's *Pericles*,[19] and with such πολυπραγμοσύνη [busybody-ness] we can identify πλῆθος πραγμάτων καὶ καινότητας καὶ μεταβολάς [a large number of activities and novelties and changes]. How often don't we see rather delicate characters, when their success has proven hopeless, abandoning their customary trade and undertaking occupations with which they are unaccustomed and inexperienced? Overwhelmed by the multitude of such occupations, they jump most unhappily, with light and heedless foot, from one kind of life to the next, constantly changing, as alluded to in the German proverb that Luther added to Solomon's margin: *Vierzehn Handwerck / funfftzehn Unglück* [Fourteen trades, fifteen troubles].

This line is commonly shared, which certainly fits here:

Τῆς πολυπραγμοσύνης οὐδὲν κενεώτερον ἄλλο.
There is nothing more unproductive than nosiness.[20]

And the weighty tetrastich is worth mentioning, with which that well-known man brought the tragic latter part of his life to an end in Prussia:[21]

Quid iuvat innumeros mundi cognoscere casus
Si fugienda facis, si facienda fugis?
Disce meo exemplo mandato munere fungi,
Et fuge ceu pestem τὴν πολυπραγμοσύνην.
[What does it help the masses to learn the world's events,
If you do what ought to be avoided, if you avoid what ought to be done?
Learn from my example to discharge your entrusted task,
And avoid busybody-ness like the plague.]

---

18. See John C. Rolfe, tr., *The Attic Nights of Aulus Gellius in Three Volumes*, vol. 2 (New York: G. P. Putnam's Sons, 1927), 336–341.

19. Cf. Plutarch, *Pericles*, Chapter 17, Section 3, where, however, most editions read κοινοπραγία, "joint enterprise, common welfare," not καινοπραγία. See e.g. Bernadotte Perrin, tr., *Plutarch's Lives in Ten Volumes*, vol. 3 (New York: G. P. Putnam's Sons, 1916), 56,57.

20. Praetorius' translation.

21. The reference is to Johann Funck (1518–1566), a court preacher for the Duke of Prussia who gained some fame for his chronology of world history. He was executed in the Kneiphof Market of Königsberg (today Kaliningrad) after getting involved in political affairs.

Some years ago, beyond my hopes and expectations, I was, out of extraordinary clemency, put in charge of directing the court choir by the Most Reverend and Illustrious Prince and Lord, Lord Heinrich Julius, Bishop of Halberstadt and Duke of Brunswick and Lüneburg, formerly my Most Clement Lord, of praiseworthy and blessed memory.[22] In preparing for this charge to which I was to apply myself, I too, venerable Maecenases, carefully weighed these and other similar things in my own limited way, and I considered how I might give my attention to music, the most prominent feature of the office commended to me, and how I might improve and adorn it with all possible faithfulness and diligence for the benefit of schools and churches. Therefore, beginning with piety, not only did I arrange German songs by the divine Luther and others and the Latin songs of the church's liturgy using choral harmonics, but also, at the wise instigation of very good friends, I did not hesitate to assume the effort and endeavor of extracting and compiling a musical compendium [*Syntagma musicum*] from both ancient and more recent writers. In this compendium, I intended to publish and present on the literary stage the theory and practice of music—ecclesiastical and pagan, sacred and profane, vocal and instrumental.

But if only I had been permitted to sacrifice to my muses auspiciously and my pursuits had never been interrupted! Certainly this present work would have made a much more polished appearance, my other musical works would have appeared in public much more easily, and additional ones filled with even more pieces. But indeed, since I was also dragged into other court responsibilities with a most unwilling disposition (I am telling the truth), I could not manage this work without taking it upon myself to enlist the supporting and subsidiary work of certain relatives and friends. I have namely been kept busy by the difficulties of various journeys, petitioners' complaints needing to be presented, the fluctuating cases of the poor, letters needing to be drawn up, annoyances arising at home, adverse physical health, and other things of the sort. Thus, let me emphasize, I have been compelled by love for justice, sympathy for the afflicted, and Christian charity to drive away threats to many people's lives, to many people's reputations, and finally to many people's prosperity. Who would be surprised if I had even abandoned musical pursuits by now? Nevertheless, since nothing is better or more important to me than the sacrosanct art of music, I have labored as zealously as possible

22. Heinrich Julius had passed away on July 30, 1613.

at improving it to the best of my ability and enhancing it as much as I could. All of this is attested by numerous other works of music that I have already produced according to my limited natural ability, with the assistance of divine grace and the help of the Holy Spirit, and by deeds of public right and use, and the *Musical Compendium* [*Syntagma Musicum*] will also make this clear.

For after I began the first volume of this compendium by having the first part on "Sacred or Ecclesiastical Music" published first—encompassing choral music, the music of the Ordinary, other liturgical music, and instrumental music[23]—I have now brought it to completion with this second part, affirmed from the records of antiquity. This part contains the history of the pagan and secular music of the ancients, in natural and liberal use and enjoyment [*usu & lusu*] outside the boundaries of the church. It is divided into two distinct sections. The first deals with both vocal music and the more general knowledge of music and frequency of its use, which was basically equal for both vocal and instrumental music. The second section deals with the instrumental music and instruments of the ancients.

But no one should think that I ὑπὲρ τὰ ἐσκαμμένα πηδᾶν (am jumping the trench or the fence, as they say) or am sending the sickle into another man's harvest if I also exhibit the music received and practiced outside the church among the pagans (in the worship and sacrificial rites of heathen gods, and in both socially festive and genteel gatherings), bringing it out onto the public stage from the testimonies of antiquity given by philosophers, poets, and scholars. It is from there that most of the light of present-day music will be conveyed—not just that of the church, which justly and piously detests that idolatrous music and out-distances it πολλοῖς παρασάγγαις [by many leagues] with its excellence, but also that of the more liberal civil realm, which rightfully and properly imitates that music, since it is hardly inferior (if at all) to present-day music in pleasant dignity and dignified pleasantness.

As was my duty, so was my desire, Magnanimous, Distinguished, Most Noble, Most Honorable Men, Maecenases most worthy of veneration, to step out into the light with the remarkable token of your names and indeed to humbly dedicate and consecrate this same modest work to your collective, most illustrious authority, being fully convinced that,

---

23. Lit.: "which encompassed psalmody, missody, liturgody, and organody." I used Praetorius' own section headings in Part 1 to render these terms into intelligible English.

under the defense and protection of Your Majesties, I will be protected from the attacks of any opponents and will easily avoid all of their poisonous bites.

Nor will Your Majesties, etc. be dishonorable for having taken up the defense of music. For although it usually only serves the pleasurable emotions and is therefore regarded as worthless by certain σκυθρώποις [sullen] Scythians, for whom the neighing of horses—and why not the hissing of bellowing Arcadian cattle?—are ever so much sweeter than harmonic singing and playing, yet I call you yourselves, Magnanimous, Distinguished, Most Noble, and Most Honorable Men—in this modest προσφωνήσει [address] I call you, I say, to the witness stand, confident that surely not one of you will deny, but that all of you will acknowledge: *Human life is not possible without the pleasurable emotions.* For what would this life be if, having been deprived of any amusement and any pleasure, it were spent in perpetual anxiety and sadness? It is precisely because we are all moved to pleasurable emotions, but few people are acquainted with decent, pure, and appropriate ones, that most people pursue unlawful, foul, and inappropriate ones and pass their entire life most deplorably in shame and vice, and still never experience genuine joy all the while. Xerxes, King of the Persians, is said to have offered a reward to those who could invent any new kind of pleasure.[24] O that wretched man, O unhappy king, who could not find the means to amuse himself in so many riches and such great wealth and abundance of all things, but who throughout his entire kingdom, which was extremely large, throughout all of Asia, abounding to the utmost with every kind of delight, was pursuing fleeting emotional pleasures! That which everything delightful and lovely that could either be looked at or used and enjoyed was unable to provide for Xerxes, the pleasure of music offers to us most abundantly, as does its loveliness. Whether as master or as servant,[25] music never lets either irritation or any tedium overtake us, or I should rather say, it is able to make the most noble joy overflow and rebound for us at all times.

In the sphere of the church, the διάνοια [discourse] on psalmody, the ὑπομνήματα [commentaries] on missody, the ἐξήγημα [explanation] of liturgical music, and the θεωρία [survey] of instruments[26] in the *Musical Compendium* [*Syntagmatis Musici*] demonstrate sufficiently (I have

24. See Cicero, *Tusculan Disputations* 5.7.20. It is also recorded in Valerius Maximus, *Memorable Doings and Sayings* 9.1, ext. 3.

25. See p. 107.

26. See n. 23 above and the corresponding text.

no doubt about this) how pleasantly music captivates the truly devoted mind, with what spiritual vigor it animates, comforts, and fortifies the heart, and how many affections of piety it stirs.

In the sphere of civil society and private life, this second part of the *Musical Compendium* will demonstrate (I think) what impulses of both mind and body natural music[27] stimulates, how vigorously it relaxes and restores the powers that have been worn down by particularly stressful dealings, and the widely varying affections and effects it conveys both at home and in the field. For what could be more enjoyable than personally witnessing the sacrifices, festive banquets, funeral rites, and undertakings of the ancients, arranged with musical singing and instruments, and listening to them as if they were taking place in the present?

That is why I was of the inclination to address the dedication of this part to no one else more than you, most benevolent Patrons and Critics of Music. For it is certain that, as often as you feel mentally worn out after arduous princely business and weighty moments of decision-making, you soothe your hearts with musical strings, sonorous instruments, and beautiful voices, thus tempering the serious thoughts of the mind with the more genteel pleasantness of music just as the philosophers, orators, and poets did, as they will be called upon to testify in this work.

Μεταβολὴ πάντων γλυκύ [A change in all things is welcome], the ancient man says.[28] And since mankind is born for toil [Job 5:7], he uses the relaxation afforded by acceptable pleasure as a remedy, so that by interchanging toil with repose he may return to his customary duties more cheerfully. Hence the entire human life, if we believe Aristotle in Book 7 of his *Politics*,[29] is divided into πόνον καὶ ἀνάπαυσιν [toil and rest]; the Latins call it *negotium et otium* [business and leisure] or *intermissionem* [intermission, i.e. from business].[30] Accordingly preceding πόνος [toil]

27. That is, the music produced by mankind apart from the knowledge of the triune God and/or unrelated to worship of him. Today we would simply call this secular music.

28. The reference is either to Euripides' play *Orestes*, line 234 (see Arthur S. Way, tr., *Euripides in Four Volumes*, vol. 2 [New York: G. P. Putnam's Sons, 1929], 144,145) or to Aristotle's *Art of Rhetoric* 1.11.20 (see John Henry Freese, tr., *Aristotle: The "Art" of Rhetoric* [New York: G. P. Putnam's Sons, 1926], 124,125), where, however, Aristotle is quoting Euripides.

29. Aristotle, *Politics* 7.13.8, or 1333b. See next n.

30. Praetorius must have been acquainted with Aristotle's *Politics* from a Latin translation and thus attempted to guess at his original Greek on his own. In fact, Aristotle's terms are ἀσχολία and σχολή, lit. non-leisure and leisure. See H. Rackham, tr.,

and work necessarily requires its corresponding ἀνάπαυσιν [rest] and repose, as a sort of perfect seasoning for work. Thus in body movement standing is rest from sitting, lying down from standing, and walking from lying down. And just as on long journeys the slope of a mountain makes the plain less unpleasant, and the roughness of the hills is diminished by the valleys beneath them, so music, more than other practical pursuits, generally breathes new life into hard work in every kind of discipline, as the examples of the poets, orators, philosophers, and others, in both peacetime and wartime, will demonstrate more fully at the proper place in this part of the compendium. It is these very men, Venerable Maecenases, that you rightfully and properly seek to imitate with a rivaling love of music, whenever you pleasantly sweeten and diligently and dignifiedly temper arduous and serious affairs with the delightful nectar and ambrosia of harmony, enjoying music not as food, but as a delicacy on the side.

The saying of Pindar is true: ὅσσα δὲ μὴ πεφίληκε Ζεὺς, ἀτύζονται βοὰν Πιερίδων ἀίοντα, that is, all the creatures Jupiter does not love are terrified when they hear the sound of the Pierides [i.e. the Muses].[31] Therefore you, patrons and protectors of music who are surely begotten of Apollo,[32] I acknowledge as most excellent men and I revere as most worthy. And thus this part of the *Musical Compendium*, packed with the singing and instruments of antiquity, I wish to devote with a faithful heart, to consecrate with a fitting vow, and to dedicate with grateful affection to the patronage of each of your names.

And so, relying on your magnificent kindness toward others who are also pupils of the Muses, I will not cease to pray and implore that you will survey with approving expressions and read with benevolent minds this trifling and meager little work produced from music's storehouse, and that you will condescend to have my studies of this kind commended to you.

If this investigation should pass the test, I am of a mind, if God is favorably disposed, to publish and make widely accessible that which will always assist what remains of the study of music and that which diligent reading will observe in the future. And if my inadequate work should result in a more ornate and attractive music in any place, it will not only be you but all supporters of music to whom such music will be more than completely indebted.

Aristotle: Politics (Cambridge: Harvard University Press, 1959), 606,607.

31. Pindar, *First Pythian Ode* 13–14; see John Sandys, tr., *The Odes of Pindar, Including the Principal Fragments* (New York: The MacMillan Co., 1915), 154–157.

32. As the god of poetry and music, presiding over the Muses

With that, farewell, Magnanimous, Distinguished, Most Noble, Most Honorable Men, Maecenases worthy of devoted veneration.

Dresden,
on the fifth day of the month of February,
of the Year of Christ:
beholD, I am comIng qVIckly qVIckly—o now, My ChrIst![33]

---

33. Praetorius indicated the year, 1615, both through the letters he capitalized in "on the fifth day of the month of February [*MensIs febrVarII DIe qVInCto*]" and through the letters he capitalized in this line, which combines Revelation 22:12 with his own responding exclamation. I only attempted to replicate the latter, though imperfectly, since in Praetorius' original, he did not have to leave any potential Roman numerals uncapitalized.

E. Prayers from the *Pol. Cad.* Part Books

In the back of most of the fifteen part books for Pol. Cad., *one can find one or more prayers and/or brief confessions of faith. These give us a glimpse not only into Praetorius' religious convictions, but also into his devotional life and the resources he used to support it. Following the prayer(s), Praetorius usually concludes with the same formula: a) one or more years in Roman numerals, b) one or more Latin religious maxims, whose letters that can double as Roman numerals add up to the year(s) indicated, c) the same year(s) in Arabic numerals, d) his initials M. P. C., which double as his motto* Mihi Patria Coelum, *and e) the initialism* F. I. I. A., *which stands for* Faxit Iehova Iesus Amen, *"May the Lord Jesus grant it or make it so. Amen."[34] For the earlier years (starting with 1609), it seems that he composed the maxim during the given year. But at some point, he must have begun composing these maxims in advance, as those in the later part books add up to years that go beyond the year* Pol. Cad. *was published (1619) and even beyond the year that he died (1621).*

Thorough Bass Part Book

None

Primus Part Book

Come, Holy Spirit,
and send forth from heaven
the ray of your light.

Come, Father of the poor.
Come, giver of gifts.
Come, light of our hearts.

Best comforter,
sweet host to the soul, [*alternate:* sweet guest of the soul]
sweet refreshment.

---

34. *Faxit* is an old third person, singular, perfect tense, subjunctive form of *facio.*
The perfect subjunctive had once been used to express wishes and prayers.

Our rest in toil,
our alleviation in turmoil,
our solace in weeping.

O most blessed light,
fill the inmost recesses of the hearts
of your faithful people.

Without your divine power,
there is nothing in man,
there is nothing wholesome.

Wash away that which is filthy,
water that which is withered,
heal that which is wounded.

Bend that which is rigid,
warm that which is frigid,
correct that which is off course.

Grant to your faithful,
who put their confidence in you,
the sacred septenary.[35]

Grant the reward of virtue, [*alternate:* Grant the asset of courage]
grant the end of salvation,[36]
grant perpetual joy.[37]

MDCIX. To my God and Jesus alone be glory. 1609
M. P. C.
F. I. I. A.

Secundus Part Book

In each line of this first group of maxims, the letters that could double as Roman numerals added up to 1613.
The world will certainly perish:

35. That is, the sevenfold gifts of the Spirit (see Isa 11:2; Rev 1:4).

36. That is, that my life may end in salvation.

37. The source of this hymn is the old Latin sequence "Veni Sancte Spiritus," which Praetorius may have copied from Musculus, *Precationes*, 60f.

Those who are righteous God will deliver from evil,
But the impious will be confounded.
Come, Redeemer, Jesus Christ.
"I am just about to come, and will not delay" [Hab 2:3].
Hairy comets,[38] stars, sun and moon bear witness to this;
Christ therefore will not tarry long.
The dead in the earth he will resuscitate,
That he may judge them all.
The dead will suddenly rise again on that day;
They will then have to give an account.
But let the judgment not frighten those who are good.
The pious believer will have life,
For the pious are saved through faith alone.
Christ has redeemed them with blood.
He has elected them; they will therefore possess the kingdom of glory.
To God alone and only let glory be rendered.

*In each line of this second group, the letters that could double as Roman
numerals added up to 1614.*
Intervene, God, and have mercy on us.
Let your tenderheartedness be shown upon us,
Even as I have put my hope in you, Lord.
He is wise who carries Jesus in his heart.
My helper is Christ.
Only to God be praise and eternal glory.[39]

My—
—fatherland is heaven.
—father is God.
—brother is Christ.
—comforter is the Spirit.
—glory is the Trinity.

38. In Latin, comets were sometimes referred to as "hairy stars."

39. This is the only part book whose back matter is completely original with
Praetorius.

Tertius Part Book

O Lord Jesus Christ, the eternal sweetness and joyful song of those who love you, the salvation and lover of penitent sinners, by whose grace I am what I am [1 Cor 15:10], by whose mercy I live, move, and subsist [Acts 17:28]—O sweetest Jesus, grant me comfort and endurance in every hour that I undergo tribulation, especially in the critical hours of my death. Hide me from the face of your wrath in the crevices of your wounds until your fury passes, O Lord [Isa 26:20]. Strengthen me for resisting the devil, the world, and flesh and blood, in order that, dead to the world, I may live to you alone. And in the final hour of my departure, receive my spirit when it returns to you, and usher me into eternal joys. Amen.[40]

MDCXIII. Come, Redeemer, Jesus Christ. 1613
M. P. C.
F. I. I. A.

Quartus Part Book

Lord God almighty, you who are three and one, the God adored into eternity, into the hands of your ineffable mercy I commend my soul and my body, my thinking and speaking, my plans and all my actions, all the necessities of my body and soul, my coming in and my going out, the passage, progress, and end of my life, my coming in, my lying down, and my getting up, together with your saints and elect into perpetuity. Teach me today and at all times to do your will. That which you hate in me drive far from me; remove from me what is harmful and supply what is beneficial. Today and always, be lenient toward my soul, be lenient toward my sins, be lenient toward my faults. Grant me a heart that fears you, a mind that loves you, an intellect that understands you, ears that listen to you, and eyes that see you. Grant me, Lord, the ability to discern between good and evil, and protect me from all evil. Merciful God, benevolent God, compassionate God, you whose mercies extend over all your works [Ps 145:9], for the sake of your holy wounds and for the sake of your bitter death, grant that I may die the death of the righteous, grant me a good and holy death, and grant that I may never die unless I am perfectly pleasing to you and after having received your most holy body and blood, so that I

40. Compiled from five prayers attributed to Bonaventure (1221–1274) in Musculus, *Precationes*, 112f, 116f, 118, 120.

may cheerfully cross over to you in correct faith and firm hope—you who are adored and worthy of praise into eternity. Amen.[41]

MDCXIV. Come, Christ our God, and have mercy on us. 1614
MDCXV. The blood of Jesus Christ has redeemed us. 1615
M. P. C.
F. I. I. A.

Quintus Part Book

None

Sextus Part Book

Love of the divine will, holy Gift imparted by the omnipotent Father and his most blessed Offspring, omnipotent Paraclete Spirit, most gentle Comforter of the mourning, flow now into the inner chambers of my heart with your mighty strength, and strike the secrets of the inner man with the javelin of your love. Give me to drink from the torrent of your pleasure, so that I may no longer derive any enjoyment from tasting the poisoned sweetness of what the world has to offer. Come, most kind comforter of the aching soul and helper in tribulation. Come, cleanser of crimes, healer of wounds. Come, strength of the weak, lifter of the falling. Come, instructor of the humble, destructor of the proud. Come, benevolent father of orphans, kindly judge of widows. Come, hope of the poor, reviver of the faint. Come, guiding star of seafarers, haven of shipwrecks. Come, singular glory of all the living, only salvation of the dying. Come, Most Holy Spirit, come and have mercy on me, conform me to yourself and graciously stoop down to me, that my smallness may be very pleasing to your greatness and my feebleness to your strength, in keeping with the multitude of your mercies, through Jesus Christ my Savior, who in unity with you lives and reigns with the Father forever and ever. Amen.[42]

---

41. Compiled from three prayers in Musculus (*Precationes*, 251,252,253,257), two of which are simply attributed to "the church." The other was taken from Pseudo-Augustine's *Meditationes*, Chapter 40 (PL 40:938,939). The author is called Pseudo-Augustine because scholarship has demonstrated that Augustine did not write these meditations. They more likely belong to Jean de Fécamp (d. 1078).

42. This is an abridged version of the prayer to the Holy Spirit in Musculus, *Precationes*, 56–57, which in turn comprises Chapter 9 of Pseudo-Augustine's *Meditationes*

MDCXVI. You, Christ, are my helper in need. 1616
M. P. C.
F. I. I. A.

Septimus Part Book

Lord Jesus Christ, Son of the living God, my most compassionate redeemer and deliverer, you who came into this world to save sinners, I
ask you for the sake of the most indulgent viscera of your mercy, amend
my life, put my habits in order, pour the multitude of your sweetness
and charity into my heart, that nothing may satisfy me without you, that
nothing expensive or attractive may please me more than you. I beg you,
let everything be worthless, let all things taken together be regarded as
of no consequence in comparison with you. Whatever is opposed to you,
may it be disturbing to me. Let it disgust me to be glad without you, and
let it please me to be saddened for you. Let your name be that which
revives me, and the remembrance of you that which consoles me. I ask
you, my hope, for the sake of all your mercies, be gracious toward my
impieties. My hope, Christ my God, dear lover of mankind, the light,
the way, the life and salvation, I plead, implore, and pray that I may live
through you, that I may make it to you, that I may rest in you. Bring me
back from ruin, O Lord, redeem me from punishment, call me by your
name, seal me with your blood, that your memorial may always be before
me and may never leave my heart, you who did not leave the cross for
my sake. O dear Christ, good Jesus, Charity my God, set me aflame with
all your fire, all your love, all your charity, that I may love you, my Lord,
with all my heart through all my life, and that I may bless and adore you
forever and ever. Amen.[43]

MDCXVII. Our Watchman does not sleep [Ps 121:3,4]. 1617
MDCXVIII. Jesus, I hope in you; let me not be confounded into eternity. 1618

(PL 40:908–9). See previous n.

   43. Compiled from four prayers to God the Son in Musculus (*Precationes*, 36–37,
40, 43–44, 46–47), which in turn were taken from Chapters 36, 7, and 18 of Pseudo-
Augustine's *Meditationes* (PL 40:930,931,907,914), Chapter 13 of Pseudo-Augustine's
Soliloquia Animae ad Deum (PL 40:874), and Chapter 10 of Pseudo-Augustine's *Man-
uale* (PL 40:956). These anonymous *Soliloquia* date to around the thirteenth century
and are not to be confused with another genuine work by Augustine titled *Soliloquia*.

MDCXVIII. May God the Lord Jesus grant it. Amen. 1618
M. P. C.
F. I. I. A.

Octavus Part Book

None

Nonus Part Book

Lord, do not treat us as our sins deserve or repay us according to our iniquities [Ps 103:10].

Lord, do not remember our iniquities of old; let your mercies go quickly before us, for we have become extremely poor [79:8].

Help us, God our Savior, and for the sake of the glory of your name, O Lord, deliver us, and be gracious toward our sins for your name's sake [79:9]. Amen.[44]

MDCXIX. When there is repentance, Christ will draw near. 1619
M. P. C.
F. I. I. A.

Decimus Part Book

Have mercy, Lord, have mercy, have mercy on me, a most miserable sinner. Help me, Lord, with my life, lest I perish in my immorality. For it was not my merits, not my charm that compelled you to create me, but your most bounteous goodness and your clemency. Let the same charity constrain you to save that constrained you to create, for it is no less now, since you yourself are charity itself, and you are always the same. Your arm is not too short to save, Lord, nor is your ear too dull to hear [Isa 59:1]. Hear, then, and save me, most compassionate Father, for the sake of your Son, our Lord and Savior. Amen.[45]

---

44. This particular combination of psalm verses appears to have comprised a liturgical prayer, seeing as other composers (e.g. Josquin des Prez) also set it to music.

45. Compiled from two prayers in Musculus (*Precationes*, 195,21), which in turn were taken from Chapter 38 of Pseudo-Augustine's *Meditationes* (PL 40:936) and Chapter 11 of his *Soliloquia Animae ad Deum* (PL 40:873). See notes 41 and 43.

MDCXX. Arise, O dead, come to the thrones of Christ. 1620
M. P. C.
F. I. I. A.

Undecimus Part Book

Come, let us jump for joy to the Lord, let us shout aloud to God our salvation! Let us preoccupy his attention with acknowledgment and shout
for joy to him with psalms. For the Lord is a great God, and a great king
above all gods. Come, let us worship and fall prostrate before him, let us
cry aloud before the Lord who made us, for the Lord himself is our God
[Ps 95:1–3, 6, 7].[46]

MDCXXI. In Jesus the redeemer are our righteousness and life. 1621
M. P. C.
F. I. I. A.

Duodecimus Part Book

Holy Father, please do this:
Impress the wounds of the Crucified
Deeply on my heart.

Grant that my heart may burn
With love for Christ my God,
That I may be pleasing to him.

Grant that I may carry the death of Christ,
That on his allotted suffering
And wounds I may reflect.

Cause me to be wounded with his blows,
To be inebriated with this cross,
Out of love for the Son.

46. This is excerpted from psalm verses commonly sung during matins.

Grant that I be protected by the cross,
Defended by the death of Christ,
Nurtured by grace.

When my body dies,
Grant that my soul be gifted
The glory of paradise. Amen.[47]
*****

King of tremendous majesty,
You who freely save those who are to be saved,
Save me, fount of kindness.

Remember, kind Jesus,
That I am the reason for your path.
Do not destroy me on that day.[48]

MDCXXII. Repent; Jesus is coming to judge. 1622
M. P. C.
F. I. I. A.

Decimustertius Part Book

Holy, holy, holy, Holy of holies, Father of our fathers, God of Abraham, God of Isaac, God of Jacob, God of the apostles, God of the prophets, God of believers, God and Father of our Lord Jesus Christ your Son, I call upon you humbly and I plead with you likewise: Please see fit to preserve the desire of my soul and the integrity of my heart, that the heart made new in the bath of salvation may remain unimpaired by carnal flaws, and that you may allow us to flourish in your holy church with uninjured faith, uncorrupted mind, strong devotion, and continuous service or love. Please impart to me a sound mind, innocence, devoted integrity, and a holy, pure, prudent, and unpolluted conscience that continues in the glorious faith amid all the world's snares. Grant us a heart fortified against the devil's threats and fleshly enticements, that we may not get

47. "Stabat Mater" (Latin hymn, thirteenth cent.), sts. 11,10,16,17,19,20, altered to put the focus on Christ rather than Mary.

48. "Dies irae" (Latin sequence, thirteenth cent.), sts. 8,9; cf. *The Lutheran Hymnal* (St. Louis: Concordia, 1941), no. 607, sts. 8,9.

caught in violent, cruel, and deadly traps,[49] and that we may bear the seal of eternal salvation unmarred to the end. Drive from me all of the world's extravagance and filth and all of the devil's persuasion, you who are seated upon cherubim [Ps 99:1] and upon thrones[50] at the right hand of the Father. Grant that my heart may desire you, in desiring that it may seek you, in seeking that it may find you, and in finding that it may love you. Extinguish in me the desires of the flesh, and kindle the fire of your love. Drive out from me the spirit of pride, and graciously grant the treasure of your humility. Remove from me the raging of anger, and kindly bestow upon me the shield of patience. Give me firm faith, corresponding hope, and continual love. Avert from me futility of the mind, fickleness, reproaches of neighbors,[51] the crimes of slander, greed for riches, the appetite for empty glory, the evil of hypocrisy, the poison of adulation, contempt for the needy, oppression of the weak, the flames of avarice, the blight of envy, and the death caused by blasphemy. O God, you who are my mercy, I entreat you for the sake of your beloved Son, give me works of mercy and pursuits of piety—to sympathize with the afflicted, to show concern for the straying, to help the unfortunate, to aid the needy, to comfort the sorrowful, to relieve the oppressed, to refresh the poor, to forgive debtors, to be lenient toward those who sin against me, to love those who hate me, to repay evil with good, not to disdain anyone but to respect them, to imitate those who are good, to beware of those who are evil, to embrace virtues, and to reject vices; patience in adversity, restraint in prosperity, control of my mouth, and a guarded door for my lips; to spurn earthly things and to thirst for heavenly things. O Lord, the power of my salvation, do not let me be numbered with those who believe for a time, but retreat in the time of testing. Cover my head on the day of affliction [cf. Ps 140:7] and guard my salvation in the time of tribulation.[52]

49. Lit. "violent and cruel deadly traps." This construction, which does not sound any better in Latin than it does in English, points to an altering of the original prayer on the part of Musculus, whether intentional or unintentional. The original prayer by Pseudo-Augustine reads: "the deadly traps of the violent and cruel enemy [the devil]."

50. Pseudo-Augustine's original prayer reads: "upon seven thrones."

51. It is unclear whether neighbors are the object or subject of the reproaches. It may have been intentionally ambiguous.

52. Praetorius changed the word "battle" to "affliction." Also, in Musculus' prayer, he left out the important word *esto* from Pseudo-Augustine's original. It should have read: "Cover my head on the day of battle. I need you to be my hope on the day of affliction, and my salvation in the time of tribulation." As a result, in his version "cover/ guard [*obumbra*]" has to be awkwardly applied to "my hope" and "my salvation."

Look, Lord, my illumination and my salvation, I have asked for the things I am lacking and have divulged the things that I fear. Give that which I seek, for the sake of your Son, our Savior, adored into eternity. Amen.[53]

MDCXXIII. Come to my aid in distress, O Christ Jesus. 1623
MDCXXIV. This Christ Jesus is my helper. 1624
M. P. C.
F. I. I. A.

Decimusquartus Part Book

Have mercy on me, Christ.
Have mercy, Son of God.
Have mercy, O merciful one,
For truly I am a sinner.
Blot out my sins,
And create a clean heart.
Give firm hope, correct faith,
and perfect love.
And grant a good end,
Which is greater than any gift,
That I may be filled with such remorse
As to be united with you, Christ.
Grant that I worthily eat
Your salutary body.
Let not your wrath weigh me down;
Let your blood likewise wash me
Beyond the body and in the heart
From sins and from uncleanness.
And when the hour of death draws near,
May your powerful angel then be at hand,
The protector you have assigned to me,
And let him place me among the righteous.

---

53. Compiled from two prayers "for obedience and newness of life" in Musculus (*Precationes*, 184–185, 183–184), which in turn were taken from a prayer attributed to Cyprian (PL 4:905–6, where, however, the attribution is to Cyprian of Antioch [d. 304], not the bishop of Carthage, though this attribution also seems dubious when the entire prayer is considered) and Chapters 1, 2, and 3 of Pseudo-Augustine's *Meditationes* (PL 40:901,902,903). See n. 41.

Though death subdue my flesh,
Do not let the second death touch me.
Though the flesh putrefy,
Let the spirit find rest in you,
That when I rise to see you,
I may remain with you always,
Never to leave you
Through infinite ages. Amen.[54]
*****

Come and deliver us, our God.
You have come, O desirable one.[55]
I have seen the Lord face to face,
And my soul has been saved.[56]

Glory to the Father, who created us. Glory to the Son, who redeemed us. Glory to the Holy Spirit, who sanctified us. Glory to the supreme and indivisible Trinity, whose works are inseparable, whose dominion continues without end. You are worthy of praise, you are worthy of hymn singing, to you belongs all honor, yours are the adoration and splendor, yours the rendering of thanks, yours the honor, worthiness, and strength, our God, forever and ever. Amen.[57]

MDCXXVII. Behold, I am coming very soon. Oh come, come now, my Christ. 1627
M. P. C.

Now in the name of Jesus Christ:
May the Lord, Jesus, and the Holy Spirit grant it. Amen.
Amen, amen, and amen.

54. "Ave Mundi Spes," a Marian hymn attributed (though with disputation) to Pope Innocent III (1160/61–1216; PL 217:919–20), abridged and altered to put the focus on Christ rather than Mary.

55. The first line appears to be an antiphon for prime (a service traditionally said or chanted at 6 a.m.). The second line appears to be taken from the Easter processional antiphon "Cum Rex gloriae."

56. Slightly altered from Genesis 32:30, which ended up comprising part of the text of Praetorius' funeral sermon.

57. Musculus, *Precationes*, 4, taken from Chapter 33 of Pseudo-Augustine's *Meditationes* (PL 40:927).

– Appendix V–

Eyewitness Account of the 1614 Princes' Convention in Naumburg[1]

SINCE NO PRINCES' CONVENTION had been held in Naumburg since the year 1587, the Most Illustrious and High-born lord, Lord Johann Georg, Elector and Grand Marshal of the Holy Roman Empire; Duke of Saxony,

Fig. 51. *Naumburg* (oriented northeast-ward), engraving in Matthäus Merian's heirs, eds., *Topographia* for Upper Saxony, Thuringia, Meissen, and Lusatia (1650). Note St. Wenceslas' Church on the right (east) side of the city.

Jülich, Cleves, and Berg; and Burgrave of Magdeburg, was most graciously pleased to hold a princes' convention in Naumburg, on March 27. He therefore notified the three houses of Saxony, Brandenburg, and Hesse. Then he most graciously charged a council here with informing the citizenry of this announcement—that they were to clean, tidy, and decorate their residences in preparation, and were to secure provisions of every kind for it, so that prominent foreigners could be entertained that much better at a suitable price. Accordingly, then, the governing burgomaster, Master Sixtus Braun, had all of this publicized to the citizenry at length,

---

1. Staffel, *Notabilia*, 36–45. This source and the others used to correct and supplement it in the footnotes will be listed and annotated at the end.

adding all sorts of good reminders and admonitions, so that the citizenry and council might not be disgraced, but might mutually acquire fame and honor from the event.

Soon thereafter the baker and butcher trades had to appear before the council. They were given orders that from now on they were to watch and be careful with meat and flour, of which they were to provide a good supply, so that, no matter what, nothing would be lacking during this function. Not only that, but they were also warned that if they failed, they would experience nothing else but to bring disgrace and shame on themselves, and a considerable penalty besides. The bakers and butchers were now to take pains to prevent this, so that no penalty would be necessary, but that they might obtain honor and fame from this event.

Soon after this had been arranged, the chamber accommodations officer [*Cammer Fourirer*] for the elector of Saxony, Augustin Felgenhauer, presented himself. He then immediately succeeded in getting the council to put Hans Koch, the town warden [*Stadtvoigt*] at the time, at his disposal. He had to inspect the citizens' houses with him and look over the stalls and other particulars with him, to see how the various princely households might best be sheltered and lodged.

And the following houses were identified and enlisted as the electoral headquarters:

- Mr. Christoph Michael's house along the Market as the elector of Saxony's quarters

- Duke August's quarters, elected administrator of the diocese of Naumburg and Zeitz, in Johann Weiss' residence

- The dukes of Coburg and Eisenach [Johann Casimir and Johann Ernst, respectively] in Tobias Harnisch's residence in the great Jacob's Lane

- The four lords and dukes of Saxony of Altenburg lineage, namely Johann Philipp, Friedrich, [Johann] Wilhelm, and Friedrich Wilhelm, in Mrs. Dr. Wacke's lodging by St. Wenceslas' Church along the Pottery Market

- Four Weimar lords, the oldest ones, namely Johann Ernst the Younger, Friedrich, Wilhelm, and Albrecht (the other four lords, Duke Ernst, Duke Bernhard, and others were not present at that time) had their quarters in the residence of Mr. Johann Lindner, the manager[2] in St. George's Cloister, at Jacob's Gate.

- The duke and elector of Brandenburg [Johann Sigismund] in Mr. Verweser's house along the Market

- His esteemed brother, Christian, the archbishop of Magdeburg, at Hans Hambruck's

- Margrave Hans Georg of Jägerndorf and Crossen at Christoph Öhler's along the Market

- Margrave Christian of Kulmbach at Christoph Seydel's there along the Market

- The margrave of Ansbach was supposed to have his quarters at the provost's residence or in the deacon's residence, but since His Grace[3] became unwell en route, he was unable to come here this time.

- The landgrave of Hesse, Otto, spent several days in Eckartsberga, but since, according to the rumors, His Grace was not at all happy with the seating arrangement that reached him,[4] his [sic] Grace did not come to this function at all,[5] but engaged in irregular activities, even mortally wounding himself with a gun and eventually fading away entirely.[6]

---

2. The German *Schösser* can also mean "tax collector, treasurer, *or* administrator."

3. German: *Ihr Gnad[en]*. Staffel uses the polite form *Ihr* (*Ihr Gnaden, Ihre Durchlaucht*, etc.) in an indirect or third person sense throughout, which was a common enough usage at the time.

4. Another possible translation: "with the seating arrangement as it pertained to him," or more idiomatically, "with the seat he was assigned." Müller explains that since Otto came with the full authority to act on behalf of his father, Landgrave Moritz of Hesse-Kassel, he wanted to have his father's seat, but was unable to obtain it (Müller, 301).

5. Since both Staffel and Müller report that Otto did not attend, and Müller also reports that he was replaced by a delegate from Kassel named Otto von Starschedel, their account is to be preferred to Bürger's, who reports that "Landgrave Otto of Hesse arrived [in Naumburg] on [March 27] after twelve o'clock [and] stayed with Burgomaster Sixtus Braun" (Bürger, 536). It was undoubtedly the second Otto who stayed with the burgomaster.

6. Staffel makes it sound as though Otto's death happened immediately after his departure from Eckartsberga. It was not until 1617 that Otto shot himself in the delirium of a fever while attempting to dispatch a barking dog that was annoying him.

Apart from this, three other margraves of Brandenburg were supposedly here and were put up in Mr. Doctor Behr's residence, but I was
unable to discover their names.

In addition, three other landgraves of Hesse arrived, of Darmstadt
lineage, namely Ludwig, Friedrich, and Wilhelm, who had their quarters
with Mr. Kretzschmar at the Three Swans.

Most of the princes who arrived here brought a considerable supply
of oats, hay, wild game, fish, hens, eggs, butter, bacon, and all kinds of
victuals here and sent them to their quarters, and many honorable men
also received a share of them, beyond their expectations. Especially the
hosts with whom the princely personages stayed suffered no loss. The
leftover wine on the dregs was almost all left behind for them. The lords
of Coburg and Eisenach, for example, gifted their hosts the makeshift
kitchen in the courtyard, which included several stacks[7] of meat, also
left a decent supply of capons,[8] turkeys, and eggs, and additionally presented them with 120 imperial thalers and honored each child and the
lady of the house with several thalers.[9]

But before they made their entrance, an Honorable Council had the
citizenry mustered into different troops, over which Mr. Johann Koch,[10]
the keeper of the Green Shield, was appointed as captain. He also had to
make a trip to Dresden on this account and pledge loyalty to the House
of Saxony on their behalf regarding a number of special points. When he
returned home, an Honorable Council assigned him three more com-
manders, Elias Mauer, Antonius Busch, and Zacharias Helmshausen,[11]
who helped him arrange the citizenry into certain divisions [Rotten] and
made other classifications. The strongest trades[12] also kept several persons ready to stand guard with armor and pikes in front of the town hall
and in the gates.

7. German: Schock, which in the narrow sense was a unit of sixty pieces, but could
also be used in the sense of "heap, pile, large quantity."

8. Castrated domestic cocks fattened for eating

9. Earlier in his notes Staffel is more specific: "The hostess [was honored] with ten
and each child with two thalers" (Staffel, 33).

10. This is different from the Hans Koch mentioned earlier, as Staffel also makes
clear towards the end.

11. Count von Beust had Helmershausen (Beust, 294).

12. Either the strongest in numbers, thus with the ability to spare some men to
stand guard, or the trades possessing men who were the strongest physically.

Eight days before March 27, the elector of Saxony's privy councilors, namely Mr. President [Caspar von] Schönburg, Mr. Chancellor [Bernhard von] Pölnitz, Mr. von Lüttich, Mr. [Esaias] von Brandenstein, Mr. von Lohss, and others made their approach into the vicinity,[13] turning in and taking lodging with then Mr. Treasurer Heinrich Metzner in the Black Bear. These lords then very diligently traveled to the town hall several days in a row, held various meetings on behalf of the Sworn Fraternity[14] and conducted mature deliberations about it. Among other things, they supposedly discussed how, if the Electoral Saxon House of Dresden, God forbid, were to pass away without any male heir to person and property, in that case the House of Altenburg would have preference for the electoral dignity.[15]

On March 27, the citizenry was summoned by the division master [*Rottenmeister*][16] at three a.m. and told that everyone should immediately betake himself in person to the gate to which he was assigned, without any excuses, and that no one should remain at home, on pain of a hefty fine. Even Mr. Burgomaster Braun's son had to line up with everyone else, as did other prominent and elderly citizens.

At this point, people were presuming as certain that[17] the princely personages would be making their appearance for the function in view, and everyone was now anxious for this event. And it happened that their eager desire was fulfilled, in that one prince and lord after the other graciously made their appearance and put on a completely princely show

13. Müller says that the councilors began arriving on Thursday, March 24; perhaps Staffel intends "eight days before March 27" in a more general sense of "the week before March 27." Müller has no record of any Mr. von Lüttich, but he has two "brothers von Lohss," Christoph and Joachim. He also documents the "others" (Müller, 274).

14. German: *Eydt-Verbrüderung*. In the opening sermon he delivered for this assembly (treated by Staffel later) and later sent to press, Head Court Preacher Hoë von Hoenegg explains this term: "Already several hundred years ago [the three houses of Saxony, Brandenburg, and Hesse] made a *pactum gentilitium* [clansmens' pact] and an alliance of succession" (Hoë von Hoenegg, *Naumburgische Fried und Frewdenport*, 3). Müller refers more than once to the *Erbverbrüderung*, "succession fraternity" (Müller, 273–275, 299, 301).

15. Müller treats these meetings in greater detail (Müller, 274–75).

16. Count von Beust had *Stattmeister*, "station master" (Beust, 295).

17. Wagner and Wünsch's edition of Staffel reads: "*Weil nuhmehr gewisse Muthmassung abhanden, dass* etc." Count von Beust has: "*Weil nunmehro gewisse Muthmasung obhanden, daß* etc." (Beust, 295). *Abhanden* and *obhanden* (synonym of *vorhanden*) are antonyms. This is one of the few times I give preference to Beust, since I cannot make any sense out of *abhanden*.

with their very remarkable courtiers and squires. There was finery on horses, on the pages and noble-boys—in short, finery could be seen everywhere. Soon came a royal messenger; now came the dukes of Coburg and Eisenach through the Salt Gate. Those in Jacob's Gate and the other gates now wished they had been waiting there and wanted to run over together and join in watching the dukes' princely entrance, but they didn't dare do it, since they constantly had to keep an eye out for the lords who would wish to enter the city through those gates. But in due course, those who were waiting in Jacob's Gate also saw the entrance made by the lords of Coburg [and Eisenach], because Their Graces turned in at the Golden Armor [*Harnisch*].[18] As they processed in, one could see beautiful plumes on the horses, as well as the noble-boys dressed in large golden chain-necklaces alongside their squires.

Before this entrance was finished, a royal messenger arrived, followed by Margrave Christian of Bayreuth and Kulmbach.[19] On account of a young lady who had recently passed away,[20] this prince made his entrance with a retinue in black.

Soon after this the four Altenburg lords, the above-named, also arrived,[21] and not long afterward the four eldest Weimar princes, who were still viewed as minors at the time. All the princes already mentioned made their appearance before midday.[22]

After midday came another royal messenger, announcing that the archbishop of Halle[23] was not far away; his carriages were already at the ferry.[24] This prince was being eagerly awaited, since he had such beauti-

18. Since Staffel already reported that the dukes of Coburg and Eisenach were to stay with Tobias Harnisch, it appears that the Golden Armor [*Harnisch*] was named after its owner.

19. Bürger reports that Duke Ernst of Eisenach arrived first, at ten a.m., his brother Duke Johann Casimir of Coburg after noon, and Margrave Christian of Kulmbach also after noon (Bürger, 536).

20. Though *Fräulein* can often be used for a prince's daughter, no daughter of Margrave Christian's had recently died. The deceased had probably been a close attendant of his wife Marie.

21. This contradicts Bürger, who says that these four dukes were the first to arrive on March 27, at 9:30 a.m. (Bürger, 536).

22. This also contradicts Bürger, who says that the "four young dukes of Saxony, of Weimar lineage," arrived at six p.m. (Bürger, 537). See also n. 19.

23. This is the same as the archbishop of Magdeburg mentioned earlier; the archbishop of Magdeburg had his residence in Moritzburg, a fortified castle in Halle.

24. The Saale River flows around Naumburg to the north. Bürger reports that the

ful, tall, princely horses with him; many people had never seen horses so large and beautiful in form their entire lives. His twelve pages and noble-boys were sitting so stylishly on their horses, dressed in white, silver, and red, as if they were nailed to them, which was no less true of his squires, courtiers, and domestics. In short, if a person just had many eyes, he could have taken in many sights.

Soon after the archbishop, Elector Johann Sigismund of Branden-burg also arrived.[25] I have never seen more canopied coaches or carriag-es at one time in my entire life, and judging by appearances, I would not have imagined that there was enough room in the city for these canopied carriages. But when the entrance was completed, sufficient room could still be seen and found.

As the evening was gradually setting in, the news came that the elector of Saxony and burgrave of Magdeburg was not coming with Lord August, his noble brother, that evening, but they were staying with their retinues in Weissenfels at the castle, and that is what happened.

During this time, while the illustrious elector of Saxony was in Weis-senfels, it supposedly happened that both princes made a wager there as to who could produce the best lead driving horses, and neither wanted to lose at this. Accordingly arrangements are made in utmost haste to have subjects and peasants of both princes trick out their horses as best they can and send them to their respective prince and lord to be used in front of his principal chamber carriage.[26] Since there can be nothing lacking for this, the best horses are procured, and it supposedly turned out that the subjects of St. George's Cloister, belonging to the diocese, having got-ten a hold of something a bit taller, are supposed to have fared better than the elector's subjects. While they were there it also happened that the stable boys and harness masters polished and cleaned themselves up extremely well. Many of them supposedly put on the following: first a yel-low goatskin garment, over that a red wool shirt of London fabric, a tan-brown London coat, over that a short black London jacket [*Mutzen*], over that a red leather,[27] and another protective overcoat besides. Now when one of the nobility saw this, who was probably standing not far from both princely personages, he says, "Good grief, five coats are simply way too

---

archbishop of Magdeburg arrived after five p.m. (Bürger, 536).

25. Bürger says he arrived at six p.m. (*ibid.*).

26. That is, the carriage in which each prince himself would be traveling.

27. The precise nature of this "red leather" is undefined, so I have left it the same.

many to wear for the peasants. Most gracious lord, would it not be alright if a couple coats were taken off? They would definitely still have enough of them." At this the lords supposedly smiled and acquiesced to his suggestion. This squire basically had the skill of Cleopas; he prophesied and it later came true here.[28] Most of the coats and horses of the subjects of both the electorate and the diocese would basically be taken away. I think that most of the noblemen's horses will not be forgotten either.[29]

Now when March 27 had receded and March 28 had dawned, everyone was very eagerly awaiting the princes who had yet to arrive, the elector of Saxony and his noble brother. Now different reports were saying that Their Graces would certainly march in through Jacob's Gate, and no one knew or suspected anything else. However, in the end it was supposedly anticipated that Jacob's Gate would be unsuitable, since the lane was not very long and most of the mounted procession of country squires would either have to halt before the gate or the carriages would end up obstructing each other. It was accordingly considered to be more convenient if His Illustriousness would make His Electoral entrance into the city through Mary's Gate, which is also what happened. Therefore some of the princely personages[30] made their way to Mary's Lane, went inside at several citizens' houses, and enjoyed themselves watching the entrance, which commenced shortly after twelve o'clock, after midday. There then appeared the illustrious elector along with his noble brother, dressed in beautiful jerkins that were elegantly trimmed with golden galloons and in many black plumes, while the counts and lords were mostly on horseback, estimated at a 1,000 horses. They rode in with considerable pomp, decked out in simple, black velvet riding jackets [Reitmutzen] with gold chain-necklaces draped across them. They were majestic and a sight to see.[31]

---

28. There is no clear point of comparison between this squire and the Cleopas of the Bible (see Luke 24:13–27). It is almost certain that Staffel misspoke and meant to say "the skill of Caiaphas," the Jewish high priest who made a prophecy pertaining to Jesus without knowing it (John 11:49–52). It is also remotely possible that Staffel did write Caiaphas and was mis-transcribed here, though Count von Beust also reads Cleopas (Beust, 299).

29. Staffel wrote this account some time after the fact, but probably not much later than 1622 when his written recollections conclude. This was well after the commencement of the Thirty Years' War, to which he is doubtless referring here.

30. Namely, of those who had already arrived

31. Bürger catalogues the "Spectacular Procession of the Elector of Saxony [and his brother August]" which, according to him, included a total of twenty-four trumpeters

Now when this majestic procession ended, all the princely personages immediately got on horseback to go visit and catch up with
each other, and there was some impressive clothing to be seen then.
Whoever was not wearing satin and velvet or gold jewelry did not count
for much. In the meantime preparations were made in St. Wenceslas'
Church for a sermon that was to be delivered on the following day by
Mr. Dr. Hoë,[32] and the different choirs[33] in which the musicians could
perform were also readied. One was in the boys' choir, the second in
the balcony of the new organ, the third near Loth's memorial slab, and
the fourth in the back choir by the baptismal font.[34] Our own cantor

---

and four kettle drummers (Bürger, 537). Müller also documents "in large part [*des
mehrern*]" the retinues of each attending prince from the "lists of the accommodations
officers and feed marshals [*Fourier- und Futter-Zedduln*]" (Müller, 275ff).

32. Matthias Hoë von Hoenegg (1580–1645) was the elector of Saxony's head court
preacher and father confessor. Since a) Staffel (p. 33), Bürger (p. 537), Müller (p. 299),
and Hoë von Hoenegg (*Naumburgische Fried und Frewdenport*, 1) all agree that the
first service was held on Wed., March 30, b) Staffel and Bürger (p. 537) both agree that
the elector of Saxony and his brother arrived on Mon., March 28, and c) this sentence
goes on to say that the preparations were made for a service to be held in St. Wenceslas'
Church "on the following day," "in the meantime" here must therefore refer to Tues.,
March 29.

33. German: *vnterschiedene Chore*. *Chor* can refer to a group of vocal and instrumental musicians, or it can refer to the space or gallery they occupy. The word, even
in context, is somewhat ambiguous here, though it seems to refer to the choir galleries
(see next n.).

34. These positions agree with those given by Bürger: "[On March 30, the Wednesday after Oculi Sunday,] the elector of Saxony caused his vocal and instrumental music
to be well heard. It was situated in four choir spaces, one in the lowest choir in front of
the altar, the second in the boys' choir, the third in the balcony of the old, disassembled
organ, which was nicely furnished with boards and tapestries for this purpose, and the
fourth on a specially assembled stage near the late Mr. Bastian Loth's memorial slab"
(Bürger, 537–538). Though the references to the organ balcony seem to be contradictory with respect to the condition of the organ, Bürger explains the discrepancy in his
general remarks on Naumburg at the beginning of his manuscript: "In the year 1612,
fourteen days before St. Michael's Day, the old organ [which had been completed almost fifty-nine years earlier, on Oct. 21, 1553] began to be dismantled, and a new one
began to be built. The organ-maker's name was Joachim Tzschock of Plauen, whom an
Honorable Council satisfied with 800 florins at first, in accordance with the contract
they had drawn up. But it was later approved to give him another 200 florins, since the
instrument to be built was taking a long time and he complained that he was having to
dig into his own pockets. During his work, two children and finally his own wife died
on him. Not until the year 1616 was the instrument completely finished except for the
painting work" (Bürger, 42; see also p. 287). So Staffel, who wrote his account years
after the fact (see n. 29), refers to "the balcony of the new organ" anachronistically,
while Bürger's description is more period correct, perhaps having also been written

Lorenz Stieffel[35] was not permitted to trouble himself with performing any music, since others were present who could perform so much better, namely Mr. Praetorius of Wolfenbüttel with the elector of Saxony's chapel choirboys, who could be heard with all kinds of instruments, kettle drums, and trumpets. I have not heard or experienced anything like it before or since. The elector's musicians were all seen in yellow satin doublets and black velvet pants and velvet jerkins.

His Electoral Illustriousness had likewise brought along twelve trumpeters similarly clothed, who had to stand at regular attention in front of his headquarters and issue dinner calls, and a special foot soldier captain was also present, who had to take turns leading some forty foot soldiers back and forth. Every one of them were stately and fine-looking fellows, who wore black, Swiss, velvet Spaniards [*Spanier*][36] with yellow feathers on their heads, black pants with yellow satin sticking out and closed above the knee, yellow stockings, and yellow satin doublets with black velvet jerkins sticking out that were inspiring to look at.

Now once preparations had been made in the church that evening, as mentioned, Mr. Dr. Hoë preached a glorious and magnificent sermon[37] on Psalm 133, "Behold, how nice and lovely etc.," in the presence of the elector of Saxony, his noble brother, Lord August, Duke Johann Casimir, Duke Johann Ernst of Eisenach, the lords of Altenburg, the lords of Weimar, and others, and in the presence of the electoral ladies of both Saxony and Brandenburg, who all stood together in the gallery, which was enveloped in black velvet tapestries. A selection, "Lamb of God, Pure and Holy etc." was then sung in four choirs with all kinds of musical instruments in such a way that a person's heart could have literally leaped for joy.[38]

---

shortly after the occurrence of the events they describe.

35. Braun reports that Stieffel passed away from phthisis the following year, on July 13, after serving "the church and school . . . very faithfully for thirty-four years."

36. The Spaniard was a round, cloth hat which, according to *DWB*, looked just like a "Leipzig doctor's hat," except it was less rigid.

37. Though it is not immediately clear in the context, this sermon was preached in the morning of March 30 (see Müller, 299). It can be found in Hoë von Hoenegg, *Naumburgische Fried und Frewdenport*, 2–26.

38. Staffel says that this piece was sung after the sermon. Müller also says that a piece was sung before both the readings (Psalms 23 and 85) and the sermon (Müller, 299). This fits with what Hoë von Hoenegg reported with his second sermon, that music was performed both beforehand and afterward (see n. 49). The "Lamb of God, Pure and Holy" mentioned is doubtless the one included in Praetorius' *Pol. Cad.* of 1619. This is proved by the following facts:

In short, I think there were many people there who had not heard such music in their lifetime.

After the completion of the service, His Electoral Illustriousness rode to the town hall along with the other lords. There a splendid banquet was served.[39] When the trumpets have solemnly issued the dinner call and the kettle drums have vigorously resonated, the banquet then commences, and all the electoral and princely personages who were here attended it. There were some curious foods to be seen, consisting of all

---

a. On the title pages of the *Pol. Cad.* part books, Praetorius describes the pieces contained therein as "solemn concertos of peace and joy [*Solennische Friedt- und Frewdens-Concert*]," which is very similar to the title Hoë von Hoenegg gave the book in which he published the two sermons he delivered during this princes' convention, *Naumburgische Fried und Frewdenport* (The Naumburg Port of Peace and Joy).

b. Praetorius dedicated the work not only to his own duke, Friedrich Ulrich, but also to Elector Johann Georg of Saxony (his de facto employer at the time) and Administrator Christian Wilhelm of the Archbishopric of Magdeburg (GA 17:vi), two of the prominent attendees of the 1614 Naumburg Princes' Convention.

c. Praetorius explicitly says in his dedicatory epistle, dated Jan. 4, 1619, that the pieces in the work are a selection of his "new compositions, which [he had] composed within the last five years by the grace God [had] bestowed upon [him] . . . and chiefly those which [had] been disposed and arranged for performing with living [i.e. vocal] and instrumental music in the presence of Your Electoral and Princely Graces in Dresden, Naumburg, Halle, Wolfenbüttel, Brunswick, and Halberstadt, etc., not just for royal, electoral, and princely tables, but also in other places, including churches" (GA 17:x–xi).

d. Finally, *Pol. Cad.* includes just one setting of "O Lamm Gottes" (GA 17:154ff), for thirteen parts in five choirs. Praetorius describes the "style" in which this piece should be performed thus: "In this . . . style, four boys must be positioned in four separate places in the church, facing each other, or wherever it will conveniently work. The first one, who is stationed by the organ, begins all by himself; the second immediately after him; then the third; and finally the fourth (who must be positioned by the full musical chorus, the ensemble chorus [see *SM* 3:133]). . . [After suggesting several combinations of instruments to accompany each of the four boys, he continues:] But when an abundance of instruments is not available, it is better to keep them [the instrumentalists] all together and put them in a separate location, and the members of the vocal chorus [who respond to the soloists in the ripienos] would also be in a separate location, like my arrangement a few years ago in Naumburg" (*SM* 3:172–74; cf. *SM* 3E:175–76). In his *Puericinium* (1621), he says the same, except at the end he has: "like my arrangement several years ago at the princes' convention in Naumburg" (GA 19:vi).

The piece sung before the readings and sermon was very likely his setting of Psalm 133, "Siehe, wie fein und lieblich," for sixteen parts in four choirs (GA 17:268ff).

39. Müller makes clear that the princes first met to conduct business in the town hall, and then stayed for a banquet in the evening, for which the women joined them (Müller, 299–302).

sorts of pies, baked goods prepared in various wonderful ways, all sorts of fish dishes and splendid confections, and even though the kitchen was set up by St. Wenceslas' Church, the citizens still had to bring all of this to the town hall in silver trays and carry it to the dance hall, which was also draped with velvet tapestries all the way around. Two fireplaces were also prepared in which a fire was kept going, so that it never felt too cold but was somewhat mild in the hall, since there was still some frost that night.

Now once this banquet was completed and came to an end in all merriness, the elector of Brandenburg sent his servants on an errand, for which several carriages were dispatched, to retrieve fir boughs. The pillars in the dance hall were then covered with them, and all sorts of fruits, consisting of oranges and lemons, were woven into them, which was a pretty sight to see. And the just-mentioned noble banquet for the lords and electors had to be continued on Friday after the sermon, once our own Mr. Parson had rendered a beautiful sermon on the apostle Paul, "Be united in the Spirit etc.," in the presence of the above-mentioned princes and princely ladies.[40] And after music had once again been performed in the same manner as before, it finally concluded and the church, where the electoral foot soldiers had to stand guard before the doors to prevent anyone from running inside, was locked.

Soon afterward the elector of Brandenburg's trumpeters began to sound the dinner call energetically, along with the kettle drummers, which lasted almost a half hour. And apart from the fact that they all had silver trumpets, they did not merit the same praise as the Saxon trumpeters.

After they had finished, the potentates betook themselves together and made their way to the table in the dance hall here,[41] where once again one could see all sorts of curious foods that were carried up. The waiters also did not have to go as far to get to the kitchen as with the Saxon kitchen,

---

40. Bürger provides more detail: "On the ensuing Friday [April 1], the electoral and princely personages again came together in the church, with the exception of the House of Brandenburg, minus the electress and her young noble-son [Joachim Sigismund, who was ten years old] and those who attended her. [In other words, these few did attend; Staffel shares an anecdote about them later.] There the elector of Saxony once again caused his music to be heard, including his trumpeters and kettle drums, and had the pastor of Naumburg, Mr. Master Caspar Bertram, give the sermon. He explained the words of St. Paul in Ephesians 4:3, 'Be careful to preserve the unity in the Spirit etc.' For his work, the elector [of Saxony] and Duke August each had him most graciously and graciously (respectively) honored with a beautiful gilded goblet" (Bürger, 538).

41. Bürger includes the seating arrangement for this banquet on pp. 538–39.

since this one was set up in the Calvinist courtyard.[42] This banquet finally ended successfully too, and some lords came away mighty inebriated.

At this point I have to mention this: The electoral ladies of Brandenburg had their stations in the gallery above the Mount of Olives[43] and diligently listened to God's word. They contracted quite a number of lice and brought them home with them. Several of them had a good laugh and surmised that this feat just had to be concocted by a prominent person, since some of the Calvinists who were unaccounted for when it came time to hear God's word were suspected in this matter.[44] Several electoral Saxon counselors recalled this affair many years later, and especially Mr. [Hans Caspar] von Körbitz, the widowed electress of Saxony's steward at the Lichtenburg,[45] who could not forget it.[46]

On the second of April, the three landgraves of Hesse, of Darmstadt lineage—Ludwig, Wilhelm, and Friedrich—who were quartered at the Three White Swans, set back out from there and departed for their own country.

On Laetare Sunday, Mr. Dr. Hoë once again preached a beautiful thanksgiving sermon in a considerably large assembly, consisting of the elector of Saxony and the princes of Coburg, Eisenach, Weimar, and Altenburg. The text was taken from the psalm, "Let them rejoice and be glad etc."[47] After he finished, not only was a heartfelt and Christian prayer of thanksgiving spoken, praising God that this commendable event had gone well,[48] but the music was also once again performed and executed

42. A reference to Elector Johann Sigismund's quarters by way of his faith; he had publicly converted to Calvinism the year before.

43. This most likely refers to artwork on the façade of the gallery.

44. The elector of Brandenburg's court was now a mixed one religiously. Even though he had converted to Calvinism (see n. 42), many of his subjects remained devoted Lutherans, including many in his court and even his wife.

45. The widow referred to is Hedwig of Denmark, who had been married to Elector Christian II of Saxony, Johann Georg's older brother. After Christian passed away in 1611, Hedwig lived in the Lichtenburg Castle in Prettin, northwest of Dresden and northeast of Leipzig.

46. Bürger shares another Calvinist-related event that took place during these days: "On the back side of our altar at the heel, where the sexton usually hangs up the surplice, a secret Calvinist adherent wrote these words: *Hic viret Daemonis ara* [Here flourishes a demon-altar.] To which another man replied and noted beneath it: *Haec scripsit Daemonis hara.* [This was written by a demon-sty.]" (Bürger, 538).

47. Psalm 5:11,12. This sermon can be found in Hoë von Hoenegg, *Naumburgische Fried und Frewdenport*, 27–46.

48. This prayer is printed in Hoë von Hoenegg, *op. cit.*, 50–52.

with all dignity by Praetorius just like before—with magnificent singing and playing on all sorts of instruments.[49]

Now once the thanksgiving had ended, the lords of Coburg and Eisenach had trumpets majestically played and the kettle drums beaten in front of their quarters and residence to issue the call to the table and to dinner. For Their Graces were not going to let themselves be heard and seen in any way inferior to the two electors.[50] And the elector of Brandenburg and elector of Saxony were also at their banquet that day, along with other princes and lords. I myself heard this banquet variously praised, and there must not have been anything lacking. Among other things, door soldiers—all those who belonged to the duke of Coburg— carried gilded partisans,[51] the likes of which could not be seen among the other princes.

On April 4, the Altenburg and Weimar lords departed for home from there, but not until honorable presents of gold gulden, on which eight young lords were stamped, had been given to the hosts with whom they had lodged.

On Thursday, April 5, the two brothers, Duke Johann Casimir of Coburg and Duke Johann Ernst of Eisenach, likewise departed. If ever princely personages conducted themselves well toward their hosts during this princes' convention, these two lords did. The innkeeper Tobias Harnisch has many times expressed the wish that he would like to have guests like them more often. And how many times have people heard him

49. Bürger briefly reports on the music for this service: "The electoral music was once again heard with great resonance [*mit grossem schall*]" (Bürger, 538). Hoë von Hoenegg editorially remarks at the end of his Laetare sermon: "After this God was once again passionately praised and glorified, accompanied by all sorts of instruments and strings, as was also done before the sermon" (Hoë von Hoenegg, *op. cit.*, 46). He also refers to Praetorius' music in a marginal note in the sermon itself. In Part II, he mentions that David shows the proper way to express our joy in the Lord in Psalms 149 and 150—by publicly praising and glorifying the Lord's name "with preaching, with singing, with psalms, with sackbuts, with cymbals, with drums, with organs, and with similar instruments." In the margin he says, "This was certainly done in Naumburg with the elector of Saxony's extremely outstanding music, to such an extent that everyone, whether in high station or low, was delighted with it and marveled at it" (p. 36).

50. I preferred Count von Beust's punctuation here (Beust, 305), since that in Wagner and Wünsch's edition did not make sense.

51. A partisan was a weapon of the sixteenth and seventeenth centuries with a long shaft and broad blade.

say during conversations how at this princes' convention he sure enjoyed an honorable one.

Finally, on Wednesday, which was April 6, the elector of Saxony and burgrave of Magdeburg also departed, as did His Electoral Grace's beloved noble brother August, the lord of our diocese, but not until both the hosts and other persons who had taken pains on their behalf were likewise presented with considerable gifts. In addition to the hosts, the head burgomaster, Mr. Burgomaster, Master Sixtus Braun, was also presented with the elector's likeness in gold.[52] Then Johann Koch, keeper of the Green Shield and captain of the town militia at the time, received a gilded goblet as a token of honor.[53] After this, Hans Koch, the town warden at the time, who was made court assessor soon afterward, also received a token of honor, a gilded harness [*Geschirr*].

This is thus the short description of the princes' convention held here in the year 1614. As for how much money an Honorable Council lost on this event and had to spend on the princely gifts for the sake of their reputation, one can obtain that information from the council's annual account for that year. And while the council did pay a sufficiently high price to obtain modest renown from this function, on the other hand it continues to benefit many an honorable man and citizen, so that they will know how to sing its praises for a good long time.

Anyone is now welcome to improve upon this, if he knows better how it happened differently and witnessed it personally.

Annotated Sources

For the complete titles and bibliographic information of each, see the Bibliography.

Staffel, *Notabilia*:

Gottfried Staffel was baptized in Naumburg on May 19, 1585. He became an official citizen of the city on February 23, 1609. On June 5, 1615, his appointment as town warden [*Stadtvoigt*] to replace Hans Koch (mentioned in this account) was confirmed; he served in this position until 1636. In 1628 and 1632 he also functioned as vice secretary to the

52. Sixtus Braun passed away later that year, on July 18, and was buried on July 21. He is described by both Staffel (p. 34) and Bürger (p. 540) as honorable, respectable, and highly learned.

53. Staffel reports that this Koch, "a robust, eminent, and upstanding man," was buried on January 29 of the following year (p. 46).

treasury. His written reminiscences cover the years 1608–1622. As for his account of the 1614 Princes' Convention, it appears from his own initial summary remarks (*Notabilia*, 33) that he first recorded his recollections in the front of a copy of Johann Becherer's *Newe Thüringische Chronica* (Mühlhausen: Martin Spiess, 1601) (in the city of Naumburg's possession?). He first refers his reader there, but then appears to have changed his mind and re-recorded his more detailed recollections at the end of his chronological remarks for the year 1614. (This convention account begins after a paragraph detailing an event dated December 23.) Did he perhaps tweak his account and/or add a few more details when doing so? (See also the comments beneath "Beust" below.) Wagner and Wünsch also included in *italics* the supplementary material and marginal notes of a certain Gottlieb Martin Buhle from the year 1796, to which Count von Beust (see below) does not seem to have had access. Though I referred to some of Buhle's material, I did not include it in my work.

Beust, *Sächsische Provinzialblätter* 6, no. 4 (October 1799):
Pages 289–307 of this issue comprise Count Johann Friedrich von Beust's edition of Staffel's account. However, he apparently did not know that Staffel was the author, since his name is nowhere mentioned. When comparing von Beust's edition to Wagner and Wünsch's (see "Staffel" above), it is unclear what von Beust was working with—an original work or a copy of the original. (Or was he perhaps working with a different original? See the comments beneath "Staffel" above). He does not seem to make any special, or at least uniform, effort to modernize or clean up Staffel's spellings, but there are still noticeable spelling differences in the two editions, and sections where material included in the Wagner-Wünsch edition is missing from von Beust's. On the whole the Wagner-Wünsch edition is to be preferred, but there are a couple places where von Beust's makes more sense.

Bürger, *Annales Numburgenses* (Naumburg Annals):
Johann Bürger was born into a cobbler's family on June 6, 1567, in Naumburg. He studied theology in Wittenberg and Leipzig, obtaining his master's degree in 1592. That same year he accepted a call to be a teacher at the Nicolai School in Leipzig, where he quickly rose to the position of conrector (or co-rector). He married a daughter of a Naumburg citizen in 1596, and the following year was issued an invitation by the Naumburg council to potentially fill the newly established third deaconate at

the Town Church of St. Wenceslas. After preaching a trial sermon, he was offered the position and accepted the call, being ordained in November 1597. He obtained full citizenship rights in 1604. He passed away on July 25, 1617. There is still some mystery surrounding the 587-page unpublished manuscript that bears his name. Although he signed the preface himself, it seems that the manuscript as a whole was not prepared in his hand. We do not know exactly what Bürger's intentions were with it. After general remarks, it covers Naumburg events from 1111 to 1616, some of them truly fascinating. Pages 536–539 cover the 1614 Naumburg Princes' Convention.

Hoë von Hoenegg, *Naumburgische Fried und Frewdenport*:
See the beginning of footnote 32. Hoë von Hoenegg was also a close friend of Michael Praetorius. He is a controversial figure (see e.g. Moser, *Heinrich Schütz*, 5), but his preaching skill cannot be denied.

Müller, *Des Chur- und Fürstlichen Hauses Sachsen . . . Annales, von 1400 bis 1700*:
Pages 273–302 cover the events related to the 1614 Naumburg Princes' Convention.

– Appendix VI –

Excerpts from Grossman's
Angst der Hellen und Friede der Seelen[1]

From the Preface

GOD PERFORMED AN EXCEPTIONALLY great kindness and miraculous deliverance for me in the year 1616 out of fatherly grace, goodness, and mercy, in exactly the way David describes in Psalm 116.[2] It was therefore my desire and duty to offer thanks to his divine omnipotence and to fulfill my vows to him in the courts of the house of the Lord in the presence of all his people[3] precisely with and from this very psalm, Psalm 116, and to do so, along with all sixteen of you gentlemen, not just sixteen times, but as long as I live, as long as I am here, and into all eternity.[4]

. . .

Equally scarce and despised are noble music and its cultivators, to which the devil is just as inimical and hostile as he is to [true Christian] love. True, music as an art, as already mentioned, has enjoyed favor, praise, and patrons at all times, even as it is given honorable mention by name in Scripture [Sir 44:1–3,5[5]]:

---

1. Burckhard Großman, ed., *Angst der Hellen / Unnd Friede der Seelen / Das ist / Der CXVI. Psalm Davids, durch etzliche vornehme Musicos im Chur: und Fürstenthumb Sachsen sehr Künstlich unnd ahnmutig uff den Text gerichtet* etc., Tenor (Jena: Johann Weidner, 1623); reprinted in Wolff, *Anguish of Hell and Peace of Soul*.

2. Psalm 116 isn't specifically attributed to David, but the biblical psalms as a whole are often called the Psalms of David because of his predominant authorship.

3. Grossman is alluding to Psalm 116:17–19.

4. Großman, *op. cit.*, fol. A iii recto; reprinted in Wolff, *op. cit.*, 5.

5. See Appendix III, n. 14.

> Let us praise the people of fame,
> and our fathers one after the other.
> [Why? Because] the Lord has done many glorious things among them,
> from the beginning by his might.
> They have ruled their kingdoms well,
> and done honorable deeds, etc.
> They learned music,
> and composed spiritual songs.

And yes, it is also true that this beautiful art has also had its Midases and ass-heads[6]—to whom I was not about to give the honor of mentioning them here, lest they gain more fame among those of their kind. Yet in our day noble music is hated even more, and that, too, among those who should most be fostering it and preserving it to the glory of God. It is so worthless to them that many of them derive greater joy, ecstasy, and even usefulness from the barking of dogs, the bellowing of bulls, and the hee-hawing of asses than from the most beautiful Orphic music, or from the truly heavenly choir music of our now blessedly departed[7] Mr. Michael Praetorius, so well-arranged and well-performed on many different occasions and in many different ways.[8]

---

6. These labels both trace back to the same myth recorded in Hyginus' *Fabulae*, in which Midas, in his poor musical tastes, judged Pan on the pipes to be superior to Apollo on the lyre. Apollo accused Midas of having the ears of a donkey, and actually caused him to sprout donkey-ears as a punishment.

7. Grossman's preface is dated Easter, April 13, 1623.

8. Großman, *op. cit.*, fol. A iv verso; reprinted in Wolff, *op. cit.*, 8. Cf. Praetorius' own remarks in his dedicatory epistle to three Christian princes, dated Jan. 4, 1619, in *Pol. Cad.*: "From all of this it is now obvious and clear as daylight that admirers of Christian music are incited and urged to such worship of God by the Holy Spirit's indwelling, according to the apostle Paul's exhortation to the Ephesians in Chapter 5, verse 19. In the same way, we can gather and conclude on the opposite side that those who advance foolish prudence, Pharisaic holiness, and Thrasonical and Catonian, yes, Stoic and stubborn seriousness are lacking the Holy Spirit's indwelling and are not urged by the good, princely spirit [the Holy Spirit], but are ridden by the wicked, evil, and worthless spirit [the devil], so that they would rather hear *hinnitum et latratum*, the neighing of steeds and horses and the howling and barking of dogs, than *vocalem et organicum aulicae et ecclesiasticae musicae concentum*, a living and instrumental music at the dining table and in church. They will eventually pay dearly for such equine and canine tastes and scorn for princely music, when those proud steeds and jealous hounds have to keep neighing and yelping, chattering with their teeth, howling and barking out a miserable and dreadful music and screams of bloody murder for all eternity, there in the burning hot chapel of hell" (GA 17:viii).

Special Foreword to Praetorius' Setting of Psalm 116

The late author of the following piece, Mr. Praetorius, in transmitting this psalm, also composed an excellent Ordinance and several variations, indicating how he wants it performed. He also wrote a most moving and spiritually enriching letter to me, in which he states that he composed this psalm not only in friendly compliance with my Christian request, but also to bid farewell to himself, and with it he intended to take his leave. Shortly after that he died a blessed death and was transferred to the heavenly ensemble. Presumably, then, he did not compose another note after this composition. It was therefore my desire and duty not to forget this final wish, farewell, and swan song of his with this piece, but to fix his Ordinance here at the head, exactly as he sent it to me in his own hand, to his blessed and eternally praiseworthy memory and in fitting gratitude.[9]

---

9. Großman, *op. cit.*, V. [Quinta] Vox, ix; reprinted in Wolff, *op. cit.*, 18 (cf. p. 255).

Major Corrections and Improvements

ALL OF THESE CORRECTIONS *and improvements correspond to asterisks in the main text of Chapters 1–6. See Translator's Preface for more.*

Chapter 1

The Father, Michael Schulteis

Par. 1

I changed "all seven of the children from this marriage" to "all of his children." See Appendix I for the reasoning.

I omitted the final two sentences, which read: "This document, however, calls Praetorius' birth year of 1572 into question, since he would have been enrolling at age four. However, we cannot pursue this further here." I establish in Appendix II that Praetorius was born in 1571.

Pars. 4–8, 10

Most of the content in these paragraphs and their accompanying footnotes is my original work. In Vogelsänger's book, his par. 3 continued: "After Luther's death (1546), the Lutheran theologians had divided into two camps with irreconcilable positions. The one, the so-called Gnesio Lutherans (from the Greek *gnesios* = genuine), continued to champion a position consistent with Luther's doctrine of faith in the grace of God as the only way to salvation. The other camp called themselves Philippists after Philipp Melanchthon, and were of the opinion that in accessory matters (the adiaphora) one could be more liberal. For them, that included, for example, the wearing of the chasuble in place of the Lutheran surplice—something completely unacceptable to the Gnesio Lutherans, since to them that would have already signified a return to Roman Catholicism." In addition to being too simplistic an explanation, even for an overview, the presented point of contention—chasuble versus surplice—is incorrect. This particular point of contention was simply over the demand that the Lutheran clergymen wear the surplice. In his original par. 4, Vogelsänger summarized how these religious questions influenced political governance and affected pastors in individual territories; I included these ideas and some of his wording in my par. 10.

Studies in Frankfurt an der Oder and Helmstedt

Par. 13

I modified Vogelsänger's original sentence: "Investigations have uncovered that Praetorius continued his studies at the university in Helmstedt, founded in 1576 by Duke Julius of Brunswick (Braunschweig) and Lüneburg." The source he cites for these "investigations" does not actually say that Praetorius studied at the university. In fact, it suggests that his studies took place exclusively under Reineccius and "could certainly only take place privately, since Reineccius was exempted from [public] teaching responsibilities at the university." I then had to rework the content that followed accordingly.

Chapter 2

Heinrich Julius (1564–1613), Bishop of Halberstadt and Duke of Brunswick-Lüneburg

Pars. 1–9

These paragraphs are a large expansion of one relatively small paragraph by Vogelsänger. I thought it worthy of mention how Duke Heinrich Julius and his territories came to be Lutheran (without which development Praetorius would never have entered the duke's service). I also thought his infamous installation ceremony as bishop of Halberstadt was worthy of inclusion. All of the accompanying footnotes except for one ("WGD, 98") are mine.

Par. 16

In the original book, this paragraph is followed by a paragraph that I have moved to the end of this section. In its original placement, it interrupted the thought of multiple paragraphs having to do with Heinrich Julius' trip to Denmark and marriage to Princess Elisabeth.

Chapter 4

Musae Sioniae (The Muses of Zion)

Pars. 6–17

This section contains my most significant revisions to Vogelsänger's text. I rearranged Vogelsänger's paragraphs to better reflect the chronology of Praetorius' production and corrected much of Vogelsänger's material. (I cite one of his errors in the Translator's Preface. He also erroneously says that the famous woodcut portrait of Praetorius and his "holy vow to the Lord" were inserted into Installment I, when they were actually first printed in *MS* Coll.) I also added to and supplemented much of Vogelsänger's material (also documented in the footnotes). I felt these additions were necessary both for understanding the nature and content of Praetorius' installments and for understanding Praetorius' character and religious background and convictions.

Par. 18

I added this material since it strengthens Vogelsänger's remarks and highlights the connection between Praetorius' love for polychorality and his organ-playing background.

The *Syntagma Musicum*, a Compendium of the Musical Knowledge of the Time

Pars. 3–4

These paragraphs represent one paragraph in the author's original (p. 41, par. 1), which I reworked considerably after translating Praetorius' dedicatory epistle for Part 2 of *SM* 1 (Appendix IV, D). I suspected (and my suspicion proved correct) that Praetorius' actual position on secular music was more nuanced than the author had presented. The author had said that Praetorius simply equated secular music with sacred music, as far as the ability of each to provide moral training, restoration, and therapy.

Michael Praetorius and Prague

Par. 5

I made adjustments to this paragraph to clarify both Jacob Chimarrhaeus' position and the nature of the congratulatory collection. The author made it sound as though this were a collection of pieces actually played at a birthday celebration, but that is disproved, among other things, by the fact that one of the composers represented in the collection, Jacob Handl, had passed away in 1591.

Par. 6

The author's original paragraph begins: "What acquaintances might Praetorius have made and what experiences might he have had during his stay in Prague in 1602? He reports on this more extensively in volumes II and III of his *Syntagma Musicum* than he does anywhere else in his numerous publications. In those volumes he mentions Prague musicians seven times, among them the imperial court music directors Philipp de Monte and Lambert de Sayve and the imperial court organist Carolus Luython." While this is technically true, it is misleading in this context in which Praetorius' 1602 stay in Prague is under discussion, since Lambert de Sayve was not an imperial court music director at the time, nor did he live in Prague. Lambert de Sayve was the court music director in Vienna for Archduke Matthias of Austria. It was not until Matthias became Holy Roman Emperor in 1612 that de Sayve became the imperial court music director, but even then Emperor Matthias did not move his court to Prague. If Praetorius ever did meet de Sayve in person, at Prague or anywhere else, it would have to have been while de Sayve's employer Matthias was visiting there with his chapel ensemble. However, as I note, Mathias de Sayve, Lambert's brother, did serve in the chapel ensemble in Prague and could have helped to acquaint Praetorius with his brother Lambert's music. I also had to make corresponding tweaks later in this section, where the author erroneously continued to associate Lambert de Sayve with the Prague musicians.

Pars. 6 (bulleted list) and 7

Here I spelled out the particulars of the knowledge Praetorius acquired in Prague in more detail than the author did.

End of par. 7

I transplanted the author's original sentence here, regarding Praetorius' thirteen-page excerpt of a Handl motet, to the next paragraph.

Chapter 5

Par. 2

I expanded this paragraph. The author simply referred to "some install-ments of his *Musae Sioniae*"; he did not specify which ones or distinguish between the addressees of the quotes from his dedications.

Par. 4

I expanded the section on the 1614 Naumburg Princes' Convention con-siderably. Gottfried Staffel's eyewitness account fascinated me early on in this project and was one of the first primary sources I was determined to translate and include with this work (Appendix V). After working so closely with his account and the other related sources, I couldn't help but spell out the specifics of this event in greater detail than the author.

Par. 12

I expanded this section for the sake of clarity. The author's original read: "But he also finds it in the Marian vespers of Claudio Monteverdi—in the hymn 'Ave maris stella' and the psalm 'Dixit Dominus'—and he writes: 'And in my opinion, this is the proper way to understand the term under discussion, ritornello.'" Without the broader context, "the proper way to understand the term" is entirely unclear.

Bulleted list

I was able to fill in more details for a number of these bullets, and to cite more sources confirming their information, by consulting Vogelsänger's own article, "Michael Praetorius – „Capellmeister von Haus aus und Director der Music" am Kurfürstlichen Hof zu Dresden (1614–1621)." Of greatest interest is the final bullet point about the Reformation centennial celebration, where the author's original final sentence reads: "An explanation for why Praetorius did not direct this music himself has yet to be found." However, in the article just cited, he writes: "Praetorius did not perform his works in Dresden himself. That's because a similar celebration was also planned at the Wolfenbüttel court for the Twenty-first Sunday After Trinity (November 9). But the celebration was then moved forward to November 2. We might guess that this decision can be traced back to Friedrich Ulrich's influence; he probably wanted to keep his music director from traveling to Dresden yet again and boosting the elector's reputation there once again with his performance." Even though he doesn't cite any sources for this information, his assertions are too specific to allow one to suppose that he simply made them up.

"Swan Song" and Death

Par. 1

I expanded this section to provide the reader with more details about the interesting circumstances of Grossman's commission. This reworking includes the first sentence of par. 2 of this section in the author's original. This expansion was inspired in part by my research for, and work in, Appendix VI.

Pars. 5–7

I included much more of Tuckermann's graveside remarks than the author. I especially thought this appropriate given the title I chose for this book.

Chapter 6

The Bequest (Will)

Last par.

I added this paragraph.

The Memorial Slab

Pars. 2–3

I added the Latin epitaph beneath Praetorius' portrait to complete the memorial slab's description. I also added the paragraph after the Latin epitaph on the basis of a) the caption for figure 47 on page 66 of the original book and b) an email message from Winfried Elsner on January 20, 2020.

Estate

Par. 7

The author gave the impression that the story of Anna Praetorius returning several thalers to Fritzsche took place after the case was settled. But this was not the case. So I put the story in its proper context and included more of Fritzsche's account, since it speaks very highly of Anna's character.

Glossary

ITALICIZED ENGLISH WORDS IDENTIFY entries in this Glossary.

Abbey

A building or buildings occupied by a community of monks living under certain religious vows; also called a monastery or cloister. Article 27 of the Augsburg Confession (1530), the first of the Lutheran Confessions, concludes: "So many godless and erroneous ideas are ingrained in monastic vows—that they justify and make a person pious in God's sight, that they constitute Christian perfection, that by taking them a person keeps both the counsels and commands of the gospel, and that they possess extra works beyond what God actually requires of a person. Since then all of this is false, empty, and made up, that also leaves monastic vows null and void." These conclusions resulted in the dwindling of the population of abbeys and monasteries in Lutheran territories, since the completely voluntary, non-meritorious nature of the vows was now stressed to everyone considering entry. In order to ensure a cloister's survival, its purpose and organization usually had to be altered; e.g. some were turned into schools, hospitals, or charitable institutions.

Cantor

German: *Cantor* (also Latin, lit. "chanter, singer") or *Kantor*. When not used more broadly for a singer in general, this term denotes the man responsible for the oversight and direction of the playing and singing of music in a city church (for the commoners, not the royalty), oftentimes composing *choral* music himself. The cantor also often had music-teaching responsibilities at one or more of the city's lower level schools.

Cathedral chapter

German: *Domcapitel* or *Domkapitel. Chapter* of a cathedral.

Chamber accounts

German: *Kammerrechnungen,* abbreviated "KR" in Vogelsänger's book and "K.-R." in WGD (see Annotated Abbreviations). The income and expense records for the court of a duke or other territorial ruler. In this book, the term refers to the chamber accounts of the Wolfenbüttel court unless otherwise noted.

Chapel ensemble

German: *Capelle* or *Kapelle,* lit. "chapel." See *Court chapel ensemble.*

Chaplain

German: *Capellan, Kapellan,* or *Kaplan.* An assistant to the pastor(s) of a church, like a deacon.

Chapter

German: *Capitel* or *Kapitel.* 1) A meeting of the members of the governing body of a religious community in which the chapters, i.e. rules and regulations, are read, concerns are discussed, and other business is conducted. 2) The place where such a meeting is held. 3) The religious governing body itself.

Choral

An adjective usually referring to any music that is sung by one or more choirs, but also used in a narrower sense referring to the singing of a melody in unison, especially in the phrase "choral and *figural.*"

Choristry

German: *Cantorei* or *Kantorei*. The choir and instrumentalists under the direction of a *cantor*. Choristry is not an established English word, but precisely for that reason it was an attractive rendering of the unique German word. Other options like (municipal) choir, (municipal) choristers, and cantorium were all more readily prone to misunderstanding or otherwise lacking.

Church order

German: *Kirchenordnung*. The church constitution for a given area (usually defined by governmental control), detailing such things as the doctrine adhered to, accepted rites, ministerial positions and requirements, the number and types of services to be held, the orders of service to be followed, the festivals to be observed, etc.

Climacteric

Latin: *climactericum*. An adjective referring to a critical epoch in human life, especially years of age that are multiples of seven. Gellius (*Attic Nights* 3.10.9) traces the origin of this concept to the Chaldeans. In English, climacteric can also be a noun referring to the critical period itself.

Consistory

A board of officers consisting of clergymen and prominent *laymen*, usually appointed or nominated by the sovereign of a territory, responsible for supervising the ecclesiastical affairs of that territory.

Consort

German: *Gemahl* (male) or *Gemahlin* (female). The husband or wife of a sovereign or princely personage.

Conventual

Latin: *Conventualis*; German: *Konventual*. A voting member of an *abbey* or monastery.

Court chapel ensemble

German: *Hofcapelle* or *Hofkapelle*, lit. "court chapel." *Kapelle* was used both for the actual worship edifice in the prince's or sovereign's palace or on the palace grounds, and for the body of singers and musicians in his employ who provided the music for the services held there. However, although the body of court musicians was primarily responsible for church music, they were also responsible for a wider variety of music at princely meals and gatherings and in the prince's private chambers. *Chapel ensemble* or even just *ensemble* often suffices, depending on what is already under discussion in the context.

Court music director

German: *Hofcapellmeister* or *Hofkapellmeister*, lit. "court chapel master"; Latin: *Chori Musici Magister*. The man who managed the *court chapel ensemble* and arranged and directed its performances, also often composing the music it played. Praetorius filled this position at the Wolfenbüttel court from 1604 to the end of his life. One shortcoming of translating *(Hof)kapellmeister* as "court music director" is that sometimes the actual word *Director* also appears, and not always as a synonym for *Kapellmeister*, but sometimes to denote someone in a position below the *Kapellmeister*, a sort of "managing director."

Diet

German: *Reichstag*, lit. "imperial convention." A regular, representative imperial business meeting for the *Holy Roman Empire*. Diets were attended by the *Holy Roman Emperor* and the Imperial Estates of the empire. The Imperial Estates were divided into three chambers—the Council of Electors, the Council of Princes, and the Council of Free and Imperial Cities. These representatives would hold discussions and make decisions pertaining to the problems, reform, and maintenance of the empire.

Duchess

German: *Herzogin*. The wife of a *duke*.

Duke

German: *Herzog*; Latin: *Dux*. Ruler of a small independent state, called a duchy or principality, making up a part of the Holy Roman Empire.

Elector

German: *Churfürst, Kurfürst,* or *Kürfürst*. One of the seven members of the electoral college (or assembly) of the *Holy Roman Empire* who were responsible for electing the *Holy Roman Emperor*; three of the electors were clergymen, and four were *laymen*.

Emperor

Latin: *Caesar*; German: *Kaiser*. See *Holy Roman Emperor*.

Ensemble

German: *Capelle* or *Kapelle*. See *Court chapel ensemble*.

Figural

An adjective (sometimes used as a noun) that, when used in phrases like "in figural" or "*choral* and figural," refers to the filling out of a melody with additional harmonizing voice parts.

Holy Roman Emperor

The secular protector and symbolic leader of the *Holy Roman Empire*, elected by the *electors* and crowned emperor by the pope. During Praetorius' employment in Wolfenbüttel, the Habsburgs Rudolf II (r. 1576–1612), Matthias (r. 1612–1619), and Ferdinand II (r. 1619–1637) reigned as emperors.

Holy Roman Empire

Also known as the Holy Roman Empire of the German Nation (German: *das Heilige Römische Reich Deutscher Nation*). A secular sphere created by the pope in central Europe in 800 AD in an attempt to unite Christian territory under one rule, which at times included Germany, Austria, Switzerland, and parts of Italy and the Netherlands.

Layman

Latin: *Laicus*; German: *Laie*. A non-clergyman. The gender neutral form is "layperson" (plural, "laypeople"), and the corresponding adjective is "lay" (e.g. lay representative). The word stems from the Greek word λαός (*laós*), "people," which could be used to identify civilians as opposed to priests and soldiers.

Monophonic

German: *einstimmig*. An adjective referring to the production of, or the ability to produce, only one sound, or to the composition or performance of music with only one part (a melody). Cp. *polyphonic*.

Nonresident music director

German: *Kapellmeister von Haus aus*; lit. "chapel master from house out." A man on loan as *court music director* to the court in question in an interim, temporary, or as-needed capacity, while still keeping his official, full-time appointment at a different court. Praetorius served as nonresident music director at the Dresden court from 1614 onward.

Ordinance

German: *Ordinantz*. When capitalized in this book, it reflects Praetorius' usage, denoting an ordered set of instructions and suggestions for the performance of a given work or collection of works.

Ordinary

When used in the context of formal Christian, liturgical worship, it refers collectively to the parts of the service, especially the songs, that remain the same from one main service (also called a mass) to another. In *SM* 1, Praetorius includes the following with the Ordinary: the *Kyrie* ("Lord, Have Mercy"), *Gloria in Excelsis* ("Glory to God in the Highest"), *Credo* (Apostles' or Nicene Creed), *Sanctus* ("Holy, Holy, Holy"), and *Agnus Dei* ("O Christ, Lamb of God").

Patrician

German: *Patricier* or *Patrizier*. A man belonging to a city's prominent and privileged class, especially belonging to a council-eligible family in a free imperial German city.

Polychorality

German: *Mehrchörigkeit*. A style of composition that employs multiple choirs that engage in musical dialogue with one another. See also *Venetian polychorality*.

Polyphonic

German: *vielstimmig*. An adjective referring to the production of, or the ability to produce, many different sounds, or to the composition or performance of music with multiple, harmonic parts. For example, Praetorius refers to the organ as a "polyphonic mechanism." Cp. *monophonic*.

Positif

A small, provisional pipe organ, or one built for a private room. It was often able to be transferred and positioned in different places, in which case it could also be called a portative.

Prebend

German: *Pfründe.* A vocational position in a church or other religious institution (e.g. an abbey), and the portion of the institution's revenues allotted to the person in that position as his stipend.

Prior

The man next in rank below an abbot in an *abbey* or monastery. Praetorius was appointed prior of the Ringelheim Abbey by 1614. It is unknown what exactly his duties entailed as such.

Rückpositiv

Lit., "back *positif.*" A separate division of a pipe organ, usually located behind the organ bench and main organ case (from the organist's perspective) in its own smaller case installed into the balcony parapet.

Quempas

Occurs in the German phrase *Quempas-Singen,* "Quempas singing," from the opening lines of the Latin Christmas hymn, "Quem pastores laudavere [The one whom the shepherds praised]." It refers to the traditional German practice of singing each line in four-line Christmas carols (such as "Quem pastores") by four soloists or choirs in turn.

Venetian polychorality

A style of composition and performance that employs spatially separate choirs singing in alternation. It originated in the mid-sixteenth century in St. Mark's Basilica in Venice as an innovation for circumventing the sound delay caused by the church's architectural peculiarities.

About the Author[1]

SIEGFRIED VOGELSÄNGER WAS BORN on September 24, 1927, in Dortmund, Germany, where he also attended school. During World War II he was conscripted into the Luftwaffe auxiliary personnel. After surviving American captivity and working in the agricultural sector, he began to learn the cabinetmaker's trade in 1946, eventually obtaining a journeyman certificate.

From 1952–1955 he studied sacred music at the Evangelical Church of Westphalia's Music School in Herford under Wilhelm Ehmann and Arno Schönstedt, eventually passing the B-Examination.[2] After studying pedagogy in Dortmund, he served as an elementary schoolteacher in Dortmund and church musician in Soest, east of Dortmund, from 1957–1961.

From 1961–1969 he was an adjunct professor and lecturer in the field of music and its education at the Pedagogical Academy (*Hochschule*) of Dortmund, where he worked with Michael Alt. At the same time, he continued his music studies at the Northwest German Music Academy in Detmold under Martin Stephani, Johannes Driessler, Irmgard Lechner, and Helmut Tramnitz, eventually passing both the A-Examination[3] and the School Music Examination.

1. This biography appears on p. 77 of Vogelsänger's book. I added the last sentence and footnotes.—Trans.

2. The B-Examination was taken at the end of a four-year course of study. A student passing this examination was considered qualified for a full-time position in sacred music.

3. The A-Examination was taken at the end of a four- to six-year course of study, or supplementary two-year course of study for those having already passed the B-Examination. This course of study included special artistic emphases, e.g. in choral work or organ playing. A student passing this examination was considered qualified for a full-time music position at a major church.

He obtained his doctorate in 1972 and his habilitation in 1974 at the Pedagogical Academy of Dortmund. From 1973–1992 he was professor of media, education, and music at the Lower Rhine Polytechnic College (*Fachhochschule*) in Mönchengladbach. He authored numerous publications in the fields of music education and social education. After retiring in 1992, he pursued studies and authored publications in the field of Praetorius research.

In retirement he resided in Belgium, then in France. Beginning in 2005 he had a second residence in Wolfenbüttel, a retirement home called the Michael Praetorius House. He is the father of two sons and a daughter. As of 2007, the former were church musicians in Brunswick and Lüneburg and the latter was a pianist in Freiburg.

Vogelsänger passed away on February 5, 2015, in Saint-Hernot, France, at the age of eighty-seven.

About the Translator

NATHANIEL BIEBERT IS THE oldest of eight children, seven boys and one girl, born to Rev. Timothy and Linda Biebert of Wisconsin. He was born and baptized in California and attended Lutheran grade schools in Wisconsin. He graduated from Luther Preparatory School (2001), Martin Luther College (BA with a minor in confessional languages, 2005), and Wisconsin Lutheran Seminary (MDiv, 2009) after serving a vicarship (pastoral apprenticeship) in New Hampshire (2007–2008). Upon his seminary graduation, he received a one-year assignment to be a dormitory supervisor and instructor at a Lutheran high school in Nebraska, where he was ordained into the pastoral ministry. In 2010, he was reassigned as the pastor of two rural parishes northwest of Wausau, Wisconsin, where he also taught religion part-time at a nearby Lutheran high school. In 2017, he accepted a call to serve a Lutheran parish in South Austin, Texas.

In 2012, God united him in marriage with Katherine née Sternberg. Among other things, they enjoy bicycling, traveling, camping, reading, watching good movies, and attending classical music concerts together. Nathaniel also enjoys hiking, fly fishing, fly tying (still a novice), and historical research, including translating German and Latin works. He and Katie have a golden retriever named Gerhardt.

Nathaniel is the author of *Luther at the Manger* (Milwaukee: Northwestern, 2017), a translation of a 1531 sermon series. He has authored articles and translations for the *WELS Historical Institute Journal, Wisconsin Lutheran Quarterly*, and *Forward in Christ*. He has also provided translations for Baroque choral concert programs for two of Austin's ensembles. He is a 2018 recipient of the Concordia Historical Institute's Award of Commendation.

Bibliography

SOURCES MARKED WITH AN *asterisk* (*) *are those not included in the original bibliography, notes, and abbreviations. See also Annotated Abbreviations.*

Abel, Caspar. *Stiffts- Stadt- und Land-Chronick / Des jetzigen Fürstenthums Halberstadt.* Bernburg: Christoph Gottfried Cörner, 1754.

Allihn, Ingeborg. "Frankfurt an der Oder." In *MGG* Sachteil 3:664–73.

Arbeitsgruppe am Francisceum Zerbst zum Melanchthonjahr 1997. *Philipp Melanchthon und Zerbst: Quellensammlung und Aufsätze zum 500. Geburtstag des Reformators.* Zerbst: Förderverein Francisceum Zerbst, 1997.

*Aufdemberge, C. T. *Christian Worship: Handbook.* Milwaukee: Northwestern, 1997.

Aumüller, Gerhard. "Lebens- und Arbeitsbedingungen hessischen Organisten während des 17. Jahrhunderts: Das Beispiel der Organistenfamilie von Ende." *Zeitschrift des Vereins für hessische Geschichte und Landeskunde* 111 (2006) 85–126.

*Bauch, Gustav, ed. *Das älteste Decanatsbuch der philosophischen Facultät an der Universität zu Frankfurt a. O.* Pt. 2, *Die artistisch-philosophischen Promotionen von 1540 bis 1596.* Breslau: M. & H. Marcus, 1901. In *Acten und Urkunden der Universität Frankfurt a. O.* Vol. 1. Breslau: M. & H. Marcus, 1907.

Becker-Glauch, Irmgard. *Die Bedeutung der Musik für die Dresdner Hoffeste bis in die Zeit Augusts des Starken.* Kassel: Bärenreiter, 1951.

*Becman, Johann Christoph. *Notitia Universitatis Francofurtanae.* Frankfurt an der Oder: Jeremias Schrey and Johann Christoph Hartmann, 1707.

*Beust, Johann Friedrich von, ed. *Sächsische Provinzialblätter* 6, no. 4 (October 1799) 289–307.

*Beyer, Heinrich, ed. "Leichensermone auf Musiker des 17. Jahrhunderts." *Monatshefte für Musik-Geschichte* 7, no. 12 (1875) 177–78.

Blankenburg, Walter, and Clytus Gottwald. "Praetorius, Michael." *The New Grove Dictionary of Music and Musicians.* 2nd ed. (2001), 20:261–66.

Blume, Friedrich, ed. *Gesamtausgabe der Musikalischen Werke von Michael Praetorius.* 21 vols. Wolfenbüttel: Möseler Verlag, 1928–1960.

———. "Das Werk des Michael Praetorius." *Zeitschrift für Musikwissenschaft* 17, no. 8 (August 1935) 321–31.

———, ed. "Lambert de Sayve und Michael Praetorius: Teutsche Liedlein zu 4 Stimmen." *Das Chorwerk* 51 (1938).

*Bodemann, Eduard. "Herzog Julius von Braunschweig: Kulturbild deutschen Fürstenlebens und deutscher Fürstenerziehung im 16. Jahrhundert." *Zeitschrift für deutsche Kulturgeschichte* 4 (1875) 193–239, 311–48.

Böhm, Oskar. *Chronik der Oberschule Torgau*. Kleine Schriften des Torgauer Geschichtsvereins, no. 12. Torgau: Torgauer Geschichtsverein, 1999.

*Bornitz, Jacob. *Tractatus Politicus: De Rerum Sufficientia In Rep. & Civitate procuranda*. Frankfurt am Main: Johann Friedrich Weiss, 1625.

Breig, Werner. "Schütz, Heinrich." In *MGG* Personenteil 15:358–409.

Brülls, Holger. "Stellungsnahme zur kunsthistorischen Bedeutung und denkmalpflegerischen Behandlung des Renaissance-Orgelprospektes von 1596 in der Stadtkirche St. Martini zu Halberstadt." Halle an der Saale: unpublished expert's report, 2006.

*Bürger, Johann. *Annales Numburgenses oder angefangene Naumburgische Chronica*. Transcribed by Karl-Heinz Wünsch and edited by Siegfried Wagner and Karl-Heinz Wünsch. Naumburg: Museumsverein Naumburg, 2014.

*Clemen, Otto. *Beiträge zur Reformationsgeschichte aus Büchern und Handschriften der Zwickauer Ratsschulbibliothek*. No. 2, 42–44. Berlin: C. A. Schwetschke und Sohn, 1902.

Deeters, Walter. "Alte und neue Aktenfunde über Michael Praetorius." *Braunschweigisches Jahrbuch* 52 (1971) 102–20.

———. "Das Lehen der Familie Praetorius." *Braunschweigisches Jahrbuch* 53 (1972) 111–26.

*Die Compenius-Orgel der St. Martini-Kirche zu Kroppenstedt (website). "Der Orgelbau in Kroppenstedt durch Esaias Compenius." https://www.compenius-orgel.de/geschichtederorgel.htm.

Die Orgel der Hauptkirche Beatae Mariae Virginis Wolfenbüttel. Wolfenbüttel: Kirchenvorstand der Hauptkirche, 1986.

*Eitner, Robert. *Biographisch-Bibliographisches Quellen-Lexikon der Musiker und Musikgelehrten der christlichen Zeitrechnung bis zur Mitte des neunzehnten Jahrhunderts*. Vol. 6 (1902) 295–96 and vol. 8 (1903) 45–49. Leipzig: Breitkopf & Haertel.

Elsner, Winfried, ed. *Michael Praetorius in Wolfenbüttel*. Exhibition booklet. 2005. Herzog August Bibliothek 55.876.

Faber, Heinrich. *Compendiolum musicae pro incipientibus*. Nuremberg: Johann Montanus [vom Berg] and Ulrich Neuber, 1548. https://books.google.com/books?id=blc8AAAcAAJ&printsec=frontcover.

Festschrift zur Einweihung der Orgel in der Stadtkirche zu Bückeburg. Bückeburg: Kirchenkreisamt Rinteln, 1997.

*Flacius, Matthias Illyricus. *Gründliche Verlegung des langen Comments der Adiaphoristen / oder der verzelung jrer handlungen*. Jena: Donatus Richtzenhayn, 1560.

*Fleming, Michael David. "Michael Praetorius, Music Historian: An Annotated Translation of Syntagma Musicum I, Part I." PhD diss., Washington University (St. Louis), 1979.

*Foerstemann, Carl Eduard, ed. *Album Academiae Vitebergensis ab A. Ch. MDII usque ad A. MDLX*. Leipzig: Carl Tauchnitz, 1841.

Forchert, Arno. *Das Spätwerk des Michael Praetorius: Italienische und deutsche Stilbegegnung*. Berlin: Merseburger, 1959.

———. "Michael Praetorius: Werk und Wirkung." *Sagittarius: Beiträge zur Erforschung und Praxis alter und neuer Kirchenmusik* 4 (1973) 98–110.

———. "Michael Praetorius und die Musik am Hof von Wolfenbüttel." *Daphnis: Zeitschrift für Mittlere Deutsche Literatur* 10, no. 4 (March 1981) 625–42.

———. "Musik als Auftragskunst: Bemerkungen zum Schaffen des Michael Praetorius." *Schütz-Jahrbuch* 27 (2005) 37–51.

———. "Musik zwischen Religion und Politik: Bemerkungen zur Biographie des Michael Praetorius." In *Festschrift Martin Ruhnke zum 65. Geburtstag*, edited by the Mitarbeitern des Instituts für Musikwissenschaft der Universität Erlangen-Nürnberg, 106–25. Neuhausen: Häussler-Verlag, 1986.

———. "Praetorius, Michael." In *MGG* Personenteil 13:884–92.

Friedlaender, Ernst, ed. *Aeltere Universitäts-Matrikeln. I. Universität Frankfurt a. O.* Vol. 1, *(1506–1648)*. Publicationen aus den K. Preußischen Staatsarchiven 32. Leipzig: S. Hirzel, 1887.

Geißmann, Friedrich. "Die Musiker am Hofe des Fürsten Ernst." *Schaumburgisch-Lippesche Mitteilungen* 20 (1969) 21–24.

Grimm, Heinrich. *Meister der Renaissancemusik an der Viadrina: Quellenbeiträge zur Geisteskultur des Nordosten Deutschlands vor dem Dreissigjährigen Kriege.* Frankfurt an der Oder: Trowitzsch, 1942.

Gudewill, Kurt. "Heinrich Schütz und Michael Praetorius: Gegensatz und Ergänzung." *Musik und Kirche* 34 (Sept.–Oct. 1964) 253–64.

Gudewill, Kurt, and Hans Haase. *Michael Praetorius Creutzbergensis (1571[?]–1621): Zwei Beiträge zu seinem und seiner Kapelle Jubiläumsjahr.* Wolfenbüttel: Möseler, 1971.

Gurlitt, Wilibald. Afterword to *De Organographia: Zweiter Teil des Syntagma Musicum*, by Michael Praetorius. Facsimile reprint. Kassel: Bärenreiter, 1929.

———. Afterword to *Syntagma Musicum III: Termini Musici*, by Michael Praetorius. Facsimile reprint. Kassel: Bärenreiter, 1958.

*———. "Heinrich Schütz. Zum 350. Geburtstag am 8. Oktober 1935." *Jahrbuch der Musikbibliothek Peters* 42 (1935) 65–83.

———. *Michael Praetorius (Creuzbergensis): Sein Leben und seine Werke.* Wolfenbüttel: Dr. Josef Floßdorf, 2008

*Hendel, Kurt K. *Johannes Bugenhagen.* Vol. 1. Minneapolis: Fortress, 2015.

*Hoë von Hoenegg, Matthias. *Chur Sächsische Evangelische JubelFrewde / In der Churfürstlichen Sächsischen Schloß Kirchen zu Dreßden* etc. Leipzig: Abraham Lamberg, 1617.

*———. *Naumburgische Fried und Frewdenport.* Leipzig: Abraham Lamberg, 1614.

*Israël, Carl. *Programm des städtischen Gymnasiums zu Frankfurt a. M. Ostern 1872.* 72–73. Frankfurt am Main: Druck von Mahlau & Waldschmidt, 1872.

*Johnston, Gregory S., ed., *A Heinrich Schütz Reader: Letters and Documents in Translation.* Oxford University Press, 2013.

*Kelsch, Wolfgang. "Elias Holweins Stadtansicht von Wolfenbüttel aus dem Jahre 1620." *Braunschweigisches Jahrbuch* 60 (1979) 165–71.

*Küttler, Detlev. "Recherche: Wer ist die Mutter von Michael Praetorius?" *Familiengeschichte Küttler* (blog), Nov. 28, 2009. http://kuettler.net/recherche-wer-ist-die-mutter-von-michael-praetorius/.

Laakmann, Astrid. ". . . *nur allein aus Liebe der Musica": Die Bückeburger Hofmusik zur Zeit des Grafen Ernst III. zu Holstein-Schaumburg als Beispiel höfischer Musikpflege im Gebiet der "Weserrenaissance."* Münster: LIT Verlag, 1998.

Leuckfeld, Johann Georg. *Antiquitates Gröningenses, Oder Historische Beschreibung Der Vormahligen Bischöfflichen Residentz Gröningen.* Quedlinburg: Theodor Jeremias Schwan, 1727.

Liebe, Georg. "Der Hofhalt des Bischofs Heinrich Julius von Halberstadt, Herzogs zu Braunschweig und Lüneburg." *Zeitschrift des Harz-Vereins für Geschichte und Altertumskunde* 28 (1895) 740–50.

Lietzmann, Hilda. "Der Altar der Marienkirche zu Wolfenbüttel." *Niedersächsische Beiträge zur Kunstgeschichte* 13 (1974) 199–222.

———. *Herzog Heinrich Julius zu Braunschweig und Lüneburg (1564–1613): Persönlichkeit und Wirken für Kaiser und Reich.* Braunschweig: Braunschweigischer Geschichtsverein, 1993.

Ludewig, Randolf. "Genealogische Forschungen zur Familie Praetorius." Graciously shared with the author in 2003.

*Mentz, Georg, and Reinhold Jauernig, eds. *Die Matrikel der Universität Jena.* Vol. 1, *1548 bis 1652.* Veröffentlichungen der Thüringischen Historischen Kommission 1. Jena: Gustav Fischer, 1944.

Möller-Weiser, Dietlind. *Untersuchungen zum I. Band des Syntagma musicum von Michael Praetorius.* Detmold-Paderborner Beiträge zur Musikwissenschaft 3. Kassel: Bärenreiter, 1993.

*Mönkemeyer, Helmut, ed. *Michael Altenburg (1584–1640): Intraden.* Vol. 1. Musica Instrumentalis 32. Zürich: Musikverlag zum Pelikan, 1982.

*Moser, Hans Joachim. *Heinrich Schütz: His Life and Work.* Translated by Carl F. Pfatteicher. St. Louis: Concordia, 1959.

*Müller, Johann Sebastian. *Des Chur- und Fürstlichen Hauses Sachsen, Ernestin- und Albertinischer Linien, Annales, von 1400 bis 1700.* Weimar: Johann Ludwig Gleditsch, 1700.

*Musculus, Andreas, ed. *Precationes ex Veteribus Orthodoxis Doctoribus, ex Ecclesiae Hymnis et Canticis, ex Psalmis Denique Davidis Collectae.* Leipzig: Andreas Schneider, 1573.

Niemann, Hartwig. "Michael Praetorius als Organist." In *Michael Praetorius in Wolfenbüttel,* edited by Winfried Elsner. Exhibition booklet. 2005. Herzog August Bibliothek 55.876.

Niemöller, Klaus Wolfgang. "Die musikalische Festschrift für den Direktor der Prager Hofkapelle Kaiser Rudolf II. 1602." In *Bericht über den internationalen musikwissenschaftlichen Kongress Bonn 1970.* Kassel: Bärenreiter, 1973.

Nolte, Rudolf August. *Chronicon Der Stadt und Vestung Wolffenbüttel, in sich haltend des seel. Herrn Ober-Amtmanns Christoph Woltereck Begräbniß-Buch der Kirchen B. M. V. zu Wolffenbüttel* etc. Helmstedt: Johann Drimborn, 1747. https://publikationsserver.tu-braunschweig.de/receive/dbbs_mods_00024200.

*Olson, Oliver K. *Matthias Flacius and the Survival of Luther's Reform.* Wiesbaden: Harrassowitz, 2002.

*Pallas, Karl, ed., *Die Registraturen der Kirchenvisitationen im ehemals sächsischen Kurkreise.* Div. 2, pt. 4, *Die Ephorien Torgau und Belgern.* Geschichtsquellen der Provinz Sachsen und angrenzender Gebiete 41. Halle: Otto Hendel, 1911.

*Pezold, Georg. *Beschreibung Der Churfürstlichen Kindtauff / und Frewdenfests zu Dreßden / den 18. Septemb. des verlauffenen 1614. Jahres* etc. Dresden: Hieronymus Schütz, 1615. http://digitale.bibliothek.uni-halle.de/vd17/content/pageview/632725.

*Praetorius, Andreas. BPABEION, *Das ist / Ehrendanck oder aller Edlestes Kleinoth.* Frankfurt an der Oder: Andreas Eichorn, 1584. http://digitale.bibliothek.unihalle.de/vd16/content/pageview/13544161.

*———. BPABEION *Ehrendanck: oder Aller Edlestes Kleinoth.* Reprint. Wolfenbüttel: Fürstliche Druckerey, 1608. http://diglib.hab.de/drucke/yv-952–8f-helmst/start.htm.

*Praetorius, Andreas (Jr.), ed., *Prodromus Lutheri, Das ist / Kurtzer Auszug des besten Kerns und Saffts / aus den Deutschen Jenischen Tomis, des Mannes Gottes D. Martini Lutheri, Christmilder gedechtnis.* Leipzig: Henning Grosse der Jüngere, 1611. https://books.google.com/books?id=ifJVAAAAcAAJ&printsec=frontcover.

*Praetorius, Michael. III. *Polyhymnia Panegyrica Michaëlis Praetorii C. Darinnen XL Solennische Friedt- und Frewdens-Concert.* Primus–Decimusquartus. Wolfenbüttel: Elias Holwein, 1619.

*———. *Leiturgodia Sionia Latina, Complectens Sub hoc Generali Titulo, Omnes Ecclesiasticas Cantiones Latinas usitatiores & selectiores, quae diebus Dominicis & Festis, In Officio Matutino, Summo, & Vespertino, per annum in Ecclesia decantari solent* etc. Wolfenbüttel: Elias Holwein, 1612. http://diglib.hab.de/drucke/2–5-7-musica-11s/start.htm.

*———. *Missodia Sionia Continens Cantiones sacras, ad Officium quod vocant Summum, ante Meridiem in Ecclesia usitatas.* Cantus. Wolfenbüttel: Officina Typographica Principalis, 1611. https://stimmbuecher.digitale-sammlungen.de/view?id=bsb00092770.

*———. *Musae Sioniae: Geistliche Concert Gesänge uber die fürnembste Deutsche Psalmen und Lieder.* Ander Theil. Cantus I. Chori. Jena: Christoff Lippold, 1607.

*———. *Musae Sioniae: Geistliche Concert Gesänge uber die fürnembste Deutsche Psalmen und Lieder.* Dritter Theil. Cantus I. Chori. Helmstedt: Jacob Lucius, 1607.

*———. *Musae Sioniae: Geistliche Concert Gesänge uber die fürnembste Deutsche Psalmen und Lieder.* Vierdter Theil. Cantus I. Chori. Helmstedt: Jacob Lucius, 1607.

*———. *Musae Sioniae Michaëlis Praetorii C. Darinnen Deutsche Psalmen und geistliche Lieder / wie sie durchs gantze Jar in der Christlichen Kirchen breuchlich* etc. Wolfenbüttel: Elias Holwein, 1607.

*———. *Musae Sioniae Oder Geistliche Concert Gesänge über die fürnembste Herrn Lutheri und anderer Deutsche Psalmen.* Erster Theil. Cantus I Chori. Regensburg: Bartholomeus Gräf, 1605.

*———. *Musarum Sioniarum Motectae et Psalmi Latini.* Cantus. Nuremberg: Abraham Wagenmann, 1607.

*———. *Polyhymnia Caduceatrix & Panegyrica. Darinnen Solennische Friedt—und Frewden-Concert.* Bassus-Generalis seu Continuus. Wolfenbüttel: Elias Holwein, 1619.

———. *Syntagma Musicum.* 3 vols. Edited by Arno Forchert. Reprint of the original 1615–1620 editions. Kassel: Bärenreiter, 2001.

*———. *Syntagma Musicum II: De Organographia, Parts I & II.* Translated by David Z. Crookes. Oxford University Press, 1986.

*———. "Syntagma Musicum II: De Organographia, Parts III—V with Index." Translated and edited by Quentin Faulkner (2014). *Zea E-Books* 24. https://digitalcommons.unl.edu/zeabook/24.

*———. *Syntagma Musicum III*. Translated by Jeffery Kite-Powell. Oxford University Press, 2004.

*———. *Syntagmatis Musici Michaelis Praetorii C. Tomus Secundus De Organographia.* Wolfenbüttel: Elias Holwein, 1619. https://reader.digitale-sammlungen.de/de/fs1/object/display/bsb10527678_00005.html.

*———. *Syntagmatis Musici Michaelis Praetorii C. Tomus Tertius.* Wolfenbüttel: Elias Holwein, 1619. https://archive.org/details/SyntagmaMusicumBd.31619.

*———. *Syntagmatis Musici Tomus Primus.* Wittenberg: Johann Richter, 1615. https://books.google.com/books?id=kO1CAAAAcAAJ&printsec=frontcover.

*———. *Theatrum Instrumentorum Seu Sciagraphia Michaëlis Praetorii C.* Wolfenbüttel: Elias Holwein, 1620. https://reader.digitale-sammlungen.de/de/fs1/object/display/bsb10527679_00005.html.

*Preus, J. A. O. *The Second Martin: The Life and Theology of Martin Chemnitz.* St. Louis: Concordia, 1994.

Ruhnke, Martin. *Beiträge zu einer Geschichte der deutschen Hofmusikkollegien im 16. Jahrhundert.* Berlin: Merseburger, 1963.

*Sayve, Lambert de. *Teutsche Liedlein mit Vier Stimmen componiret.* Cantus. Wolfenbüttel: Fürstliche Druckerei, 1611. https://gdz.sub.uni-goettingen.de/id/PPN100225518X.

*Schäfer, Wilhelm, ed. "Einige Beiträge zur Geschichte der Kurfürstlichen musikalischen Capelle oder Cantorei unter den Kurfürsten August, Christian I. u. II. u. Johann Georg I." *Sachsen-Chronik für Vergangenheit und Gegenwart.* Erste Serie (1854) 404–51.

*Serauky, Walter. *Musikgeschichte der Stadt Halle: Von Samuel Scheidt bis in die Zeit Georg Friedrich Händels und Johann Sebastian Bachs.* Halle: Buchhandlung des Waisenhauses, 1939.

SL. "Zerbst." In *MGG* Sachteil 9:2380–82.

*Staffel, Gottfried, et al. *Notabilia: Naumburger Denkwürdigkeiten aus dem 17. Jahrhundert.* Transcribed and edited by Siegfried Wagner and Karl-Heinz Wünsch. Naumburg: Museumsverein Naumburg, 2005.

*Tuckermann, Peter. *Leichpredigt. Des Ehrnvesten/ Achtbarn vnd Kunstreichen Herrn. Michaelis Praetorii* etc. Wolfenbüttel: Elias Holwein, 1621. http://diglib.hab.de/drucke/j-276-4f-helmst-7s/start.htm.

Vogelsänger, Siegfried. "Michael Praetorius – „Capellmeister von Haus aus und Director der Music" am Kurfürstlichen Hof zu Dresden (1614–1621)." *Schütz-Jahrbuch* 22 (2000) 101–28.

———. *Michael Praetorius: "Diener vieler Herren."* Aachen: Edition Herodot, 1991.

———. "Michael Praetorius: Festmusiken zu zwei Ereignissen des Jahres 1617: zum Kaiserbesuch in Dresden und zur Jahrhundertfeier der Reformation." *Die Musikforschung* 40, no. 2 (April–June 1987) 97–109.

———. *Michael Praetorius beim Wort genommen: Zur Entstehungsgeschichte seiner Werke.* Aachen: Edition Herodot, 1987.

Waczkat, Andreas. "Mancinus, Thomas." In *MGG* Personenteil 11:954–56.

*Walther, Johann Gottfried. *Musicalisches Lexicon.* 491–94. Leipzig: Wolffgang Deer, 1732. https://reader.digitale-sammlungen.de/de/fs1/object/display/bsb10600439_00007.html.

Werckmeister, Andreas. *Organum Gruningense redivivum.* Edited by Paul Smets. Reprint of the original 1705 edition. Mainz: Rheingold-Verlag, 1932.

*Wetzel, Johann Caspar. *Johann Caspar Wetzels Historische Lebens-Beschreibung Der berühmtesten Lieder-Dichter.* Pt. 2, 315–16. Herrnstadt: Samuel Roth-Scholtz, 1721. https://reader.digitale-sammlungen.de/de/fs1/object/display/bsb10592986_00001.html.

*Wolff, Christoph, ed. *Anguish of Hell and Peace of Soul: A 1623 Collection of Sixteen Motets on Psalm 116 by Michael Praetorius, Heinrich Schütz, and Others.* Harvard Publications in Music, 1994.

*Zimmermann, Paul, ed. *Album Academiae Helmstadiensis.* Vol. 1. Hannover: Selbstverlag der Historischen Kommission, 1926.

———. "Zur Biographie des Kapellmeisters Michael Praetorius." *Jahrbuch des Braunschweigischen Geschichtsvereins* 2, vol. 3 (1930) 91–101.

*Zywietz, Michael. "Sayve, Mathias (I) de." In *MGG* Personenteil 14:1052.

Index

(*Italicized* page numbers refer to an illustration.)

Made in the USA
Monee, IL
26 September 2020